Praise and Lament in the Psalms

PRAISE AND LAMENT IN THE PSALMS

CLAUS WESTERMANN

Translated by Keith R. Crim and Richard N. Soulen

John Knox Press
ATLANTA

Library of Congress Cataloging in Publication Data

Westermann, Claus.
   Praise and lament in the Psalms.

   Translation of: Lob und Klagen in den Psalmen.
   Bibliography: p.
   Includes index.
   1. Bible. O.T. Psalms—Criticism, interpretation,
etc. 2. Praise of God—Biblical teaching.
3. Laments in the Bible.
BS1430.2.W3913   223'.206   81-13753
ISBN 0-8042-1791-2   AACR2
ISBN 0-8042-1792-0 (pbk.)

© copyright M. E. Bratcher 1965 and John Knox Press 1981
10 9 8 7 6 5 4 3 2 1
Printed in the United States of America
John Knox Press
Atlanta, Georgia 30365

CONTENTS

Explanations of the Abbreviations

1

IR, IIR, H. Rawlinson, *Cuneiform Inscriptions of Western*
etc.: *Asia,* London
VAT: Vorderasiatische Abteilung der Museen zu
Berlin, Tontafelsammlung

OTHER ABBREVIATIONS

A.T.: Old Testament (in German works)
O.T.: Old Testament
N.T.: New Testament
ZAW: *Zeitschrift für die alttestamentliche Wissenschaft*
BZAW: Beihefte of the ZAW
BWANT: *Beiträge zur Wissenschaft vom Alten und Neuen
Testament*
HSAT: *Die Heilige Schrift des Alten Testaments,* eds.
Feldmann and Herkenne, Bonn
KHSAT: E. Kautzsch, *Die heilige Schrift des Alten Testaments,* 4th edition, ed. Bertholet
OTS: *Oudtestamentische Studien*
HAT: *Handbuch zum Alten Testament*
RGG: *Die Religion in Geschichte und Gegenwart*
ThB: *Theologische Bücherei*
VT: *Vetus Testamentum*

Translator's Preface

The Praise of God in the Psalms appeared in German in 1961 and was translated into English by Keith R. Crim in 1965. That translation is reprinted here unaltered. The fifth edition of *Das Loben Gottes in den Psalmen* was published in 1977 by Vandenhoeck & Ruprecht under the title *Lob und Klage in den Psalmen,* having been augmented by two essays on the lament and another on the formation of the Psalter.[1]

In translating the technical vocabulary of these essays, it seemed best to follow the course chosen by Professor Crim rather than to devise new English equivalents, however justified they might be. The final essay, however, entitled "The Role of the Lament in the Theology of the Old Testament," represents an exception to this rule. It first appeared in *Interpretation* 38 (Jan. 1974) and is reprinted here essentially unaltered. In that translation I chose to translate the German word *Volksklage* as "the lament of the nation"; in the essays which now precede it, the term is rendered "the lament of the people."

Richard N. Soulen

---

1. "The Structure and History of the Lament in the Old Testament" appeared as "Struktur und Geschichte der Klage im Alten Testament," *Zeitschrift für die alttestamentliche Wissenschaft (ZAW)* 66, 1/2/1954, 44–80, Berlin: Verlag Alfred Töpelmann. "The Re-presentation" of History in the Psalms" appeared as "Vergegenwärtigung der Geschichte in den Psalmen," *Zwischenstation. Festschrift für Karl Kupisch zum 60. Geburtstag,* 1963, pp. 253–280, München: Chr. Kaiser Verlag. "The Formation of the Psalter" appeared as "Zur Sammlung des Psalters," *Theologia Viatorum* 8, 1961/62, 1962, pp. 278–284, Berlin: Walter de Gruyter & Co.

Preface

In the present transitions and disasters the church has been confronted anew with the question of the praise of God. Praise has played a limited role in the relationship of modern man to God. The last time it had real significance was in the period of the enlightenment, but it was then essentially praise of the Creator. Only recently, and only in those places where the church was under severe trial has the praise of God been again awakened. A collection of letters from pastors of the confessing church, which were illegally printed during the church struggle, bore the title: . . . *And They Praised God.* A pastor collected poems from the years of the church struggle and the war in a volume: *Praise Out of the Depths.* At about the same time there appeared outside the church a volume of poetry from the same period with the title: *De Profundis.* In many places, even including the gathering of a congregation at the side of the grave, this new tone can be heard.[1]

Here and there under the heavy burden of what was happening to them, members of the congregation discovered that they were not only learning patience and self-discipline under that which had been given them to bear, but that *under* the burdens, despite all trials, they were able to praise God. For all who experienced it, it was a real discovery that this was possible.

In such praise out of the depths, their need, the sorrow through which they had to struggle all alone, was no longer merely their own concern. It was not *merely* a test and confirmation of their piety, a happening that took place between God and their soul, but it was an occurrence in the congregation.

1. K. Barth, *Credo*, p. 124: "Praise of God is the most endangered and the most dangerous undertaking of the church. Everyone can praise, even the heretic! Thus it must be that at certain times one speaks but little or not at all of the praise of God, that there are special times when it awakens with power and then is neither endangered nor dangerous."

5

Whenever one in his enforced separation praised God in song, or speech, or silence, he was conscious of himself not as an individual, but as a member of the congregation. When in hunger and cold, between interrogations, or as one sentenced to death, he was privileged to praise God, he knew that in all his ways he was borne up by the church's praise of God. By this it became an element of what was going on between God and the world. At all times and in many places there have been men who suffered and died for their convictions. In the accounts of the Acts of the Apostles it is clear that the strongest outward impression is made by the fact that the witnesses of Jesus Christ sing and praise God in prison. By this they make known that God acts, whatever may happen to them. Something of this forensic[1a] character of the praise of God has again broken through in our time. This praise out of the depths has become an argument that speaks louder than the arguments that we have been accustomed to bring forth for "Christendom." As such it became a sort of exegesis of Holy Scripture. (Compare Gerhard Ebeling, *Kirchengeschichte als Geschichte der Auslegung der Heiligen Schrift* [Church History as the History of the Exegesis of Scripture], Tubingen, 1947. See especially p. 24.) The church is to be open at this point, to ask and to hear. What about this praise out of the depths, what about the praise of God in any case?

The question concerning the praise of God has yet another side, which is posed for the church in a wider horizon by the liturgical movement, in interconfessional contacts and discussions. It is the whole question of cult. Both questions, that of the praise of God in the trials of the church and that of the praise of God in the "liturgy," have encountered each other in a strange way in recent German church history. In part they run along beside each other, and in part they are remarkably intertwined with each other.

The great number of questions that are here only alluded to are to be attacked exegetically at one point: What is the praise of God in the Psalms?

1a. "Forensic" is used here in the simple meaning, "public, occurring in public."

Their proper "Yes" to God, which they have in common in contrast to that which is today historically powerful, the existential (in the pregnant meaning of the word) "No" to God, is not primarily to be found where someone says something about God or his relationship to God, but where he turns to God.

In the introductory paragraphs of his *Old Testament Theology*, L. Köhler says of God's being, "The deeper one descends through the centuries into the breadth of the Old Testament writings, the louder the praise and laud of God can be heard. But they are not lacking even in the oldest pages, and each act of praise is a confession of the ever-present sentence—that God is" (pp. 1 ff.).

Today our history bids us inquire about it anew. The following undertaking which investigates the praise of God in the Psalms is intended to help in this inquiry.

Preface to the Second Edition

Since the book is out of print and there is still demand for it, it is now appearing, thanks to the friendly willingness of the publisher, essentially unaltered in a second edition. A lack of time prevents me from undertaking now a revision that would take into consideration the literature that has since appeared (especially the Psalm commentary of H.-J. Kraus, which was published in the interim), or to deal with the objections which have been raised. I would not need to change anything on the essential lines which the work follows. The objection has repeatedly been raised that the designations "declarative" and "descriptive" Psalms of praise (instead of "song of thanks" and "hymn") are too complicated. I readily admit this, but so far no terms have been suggested to me that are simpler or more accurate. I am not concerned with the designations as such; the traditional ones may simply continue to be used. My essential concern is to make clear through these terms that they are both categories of the praise of God, but that they are to be clearly distinguished from each other as different ways of praising God. I have found wide agreement that what takes place in the declarative Psalms of praise cannot be unambiguously reproduced with our word "thank." If F. Mand ("Die Eigenständigkeit der Danklieder als Bekenntnislieder," *ZAW*, 1958, pp. 185-199) wants to take the songs of thanks as "songs of confession," I will agree with him that the Hebrew *hōdāh* contains the element of confession. I once suggested that one could say confessional praise instead of declarative. Nevertheless, because of the entirely different sound of our words "confess" and "confession," it must be clearly expressed that *hōdāh* in any case contains that element which we can reproduce only with "laud," "praise."

To be sure, the group of Psalms that I have brought together

9

as "descriptive Psalms of praise" have throughout that characteristic that is meant by this designation and are thereby clearly distinguished from the "declarative"; still there is need for a more
exact differentiation (according to an oral suggestion from R.
Rendtorff). In this area further work has been done on individual
Psalms in the interim. An exact grouping of these Psalms, which
would take into consideration both their particular function for
worship and the elements of tradition which are recognizable in
them, has not yet been made. What has been said in my work of
this whole group of Psalms of praise was intended to bring out
only a few lines which are important for their exegesis, but it is
not adequate for the exact determination of the individual
groups and types. Now as before, I regard the way in which this
whole complex of Psalms of praise is throughout determined by
the polarity of the majesty and the condescension of God as the
essential matter. Illustrations of this can be freely multiplied
from Second Isaiah, Job, and many individual passages.

The literature which has appeared in the meantime in the
treatment of this research cannot be cited in detail. Rather
reference should be made to the bibliography in the Psalm
commentary of H.-J. Kraus, which appeared in 1960 (*Biblischer
Kommentar*, Neukirchen, Vols. 1 and 2). This material is collected at the end of the introduction, and then is also found in
connection with the various Psalms. In addition, reference should
be made to the very valuable collection by J. J. Stamm, "Ein
Vierteljahrhundert Psalmenforschung" (*ThR*, NF 23, 1955, pp.
1-68).

C. Westermann
February, 1961

Preface to the 1977 German Edition

Since my two larger works on the Psalms are out of print (*Das Loben Gottes in den Psalmen*, 1954, 1968; and "Struktur und Geschichte der Klage im Alten Testament," *ZAW* 66, 1954, 44–80, reprinted in *ThB* 24, 1964, 266–305), they are presented here once again together with two additional works on the Psalms which are also no longer available, "Vergegenwärtigung der Geschichte in den Psalmen" and "Zur Sammlung des Psalters" (*ThB* 24, 1964, 300–335 and 336–343). I wish to thank the publishing house of Vandenhoeck & Ruprecht for being prepared to undertake this new printing.

In my years of work on the Old Testament, particularly on the Psalms, it has become increasingly clear to me that the literary categories of Psalms of lament and Psalms of praise are not only two distinct categories among others, but that they are the literary forms which characterize the Psalter as a whole, related as they are as polar opposites. Thus juxtaposed, they tend to encompass the whole of human existence, its development from birth and its movement toward death. Praise of God gives voice to the joy of existence ("The living, the living, he thanks thee, as I do this day," Isa. 38:19); lamentation gives voice to sorrow. As the language of joy and the language of suffering, praise and lament belong together as expressions of human existence before God. As such, praise of God and lament alike run through the entire Old Testament, from primordial history to apocalyptic. The Psalms of praise and the Psalms of lament, shaped by corporate worship, form the center of a very much broader, even a very much richer body of texts that include the words of lament and the words of the praise of God as they grew out of the suffering and joy of everyday life.

For us, in the course of a long tradition, the polarity of lament and praise have been replaced by that of petition and thanksgiving. But through the upheavals of the decades that lie behind us, we have grown to understand why the elementary polarity of lament and praise is the decisive one in the Psalms of the ancient people of God. In the Preface to the first edition of *The Praise of God in the Psalms,* I drew attention to the fact that during the church struggle the praise of God was rediscovered. I would now add that in the great catastrophies of our time, for those who suffer, the lament quite of itself has again appeared in its positive and necessary function, as is particularly evidenced by the plethora of witnesses from the younger churches.

For the Psalms of praise I have suggested the designations "declarative" and "descriptive Psalms of praise" instead of the usual "Psalms of thanksgiving" and "hymns." This was done in part so that the terms themselves might help clarify the polarity of lament and praise which is determinative of the whole Psalter.

In the essay "The 'Re-presentation' of History in the Psalms" I have endeavoured to show how in ancient Israel the consciousness of history and the understanding of history grew directly out of Israel's relationship with God. I have also attempted to show, from brief linguistic forms like the vow of praise to the great historical summaries, that both the experience and the perception of the contingency of historical events were at the same time the experience and the perception of something going on between God and man.

The essay entitled "The Formation of the Psalter" presents something I came to recognize in my biblical studies with students: in the structure of the Psalter, many more interconnections are to be found among them than is commonly assumed in Introductions to the Psalms.

The chapters of this volume have been left in their original form. The bibliography lists literature used at the time. In an addendum I have cited a number of the most important recent works containing comprehensive bibliographies.

This new edition of my studies on the Psalms is accompanied by the wish that they may be of help in better understanding the Psalms in terms of their world and in letting them speak anew in our world.

Claus Westermann

BOOK ONE

THE
PRAISE
OF GOD
IN THE
PSALMS

Translated by Keith R. Crim

PART ONE

The Categories of the Psalms

What does it mean in the Psalms to "praise God"? An exhaustive answer to this question cannot be found simply through an investigation of the vocabulary of praise as it occurs in the Psalms.[2]

Indeed, this investigation must take second place. The words for praise are to be found to an astonishing degree, more so than any other verb in the Bible, in the imperative (including the voluntative, cohortative, and jussive). The greatest part of this vocabulary, therefore, exhorts to praise.[3]

Praise takes place in words. This can occur in two ways. A teacher who wants to praise a pupil can say to him, "I praise you!" But we immediately feel that this is not the real way to praise. It sounds wooden, stiff, pedantic. But the teacher can also say, "That was well done!" This is the real way to praise (of course there are many possible forms it may take). In that sentence, then, praise *occurs*.

This real way of praising, in words or sentences that do not even contain the word "praise," is also present in the Psalms. We thus are confronted with the question, which are these words or sentences in the Psalms in which God is praised? What do *they* say to us about the praise of God in the Psalms?

This is the question concerning the categories in the Psalms: In which Psalms is God praised? Only in recent times has re-

2. This must be reserved for special investigation.
3. The expressions "I praise . . ." or "we praise . . .," which are frequent in our liturgies and hymns, are not encountered in the O.T. prior to the work of the Chronicler.

15

search into the categories become a serious undertaking. At the end of this development stands Gunkel's *Einleitung in die Psalmen*, which, after his death, was completed and published by Begrich (Göttingen, 1933). In this book the results of the form-critical work on the Psalms are united in a masterful whole, which enables us to see all the comprehensive range of the structure of the Psalms in their various categories, from the basic forms to the most distant branches, which grow out of the given elements of form into ever new variations.

According to Gunkel (pp. 27, 30), the major categories of the Psalms are the following:

Hymns
Laments of the people
Laments of the individual
Songs of thanksgiving of the individual
"Spiritual poems" ("the real treasure of the Psalter").

In addition there are smaller categories, including the "songs of thanksgiving of Israel" and the "Torah."

With this may be compared Kittel's "Introduction" (D. R. Kittel, *Die Psalmen*, 1929); he was already acquainted with and approved of Gunkel's earlier work:

The hymn (song of praise)
The prayer of thanksgiving
The prayer of petition
The didactic poem
The spiritual song (as highpoint of the poetry of the Psalms).

The distribution is, apart from minor differences, identical. Some typical examples of earlier attempts to divide the Psalms into classes are given in Gunkel's work ("Introduction," pp. 8 f.).

In Gunkel, as also in Kittel, Hempel, and others, the "hymn," the Psalm of praise, stands in the first position. This is not entirely obvious. At first glance the Psalms of petition are certainly more numerous (Kittel: "prayer petitions"; Gunkel: "laments of the people," and "of the individual"). Gunkel occasionally refers to the great significance which the "hymn" apparently had (pp. 83, 433: the hymns are "the most important part of the collection"). This is seen especially in that this category had the greatest influence on other—actually on *all* other—categories, although Gunkel does not specifically establish this. Later it must be asked whether this formulation entirely fits the facts. In any case Gunkel asserts again and again throughout his entire work that the "hymnodic" (can one say this?), hymnodic elements, small hymns, are encountered everywhere in the other categories. This wide-reaching influence cannot be established for any other category. Thus here the priority of the "hymn" over all other categories is clear. In the survey it stands with good cause in the first place.

Now, however, the unbiased reader of Gunkel's "Introduction" notices a remarkable irregularity. Why is it that songs of thanksgiving are not divided into those of the people and those of the individual as the laments are? Gunkel has a category "songs of thanksgiving of Israel" (pp. 64, 265, 315) and includes it among his "smaller categories" (p. 315, no. 28). On page 315 he explains their small number by the tendency of the human heart, which, after deliverance, forgets to thank the helper.[4]

The same reason also explains to him why the songs of thanksgiving of the individual are so much fewer in number than the laments (p. 235). The remark, however, that the "songs of thanks of Israel" are related to the hymns, leads in another direction. Indeed, "such songs of thanks and hymns merge into one another: Pss. 65:1-8; 66:5-12; 67; 75" (p. 64). This agrees with the presentation of the "songs of thanks of Israel" individually and as a special group among the enumeration of the hymns, p. 32. So Gunkel too really counts them as hymns.

In the same way, the boundary between the "songs of thanksgiving of the individual" and the hymns is a fluid one. The definition on page 272, "To sing a song of thanks means to proclaim

4. Essentially the same reason is given by Balla, *Das Ich der Psalmen*, Göttingen, 1912, p. 66, and is taken up by Joh. Döller, *Das Gebet im Alten Testamente*, Wien, 1914, p. 51.

Yahweh's grace before all the peoples," defines, as will become clear, precisely not a song of thanksgiving, but a hymn! Gunkel deals explicitly with the mixture of style with that of the hymn on pages 272-274. The remark on page 276 is decisive: "The difference is that the songs of thanks shout for joy (note this verb!) over the specific deed which God has just done for the one giving thanks, while the hymns sing the great deeds and the majestic attributes of God in general" (cf. p. 83).

Does not this observation say quite clearly that there exists between hymn and song of thanksgiving really *no* difference of type, or category, and the song of thanks, of the individual and of the people, is really another type of hymn? The result is then, that in the Psalter there are two dominant categories, the hymn (including the Psalm of thanks) and the lament.[5]

5. This comes very close to an old division of the Psalms represented by Hupfeld's work (Hupfeld[2]-Riehm, *Psalmen* I[2], pp. 3 ff.: songs of praise and thanks, songs of lament and petition, didactic songs).

Merely in order to present material for reflection, I will here show at a few points that Gunkel has not succeeded in clearly separating the two categories from each other.

The real meaning of the hymn is most clearly expressed on p. 70: "The hymn is sung for God alone." Similarly on pp. 71, 72, 39, 41, etc. The meaning of the hymn is lauding, praising, glorifying God. In the context where Gunkel recalled the biblical term *tehillāh* (pp. 58 f.), he himself said once, "song of praise." And to be sure, in a song of praise it is a matter of "the whole fullness of the majesty of God," p. 41. The difference between hymn and song of thanks is described well and clearly on p. 276. (Cf. the last quotation before this note.)

According to this the two categories are clearly designated and distinctly separated from each other. The "song of thanks" refers to a specific, unique act of God that has just been experienced by the singer; the "hymn," to "the great deeds and glorious attributes *in general.*" The two categories are distinguished, not by the difference of the predicates but by the objects. It is not a question in them of different forms of speech, as asking and giving thanks are different, but the difference lies in that which is spoken of. In any case it is thus clear that "hymn" and "lament" are to be distinguished from each other in a different way than are "hymn" and "song of thanks."

The designations of the categories, however, give the impression that they are intended to distinguish here and there the way of speaking. Here it should be asked further, what then is the difference between "praising" and "giving thanks," and what do they have in common? But this question does not permit the term "hymn" to appear. In reality, Gunkel's way of speaking is determined generally not by that good and clear distinction, but by the fiction of a "hymnodic" expression which is differentiated from giving thanks. Here the hymn is raised to a higher plane. It belongs to the hours of pious solemnity; again and again the word "mood" was used (pp. 34, 68, 83, 178, 243, 276, 280, etc.), or "inspiration" (pp. 37, 48, 70, etc.), or "awe and reverence" (p. 75). All these modern concepts are contained *in* the vocabulary of praise. All these things exist for the men of the Old Testament only in this total turning of man to God. The vocabulary and the phrases of the praise of God are still strong enough to express this for him. But here Gunkel became involved in insolvable difficulties.

On pp. 79 and 84 the definition of "song of thanks" serves almost word for word

But just what is a hymn? In what realm does it belong? There are three possible answers to this question: It is a literary unit, or a cultic unit, or a mode of prayer.

In the various realms and phases of research that are concerned with the "hymn," one of these answers is always tacitly presupposed, without a real clarification having been reached. In Heiler's great work[6] the hymn is one of the types, or main forms, of prayer. In this the literary hymn is understood as a development of the priestly cultic hymn, which was in turn preceded by the "primitive song of prayer." (It is significant that the concept "hymn" is avoided for this first step; apparently this means that only the song of prayer that has developed into a cultic or literary stage can be called a hymn!)

In literary investigations, the hymn is generally understood as primarily a literary form, as, for example, Hempel considers it.[7]

In Gunkel's introduction the literary and the cultic designation of the hymn are brought together. The hymn, as it is found in the sources, is first of all a literary document, and to this extent the term "hymn" designates a literary category. This category,

---

as that of a hymn. On p. 79 Exod. 15:21 is dealt with among other passages. On what grounds is this called a hymn? It corresponds exactly to his own definition of a song of thanks, which had just been cited. To be more exact, Exod. 15:21 belongs under the correct definition of a song of thanks of the people, p. 316, which agrees in the important particulars with the definition on p. 276. (I can only imagine that he let himself be misled through the introductory word *šírū*, which is really the introduction of a "hymn." But the song also has been transmitted with another introduction, Exod. 15:1, "I will sing." [LXX reads, "Let us sing."])

At the beginning Gunkel said that the category could be recognized most clearly by the introduction (p. 25), but according to p. 83 the hymn and the song of thanks generally agree in the introduction and in the conclusion. (This is said more sharply on p. 267.) This confusion could have been avoided if Gunkel had maintained the distinction, according to which the two types can be clearly distinguished in the main part of the song. The "song of thanks" reports one specific action of God, and the "hymn" praises God's activity and his being for us in their fullness. In other respects Gunkel's assertion is only partially valid in the introduction, and in the conclusion only in rare and exceptional cases.

In other places where Gunkel spoke of the relationship of hymn and song of thanks to one another, the same thing happened. He spoke almost only of what they have in common. "Song of thanks and hymn have the same rules of form" (p. 251). He spoke often of their agreement in form (pp. 267, 274, 275, 276), and on p. 285 said the same thing of the Babylonian psalms. (1 Sam. 2 is called a song of thanks on p. 5, and on p. 32 it is included among the hymns.) But he also said that hymn and song of thanks agree in their basic mood (pp. 275, 267, 276). They are related to each other, p. 42, and they merge with each other, p. 64.

6. Fr. Heiler, *Das Gebet*, fifth edition, 1923.
7. "Die althebräische Literatur," Potsdam, 1930, pp. 30 ff.

however, does not have its real position in literature. Gunkel goes behind the literary stage and looks for the "Sitz-im-Leben": "What then was the Sitz-im-Leben of the Psalms? Judaism made use of them in the cult, as the term *tehillīm*, i.e., hymns, shows. The Babylonian psalms belong together with certain cultic practices. . . . Thus we may venture the supposition that they were originally derived from the Israelite cult." What is said here in the beginning of the Psalms in general, Gunkel said specifically for the hymns, p. 59, and for the other categories, pp. 175, 181, 182, 117, 260. Mowinckel then carried the cultic interpretation of the Psalms far beyond this approach of Gunkel's in a comprehensive investigation of the cultic bases of the Old Testament Psalms in their environment.[8]

This became the starting point for a new direction in research that explained not only the Psalms out of the cult, but also in addition vast areas of the Old Testament writings. For the Psalms, reference should be made on the one hand to Aage Bentzen's work (see the bibliography) for the development of this line of research in Scandanavia, and on the other hand to A. Weiser's introduction to his exposition of the Psalms in the new Göttingen commentary series as a representative example.[9]

This whole line of research has taken a road that has as good as forsaken the original question that was raised by Gunkel. In the foreground there now appeared the question concerning the cultic myth or the cultic ideology which generally stood behind the texts which were explained in terms of the cult. In contrast to Gunkel, who sought to grasp each of the Psalm categories in its peculiar character and its many-sided existence, a tendency became dominant which tried to fit everything into the same mold. It began with Mowinckel, who attributed about a third of all the Psalms (of the greatest variety of categories) to the en-

8. S. Mowinckel, *Psalmenstudien*, I-VI, Kristiania, Schriften der Wissenschaftsgellschaft, Histor.-philos. Klasse, 1921-1924. Cf. now S. Mowinckel, *The Psalms in Israel's Worship*, tr. D. R. Ap-Thomas, Oxford, 1962 (2 vols.).

9. An example of the cultic explanation of a complex from the historical books is to be found in Pedersen, *Israel, Its Life and Culture*, III-IV, London, 1940, Appendix I, pp. 728-737, where the account of the exodus from Egypt is explained as the historicizing of a cultic legend. An example of the invasion of the prophetic books by this explanation is Engnell, *The Call of Isaiah*, 1949, a study in which the author seeks to explain the call of Isaiah in terms of purely cultic elements. For further literature, see the surveys mentioned in the bibliography.

thronement festival which he discovered. And in Bentzen's area
of research it led to the extreme results, wherein on the one
hand practically all Psalms became royal Psalms, and on the
other hand fundamental significance was ascribed to a cultic pattern which was held to be valid for the whole of the ancient
East, and to be widely determinative for Israel's Psalms. The
same tendency, moreover, is to be seen at work in milder form
in Weiser's introduction to *The Psalms,* when he observes "that
the cult of the covenant festival is to be assumed as the Sitz-im-
Leben of the vast majority of the individual Psalms and their
categories" (p. 18), and when he regards as the central point of
this covenant festival the dramatic presentation of the theophany, reflexes of which are to be found in a large number of the
Psalms.

This whole tendency to explain as many as possible or even
all of the Psalms either by the "ideology" of a specific (and only
just discovered) festival, by a cultic schema, or by the connection
of a basic myth with a specific ritual (Hooke), seems to me, in
spite of all the effort that has been expended on it in the last
thirty years, to have produced meager results for the understanding of the individual Psalms. The concept "cult," which
is basic for all the branches of this line of research, became in
the process more limitless and confused. It is high time finally
to ask soberly what is regarded as cult in the Old Testament
and what the Old Testament says about cult. It will then be
impossible to avoid the fact that in the Old Testament there is
no absolute, timeless entity called "cult," but that worship in
Israel, in its indissolvable connection with the history of God's
dealings with his people, developed gradually in all its various
relationships, those of place, of time, of personnel, and of in-
strumentality, and that therefore the categories of the Psalms
can be seen only in connection with this history. All the work
on the Psalms along the lines which Mowinckel indicated cannot excuse us from taking up again the task set for us by Gunkel
of research into the individual Psalm categories in their development and in the history of their various component parts.

It is impressive to observe in Gunkel's work the way in which the texts of the Old Testament resist with a strength of their own our occidental concepts, which are the products of entirely different situations. For there, where Gunkel inquires into the origins of the hymn which has its place in the cult, this concept and this definition both fail him. Heiler also avoided the name "hymn" for the earliest stage; he spoke there of a "prayer song." In reality it is not a question here of a literary or of a cultic hymn. Rather it becomes clear what the hymn is in its original significance: praise of God.

On p. 89, in a section that begins with the assertion that hymnody grew out of worship, Gunkel gave as three of the oldest examples: the Song of Miriam, the Song of Deborah, and the Song of the Seraphim in Isaiah 6. No one of these three can be called cultic in the strict sense. The Song of Miriam and the Song of Deborah (the latter belongs to the special category of songs of victory) show, rather, with unmistakable clarity what the Sitz-im-Leben of the hymn is: the experience of God's intervention in history. God has acted; he has helped his people. Now praise *must* be sung to him.

Isaiah 6:3 is also no cultic song in the strict sense, but it is nevertheless nearer to what is called cult. In what way is it different from the other two examples? The difference is clear and almost leaps out at the reader: there it is a specific, single intervention of God in history which calls forth praise; here in Isaiah 6:3 it is God in the fullness of his being and his dealings with the world. Those two have the structure, "Yahweh has done," and this, "Yahweh is."

Here Gunkel, without realizing it, placed side by side the two basic types of the Psalm of praise in their earliest and simplest forms: the declarative and the descriptive Psalm of praise. They have in common the essential fact that in them God is praised. There he is praised for a specific, unique intervention, and here for the fullness of his being and activity.[10]

It is already clear in these two examples that the descriptive

10. This is precisely the distinction which Gunkel makes on p. 276 between a hymn and a Psalm of thanks. See above.

Psalm of praise has a clearer affinity to that which is really cultic than the declarative does. The latter very clearly has its location "out there," in the midst of history, yes, while still on the battle-field—in the hour and the place where God has acted. It might be said that both were sung in a service of worship which was held after the battle, but it is obvious that such a service of worship has a different character from that which shines through Isa. 6:3. If these are both called "cultic," then this distinction is erased and the concept of the cultic, which was intended to include both, is already unusable from the start.

At the end of the same section, p. 89, Gunkel assumed "that Israel learned the art of hymnody as it gradually came to be at home in Canaan." After the three above-mentioned examples this sentence sounds very strange. In order to utter the words in Exod. 15:21 or Isa. 6:3 is it necessary to be instructed by another nation? Apparently Gunkel means here not these words but the great songs of praise, as for example, Judg. 5. It is certainly to be assumed that they were influenced by Babylon and Egypt, probably by way of Canaan.[11]

But in such statements the decisive element has been over-looked. It is not necessary to study how to praise God. The fact here is that a great deal depends on the terminology. Hymns can be learned. When this word is used one almost inevitably thinks of a fine, cultivated, artistic creation with harmony and euphony, that is, of a literary unit. Is that, however, what either of these two examples is intended to be? Is it not actually in-admissible to designate such a single, short sentence by the liter-ary term "hymn"? It is intended to be praise of God and nothing more. And the fact that the praise of God is something that can-not be learned is certainly an essential feature of this praise. To a certain degree the form that is given to the words can be taken over and learned, but the simple act of praise that can be comprehended in a single sentence would lose its genuineness and its significance if it were borrowed.

11. Gunkel's surmise was validated in relation to the Song of Deborah by the dis-coveries at Ras Shamra. Cf. N. H. Snaith in *The O.T. and Modern Study,* p. 94. Additional literature is listed there.

In another place Gunkel too sees that. Where he speaks of the Psalms, not as literary or cultic creations, but as prayers, he does not recognize such a literary or cultic dependence. On p. 261 Gunkel says of the question of the dependence of the Israelite Psalms on the Babylonian psalms, which agree with them so astonishingly, "Should we believe that before the time of the Babylonian influence in Canaan no one prayed to God amid the exigencies of life? Everywhere where a man raises his hands in prayer, the same component parts of prayer and the same sequence of these components appear. . . . Thus regarded, the relationship rests . . . on the peculiar nature of prayer as such."

Is that, however, not also valid for lament and petition? On pp. 282 f. Gunkel speaks of the relationship of the songs of thanks to the laments and says they "correspond to one another like the shells of a mussel," and after he has developed that, on p. 284 he says, "In the alternation between lament and song of thanks there unrolls the whole life of the pious." With this may be compared p. 181, ". . . they transport us into the midst of life, but not into the service of worship."

In these two sentences, which are astonishing in the light of Gunkel's basic thesis, recognition begins to dawn that somehow the observation that the life situation of the Psalms is the cult really cannot be right. For that which really, in the last analysis, occurs in the Psalms is prayer. Gunkel himself sees that here. There is a good reason why this recognition to some extent appears only in an occasional flash and then disappears again. What takes place in these Psalms as men turn to God is in essence something different from what we of the present day name prayer (thus Gunkel p. 47). It must be conceded that Gunkel was right in this. That which he designates as "hymn" somehow does not fit into our general concept of "prayer," for our concept of prayer is actually determined in its essentials by thanks and petitions. Does, however, Gunkel's statement which was just quoted, fit for the Psalms or for the entire O.T., where the whole life of the pious is passed in the alternation of songs of lament and of thanks? If so comprehensive a statement may be attempted, would it not be truer to the O.T. to say, between lament and *praise?* This would mean then that precisely in the place of our contrast of petition and thanks there stands in the O.T. the contrast of lament (supplication) and praise.

Therefore we must inquire into the relationship of thanks and of praise to each other.

PRAISE AND THANKSGIVING

The fact that there is no word for "to thank" in Hebrew has never been properly evaluated. The ignoring of this fact can be explained only in that we live so unquestioningly in the rhythm between the poles of thanks and request, of "please!" and "thank you!", and the thought does not occur to anyone that these concepts are *not* common to all mankind, have *not* always been present as a matter of course, do *not* belong to the presuppositions of human intercourse nor to those of the contrast of God and man. We are compelled to imagine a world in which petition plays a thoroughly essential and noteworthy role, but where the opposite role of petition is not primarily thanks but praise. And this praise is a stronger, more lively, broader concept which includes our "thanks" in it. Thanking is here included entirely within praise.

Perhaps it will be easier to understand this if we remind ourselves that even today none of our children learns on his own to express thanks. He has to be told a hundred times, "Say thank you!", and he still does not say it without being reminded. In addition, where the polish of good upbringing disappears, the expression of thanks soon falls by the wayside. In male society, the harder the life is, the less expression of thanks there is. I have established this point again and again in the war and as a prisoner. Even under the worst circumstances someone will always beg a cigarette, but he very quickly forgets to say thank you.

At the basis of this there is a linguistic process that has long been known, but which has a much greater significance than has generally been assumed. In primitive languages all the force and intensity of linguistic formations is found in concrete expressions. In the African languages there is an amazingly large number of verbs for the way a man walks, and they represent the many nuances of meaning in walking. On the other hand our so-called abstract words are here essentially more complex, for the differentiation is secondary. For example, "good" and "beautiful" have not been differentiated in טוב, and depending on the context it can mean either. There are, however, other passages where the meaning should not be differentiated (as in Gen. 1). The same unity is still to be found today in the Russian хороший. In our modern languages there are whole lists of words for which there is, in Hebrew for example, no single corresponding word (for example, "modest"). And among these is "to thank." This word developed from a secondary differentiation of meaning, and what we mean by it was once contained in a verb that appears to us as complex. This is not hard to understand. A glance at our languages shows at once that this verb is not a primary formation. The German word is a variant of the verb *denken* (to think), and so is the English. In Latin it is a nominal formation, and in Greek a denominative from the corresponding noun (*gratia-χάρις*), which basically has a different meaning. At this point the Russian language is again interesting, where there is still used to express thanks a word that properly means "to give honor," благодарить. These references are enough to show that "to thank" is clearly a secondary formation in many languages. (I know of no language in which "to thank" has its own root.) It would appear then that it became an independent verb by a later development out of a more complex verb.[12]

In the Old Testament this differentiation has not yet taken place, and there is as yet no verb that means only "to thank." *Hōdāh*, which is usually translated as "to thank," is not used in the Old Testament a single time for an expression of thanks

---

12. H. Schurtz, *Urgeschichte der Kultur*, Leipzig-Wien, 1900, p. 186, refers to the primitive languages in which there is no word for "to thank." This is cited by Heiler, p. 44, where we read further, "This reminds one of the rich vocabulary of the Rigveda in which there is no word for thank."

between men. Thus it is clear from the start that this *hōdāh* cannot be equated with our "to thank," which can be directed equally to God or to man. In those places in the O.T. where our "thank" as something taking place between men is most clearly found, the verb used is *bērēk*, which does not have the primary meaning of "praise" but means "bless."[13]

In view of these facts, it is clear that the O.T. does not have our independent concept of thanks. The expression of thanks to God is included in praise, *it is a way of praising*.[14]

Thus Wendel in his investigation of lay prayer in Israel contrasts the prayer of petition or lament not with the prayer of thanks, but with the prayer of praise (p. 170).

Those elements which characterize modern thanks, now independent of praise, may be characterized briefly.

1. In praise the one being praised is elevated *(magnificare)*; in thanks the one thanked remains in his place.

2. In praise I am directed entirely toward the one whom I praise, and this means, of necessity, in that moment a looking away from myself. In thanks I am expressing *my* thanks.

3. Freedom and spontaneity belong to the essence of praise; giving thanks can become a duty.

4. Praise has a forum and always occurs in a group; giving thanks is private, for it need concern no one except the one thanking and the one being thanked.

5. Praise is essentially joyful; giving thanks can take on the character of something required. Praise can never, but thanks must often, be commanded.

6. The most important verbal mark of difference is that thanking occurs in the speaking of the words, "thank you," or in shortened form, "thanks"; genuine, spontaneous praise occurs

13. Examples are Deut. 24:13; 2 Sam. 14:22; Job 31:20; Neh. 11:2. The falling down of one person before another can have the meaning of thanks: Gen. 23:7, 12; 2 Sam. 9:8; 14:22; 16:4; 1 Kings 1:31; Ruth 2:10. Before God: Gen. 24:26, 48, 52; 47:31 (?); Exod. 4:31; Judg. 7:15.
14. B. Jacob, "Beitrage zu einer Einl. in die Ps.," *ZAW* 17, pp. 263-279. P. 276, "Finally it is very questionable whether *tōdāh* ever means thanks, but rather it always means praise, recognition, confession." According to Jacob, a proof for this is to be seen in that Modern Hebrew felt required to form a special word for "thanks": הוֹדָיָה or הוֹדָאָה. So also Quell, *op. cit.*, p. 94, note 3: "There is no proof that in the Old Testament *tōdāh* meant thanks; cf. LXX αἴνεσις."

in a sentence in which the one being praised is the subject, "thou hast done," or "thou art . . ."[15]

What was it that led to this differentiation of thanks from praise? Thanking presupposes that the community is no longer primary and no longer self-evident. It presupposes that the community is no longer prior to the individual. The differentiation of thanks from praise presupposes a certain development of individualism. In the giving and receiving of thanks, the man who has become an individual must continually be assured of community. It would therefore be foolish, on the basis of the late differentiation of thanks or of the fact that there is no single word for it in the O.T., to draw the conclusion that in our dealings with one another we might replace thanks by praise. A change, however, takes place in our evaluation of things when it becomes clear that in its essence thanking is something secondary, one way of praising. What makes this word so valuable to modern man is just that element in which it differs from praise or goes beyond it. We speak of "thankfulness," and this is the main thing. Spoken thanks is only an "externality," the expression of the feeling of thankfulness. The important thing is the thankful attitude. All this cannot be expressed by the vocabulary for praise. Surely the main difference lies here. The thankful attitude has its origin in a gift or in a helping or saving deed which someone does for me. It can then be expressed in a great variety of ways, by a word, or by a deed, but the decisive factor is the permanence of the thankful attitude. In primitive thought it is otherwise. For us thankfulness stands in a line; for the primitive man only the first and last points of this line are of interest. Both of these appear more sharply in primitive thought. That is, the beginning and end of what we

15. This distinction between "thanks" and "praise" and the relation of the two words to one another has received very little attention in research. Reference may be made to the work of Frants Buhl, "Über Dankbarkeit im A.T. und die sprach- lichen Ausdrücke dafür," *Baudissin-Festschrift*, Giessen, 1918, pp. 71-82. Here our concept of thanks was the starting point; it was assumed without reservation for the O.T. and passages were cited for reference. The same uncritical attitude toward the concept is seen in a statement of Mowinckel (*Ps. Studien*, II, p. 143), "Deepened and spiritualized, humble thankfulness becomes worship."

call thankfulness are contained in the vow and the performance of the vow.[16]

This occurs from time to time in a relationship; thankfulness, the line between these two points, is something that I have, or that I have in me; it is something that I possess as a feeling or as an attitude. For primitive man an attitude does not exist except in its expression, for man does not exist "in himself," but only in community with other men (the Hebrew *'ādām* means "mankind"). The same holds true for the relationship of man and God. Modern individualistic thought has interpreted the rejection by the prophets and many of the Psalms of specific cultic acts as meaning that it is not a matter of outward works, but of the "attitude of the heart." This interpretation does not have any basis in either the prophets or the Psalms. In the place of sacrifice the Psalms placed praise and obedience, not an attitude, but activity directed toward God. In relation to God, the concept of thankfulness and that of giving thanks are liable to be misunderstood when they are divorced from the concept of praise. The vocabulary of praise never expresses anything like an attitude or a feeling of gratitude. Where a worshiper in the Psalms says, "I will praise the Lord . . . ," he does not mean, "I will be thankful to God," but, "I will respond to him for what he has done for me."[17]

It comes to this, that in the vocabulary of thanks man remains subject, while in the sentences of praise God is subject: "Thou hast done . . . thou art . . . God is . . ."

Thus today when we translate Psalm 118:1 as "O give thanks to the LORD, for he is good; his steadfast love endures for ever!" this sentence must of necessity be understood in a false manner. An uninstructed member of the congregation can scarely understand this in any other sense than that because God is good, and his steadfast love endures for ever, we are called upon to

---

16. This is the reason why the vow at the end of a petition is an essential, inseparable part of the prayer. This is so not only in the O.T., but also in Babylon and in primitive prayers, while in our prayers it is wholly or almost wholly absent.

17. Wendel, *op. cit.*, p. 172: "Thanks as a thankful attitude that is not expressed is unknown to the O.T."

thank him. That is, (a) we should be grateful to him, (b) we should express our thanks for what God has given us: "I thank thee, O God, that thou . . ." This is not what is meant. Where is there to be found in the entire Psalter a prayer of thanks with this type of structure? What there is in the Psalter, however, seems at first to be a minimum, but it strikes deep. With this *hōdū* we are not called to a sentence in which *I* am the subject, but to one in which *God* is subject. There is such a sentence in the same Psalm a few lines later in verse 5. This difference, that in the thanks of the Psalter God is always the subject, but in our thanks almost always "I" or "we" is the subject, can scarcely be overestimated.

The third factor is that all the vocabulary of praise contains a forensic element. This is particularly expressed in the vow of praise, "I will tell of thy name to my brethren; in the midst of the congregation I will praise thee" (Ps. 22:22). That is what we are called on to do in Ps. 118:1. This is a further reason why the translation "give thanks" is false here, for today no one considers this element to be a part of giving thanks. How different it would be, if everywhere, where in our translations of the Psalms we are called on to give thanks, the forensic element were also heard. Then it would be clear that this call, "give thanks . . . ," has been truly heard only by the one, who in addition to having a deep feeling of gratitude in his heart and to thanking God in private, also tells *in public* what God has done for him.

SUMMARY AND CONCLUSIONS

We began with the question, What is a hymn?, and then considered the three possible answers. We have seen from this that it cannot be completely comprehended under any of the three main concepts. It is only secondarily a literary unit, and for the most ancient and very short hymns the concept of a literary unit is not at all appropriate. On the other hand it cannot simply be said that it is cultic, that its Sitz-im-Leben is the service of worship, even though this is certainly true of the great hymns of the postexilic era, for example, Ps. 136. Certainly the Song of Miriam cannot be so described. The general concept "prayer" fits best that which occurs in a hymn, but the caution must be made that our modern concept of prayer cannot be simply applied to the content of those passages in the Psalms. This is conditioned above all by the fact that in the Psalms, as in the O.T. generally, giving thanks is surrounded by praise, is contained within praise, that therefore instead of our contrast of thanks and petition, there stands in the Psalms the contrast of praise and lament (supplication).

It will be then necessary to replace the designations "hymn" and "song of thanks" with other terms for the categories of the Psalms. In view of the present status of Psalm research this demand must be made unconditionally, for it exists quite apart from the results and proposals of this present work. Both these concepts are inadequate. I do not believe it is possible to avoid recognizing this. "Hymn" is determined by form, "song of thanks" (or Psalm of thanks) by content. Hymn is a literary (or cultic) designation; giving thanks is a means of prayer. The designations of the categories as such would not be so important if certain preconceptions were not already contained in them. The inadequacy of the designations of the categories has been an important contributing factor to the failure to let the appropriate categories and their relationship to each other be seen clearly.

Since the essential occurrence in both of these groups of Psalms is the praise of God, I propose to call them both Psalms of praise. The difference between the two groups lies in the fact that the so-called hymn praises God for his actions and his being as a whole (descriptive praise), while the so-called song of thanks praises God for a specific deed, which the one who has been delivered recounts or reports in his song (declarative praise; it could also be called confessional praise).

The term "declarative praise" is simply a reproduction of that which actually lies before us in this group of Psalms. Gunkel too saw this, although he retained the traditional terminology:

". . . the song of thanks of Israel, like the song of thanks of the individual, was originally a report of God's help" *(Einleitung,* p. 318). Declarative praise corresponds to the Hebrew verb *hōdāh.*[18] The other mode of praise, descriptive praise, corresponds to the Hebrew *hillēl.* It does not praise a unique act of God that has just occurred, but summarizes his activity in its fullness and praises God in the totality of his dealings with men and of his being. It does not have, like declarative praise, a specific, unique occasion; it is not a confession of the one saved, but it looks at the "mighty God's great deeds" in all times and in all places and praises him for them all. This designation is also derived from the actual content of this group of Psalms.[19, 20]

18. Cf. H. Grimme, "Der Begriff von hebräischem hōdāh und tōdāh," *ZAW* 58, 1940/1941, pp. 234-240. "The basic meaning is confess; this is to be divided as follows:
(a) confess, i.e., recognize.
(b) confess, i.e., declare, make known."
(That these two meanings originally belonged together is shown by Horst in relation to Josh. 7, "Die Doxologien im Amosbuch," *ZAW* 47, 1929, pp. 45-54: "Doxology and confession thus belong here of necessity to the public, legal act." See also Wendel, *Laiengebet,* p. 164.)
I agree with Grimme's main thesis: the basic meaning of *hōdāh* is to confess, to affirm. Still, it does not seem to correspond to the vocabulary of the O.T. to say with Grimme that in relation to God, confession is primarily a "confession of the existence of Yahweh," to which is added then a "confession of his principle attributes" (can one confess attributes?). A further development would then be the citing of individual passages where these attributes are mentioned (p. 236). In my opinion it can be clearly proven that confession originally had as its object an act of God, just as the confession of sin (Josh. 7 or Ps. 32:5) had as its object an act of man. The strongest proof of this is the fact that *hōdāh* as used in the Psalms originally belonged to declarative praise, not to descriptive. When Grimme himself equates this "confess" with "proclaim" he thereby indirectly confirms what has been said here. In any case proclamation always has as its primary object an occurrence, an event; not, however, being or attributes, which can be called events only when accurate usage has decayed. A later reference of Grimme's is, however, to be noted, in which he says, pp. 239 f., that *hōdāh* often stands in the O.T. in places later taken over by the concept of faith.
19. The distinction between declarative and descriptive praise is seen also outside the Psalter in the Israelite personal names. (Cf. the work of Martin Noth, *Die israelitischen Personennamen,* Stuttgart, 1928.) In the names that express praise the two groups are clearly distinguished: names which report an act of God (or confess an act of God), such as Elnathan, Jochanan, and names which describe God, such as Abram, Tobijah, Achihud. Declarative praise is much more common in names. A more thorough comparison between the praise of God (and the confession of confidence) in names and in the Psalms is needed. As far as I know, there is no motif from the Psalms that is not reflected in personal names also.
20. This distinction between declarative (or confessional) and descriptive praise is also of significance for the history of Christian hymnology. It is not accidental that Luther's songs have for the most part the character of confessional praise. The hymn of the Reformation, "Nun freut euch . . ." ["Dear Christians one and all

In order to see the total picture, let us look at the changes that would result in the categories of the Psalms. All "thou-Psalms," that is, all that speak to God in the second or third person, are governed by the polarity of petition and praise. These are further divided into Psalms of praise and Psalms of petition.

The Psalms of petition may be divided according to subject as follows:

Lament or petition of the people. (LP)
Lament or petition of the individual. (LI)

Here an observation is necessary concerning "petition." Since in the place of our contrast of petition and thanks there is in the Psalms another, that of petition and praise, "petition" must then be understood somewhat differently from our present concept. It would be more accurate to designate the contrast as that of supplication and praise. In "petition" two elements are present which are clearly distinguished in Hebrew: (a) The (transitive) petition for something (šā'al). This petition voices specific requests. A prayer of petition (tautology!) is generally understood as the listing of various requests. There is nothing like this in the Psalms. Occasionally a single request for something (e.g., intercession for the king) is added to a Psalm. There is never a prayer of petition that summarizes various requests: (b) Supplication in time of need (intransitive) is something entirely different (Hebrew hithpallēl).[21] This supplication does not have an object like that of a petition, but is always supplication for salvation. The "object" of supplication is determined by the situation of the suppliant. We might also say that the

---

rejoice . . ."] corresponds to the structure of the declarative Psalm of praise. (See below, p. 110.) Moreover his Christmas hymn, "Vom Himmel hoch . . ." ["From Heaven Above to Earth I Come"] is declarative praise. On the other hand, the hymns of the Enlightenment, insofar as they are praise of God, are almost entirely descriptive praise, usually very reflective, nearer to the Psalms of the Apocrypha than to those of the Psalter; e.g., "Wenn ich, o Schöpfer, deine Macht . . ." (Gellert). The descriptive songs of praise of the Middle Ages, however, are much nearer the canonical Psalms, as for instance the song of Meissner, "Gott ist gewaltig, vielgestaltig . . ." (musical setting of Albert Becker, "Ein neues Lied").
21. The word originally meant "to make intercession."

"object" of this supplication is the lament. Thus lamentation is a necessary part of this supplication. It is not every request for something, but this supplication in time of need, that is the opposite pole of praise.

Thus in the interest of accuracy one should always say "supplication" instead of "petition" in the Psalms. Since, however, our word "petition" includes both concepts it would be very difficult to displace entirely the terms "petition" and "Psalm of petition."* They will therefore be retained with the reservation expressed here. From this point of view the designation "Psalm of lament," which has gained general acceptance in O.T. studies, has a certain justification. The petition which is meant here receives its distinctive character from the lament. Even though the core of all these Psalms, their σκόπος, is not lament but petition (or supplication), the justification of the customary designation "Psalm of lament" cannot be disputed. I shall follow this designation in the abbreviations which I use in this work.

The petitions of the individual constitute by far the largest category in the Psalter. Here however a further classification is necessary; for a large number of petitionary Psalms this designation is no longer accurate, for they are not *merely* lament and petition but petition that has been *heard*. At the end of these heard petitions there is a part that breaks over into declarative praise.

The *Psalms of praise* fall into two groups on the basis of the two different modes of praise (see above p. 31):

Declarative praise (God has acted);
Descriptive praise (God is . . . does) (P).

Of these, only the declarative Psalms of praise may be distinguished by categories:

The declarative Psalm of praise of the people (PP);
The declarative Psalm of praise of the individual (PI).

* Translator's note: "Petition" as a noun and as a verb has been adopted as the translation of the German "Bitte" and "bitten," and "supplication," etc., for the German "Flehen." Although these terms do not reproduce all the connotations of the German original they seem to be more adequate than any others.

In the descriptive Psalm of praise, the praise of the people (or of the congregation) and the praise of the individual are combined. Only a few of these Psalms can be distinguished by subject, and this distinction cannot be made on the basis of categories.

All the "smaller categories" are not to be placed alongside these two great categories, but are to be included in them or can be derived from them. That is to say, in them a motif from one of the two major categories has become independent. (These smaller categories must be omitted from this discussion.)

In this analysis of the Psalms, "category" is primarily neither a literary nor a cultic concept. It is both of these, but only secondarily. This analysis is determined by the two basic modes of speaking to God: praise and petition.

This basic thesis is not derived from the exegesis of the O.T. Psalms alone, but from the larger environment of which they are a part, and out of the study of which the history and distinctive character of the O.T. Psalms become clear. This can be shown first of all by an investigation of the praise of God in the Babylonian-Assyrian psalms.

PART TWO

The Structure of the Babylonian Psalms

The Babylonian psalms have one essential in common with those of the Bible: they speak to God in terms of petition and praise. In Babylon as in Israel, praising God and supplicating him were an essential part of life.

Basic to the Babylonian psalms is a structure in which five major parts may be recognized:[1]

    I. Address[2]
    II. Praise
       (Stummer: "depiction of majesty." Cumming: "ascription of praise.")[3]
    III. Lament[4]
    IV. Petition[5]
    V. Vow of praise[6]

1. This structure was primarily worked out by Stummer, *Sumer.-akkad. Parallelen,* 1922, p. 9. Stummer listed a further element, "self-introduction of the prayer." Subsequently the structure of the Babylonian psalms was further worked out. See especially Falckenstein, "Die Haupttypen der sumer. Gebetsbeschwörung," *LSSt,* NF, 1931, and W. G. Kunstmann, "Die babyl. Gebetsbeschwörung," *LSSt,* NF, 2, 1932, especially p. 7.
2. In reference to the address, cf. Kunstmann's summary, pp. 7 ff., for the category of adjuratory prayers. On p. 68 of the same work there is listed further literature for the investigation of the address to the various gods. Cf. Cumming, *op. cit.,* pp. 56 ff.
3. I have not found a single Babylonian psalm in which praise was entirely lacking (except for fragments). There are however extreme differences in the type and extent of praise. Two extremes are as follows: in a song to Marduk praise consists of only one sentence with two relative clauses (Zimmern A, p. 17): "Mighty Marduk, whose wrath is a deluge, but who is a merciful father to those reconciled to him." On the other hand, the great hymn to Shamash is composed entirely of praise (Zimmern B, 23-27).
4. Pp. 17 ff. For the forms of lament, cf. Kunstmann, *op. cit.,* pp. 17 ff.
5. Examples for the petition: Zimmern A, p. 17; King Mag 27:15 ff., 18; *KM* 27:19 ff.; Z 42; Z 80; Zimmern A, p. 22 ff.; Zimmern B 4; Z 19. Address of praise: Z 20, "I have sacrificed to thee," Z 21. Petition: Zimmern B 17, Z 14 ff.; Zimmern B, p. 19. Cf. Kunstmann, *op. cit.,* p. 25 for further examples.
6. Examples are given by Stummer, *op. cit.,* pp. 103 f., and Kunstmann, *op. cit.,* pp. 39-42.

Naturally this structure does not appear in schematic form in each psalm,[7] and there are a great many variations of it. Nevertheless the order of the various parts is almost always preserved.

Even in these five principal parts the Babylonian psalms correspond with those of the O.T.

1. The most significant distinction is that in the Babylonian psalms these five motifs constitute one psalm. In the O.T., on the other hand, these five motifs are divided among two psalm categories. The caesura comes between the second and the third parts. A division of psalms of petition and praise on the basis of categories is unknown in the Babylonian psalms. Praise of God has here a much broader field than it has in the Psalms of the O.T., but it is primarily introductory and at the same time preparatory for petition. The same is true of the Egyptian psalms.

(a) In the Psalms of lament in the O.T. the lament or petition follows directly after the address, and these are never introduced or anticipated by detailed praise (Neh. 1:5 ff.; 2 Macc. 1:24 ff.). The address is almost never expanded by honor-giving predicates such as are encountered in great number in Babylonian psalms (as many as 36 in one psalm[8]).

(b) Address and praise, that is, parts I and II, constitute in the O.T. an independent Psalm category, that of descriptive praise. At the same time, something entirely new has been added to the Psalms of praise of the O.T.: the imperative exhortation to praise. This imperative call to praise is never encountered in the Babylonian psalms.[9]

7. Ebeling I, p. 18 to Nabu, *KAR* 1, Nr. 25, 23.
   Ebeling I, p. 19 to Marduk, *KAR* I, Nr. 23.
   Ebeling I, p. 44 to Shamash, K 2132, VAT 8242.
   Ebeling I, pp. 70-72 to ? (fragment), *KAR* III, 129.
   Ebeling II, p. 14 to Tamuz, VAT 8261.
   Ebeling II, pp. 17 f. to Tamuz, VAT 10034.
   Ebeling II, p. 37 to Ishtar (Vows of praise, preserved in fragmentary condition).
8. Cumming, *op. cit.*, p. 61. "It was easy to expand indefinitely the invocation from its natural length of four to six lines until the invocation becomes itself hymnal praise of the god." (Sin 5, invocation 23 lines!). See also Begrich, *op. cit.*, p. 233.
9. This fact is mentioned by Stummer, *op. cit.*, p. 26, and Cumming in the conclusion of his work, *op. cit.*, p. 155.

2. Another difference is closely related to this one. In the Babylonian psalms praise of God is almost exclusively descriptive praise. The being of the god and his actions in general are praised. From this Stummer took his term "description of majesty" (*Herrlichkeitsschilderung*). Praise on the basis of a single act of God (declarative praise) is almost entirely absent.

3. That the god whom this praise exalts is one god among others has quite definite consequences.

(a) The emphasis of praise does not lie on what occurs between God and man, but on what occurs among the gods. (Here praise can even pass into mythical accounts, as, for example, "Flute Lament for Adad," Zimmern B, p. 7, or "Ishtar's Elevation to Queen of Heaven," Gressmann, *Texte*, pp. 252 ff.) One might wonder whether mythical accounts did not develop out of praise of the god.

(b) The one praying must keep in mind not only the god to whom he is praying, but the other gods as well. On the one hand, in his praise he must elevate high above the others the god on whom he calls (thus the often extremely exaggerated language of this praise), and on the other hand he must include them in intercessory petition[10] and praise. The intercession of the saints for which one prays in the Roman church has its exact prototype in the intercession of the other gods, which the suppliant of the Babylonian psalms requests. Especially significant is the fact that the praise of the one praying was to be reinforced by the praise of the other gods. For example, "May my god honor thy might, my goddess proclaim thy greatness" (BMS 12, King).[11] One's own petition and praise needed strengthening through an intermediary. In the matter of conjuring, the tendency goes even further; the gods even need their own (divine) priestly conjurer.[12]

4. The relationship of the Babylonian psalms to those of the O.T. becomes especially clear in the vow of praise. In both in-

10. Ebeling I, 7-8: "May the other gods regard him favorably." Ebeling I, 5-6: "Say a good word to Enlil."
11. Conjuration for Shamash, Zimmern 1, p. 15, and Ebeling I, 10-11 for Marduk.
12. Weber, "Dämonenbeschwörungen bei den Babyloniern und Assyrern," p. 7.

stances it is an essential component of prayer.[13] In both it occupies the same position, following the petition (i.e., at the end of the psalm). In form and content the vow of praise in the Babylonian psalms is essentially identical with that of the O.T. For example,

> I will praise and laud thee to the astonishment of later days,
> I will proclaim thy majesty to those who are widely scattered.[14]

In the vow of praise of the Accadian psalms it is quite clear that the opposite pole of petition is not thanks but praise. It is not thanks that is offered but praise, laud, honor, majesty, and service. (Professor Baumgartner has informed me orally that there is in Accadian no differentiated term for "thanks.") As in the Psalms of the O.T., the forensic element is often stressed in those of Babylon. It is a part of praise that others, even many others, hear it.

The vow of praise at the end of the psalm is not merely conclusion. It is more a beginning than a terminus. In it something is promised, something is held in prospect. That which is promised here occurs in Part II, in the ascription of praise.

In the Babylonian psalms there are two developments at the end and at the beginning that say this unambiguously.

(a) In two songs to Ishtar praise follows the vow of praise at the end:

> Among the black-headed ones I will glorify thy deity and thy might.
> Yea, Ishtar is exalted, Ishtar is queen . . . there is none like her . . .

(b) The expansion is more frequently encountered at the beginning. There is a whole group of psalms that begin with clauses that correspond exactly to the vow of praise, but which at the beginning of the psalm can only have the meaning of a

13. Stummer, *op. cit.*, p. 102: ". . . in the Babylonian psalms very frequent, almost regular."
14. K ALL 1 and K 6475.

declaration.[15] It can be shown that these sentences are secondary matter in the introduction. Once an introduction which announces praise of God is followed directly by lament and petition. This introduction then became a stereotyped formula.[16]
A song to Ishtar:

> ... my Princess, above and below
> Thy goodness (?) will I proclaim,
> The splendid Ishtar, in her will I exult,
> Princess, elevated to heaven,
> Ishtar, thou art great!
> Lady Ishtar, thee will I honor,
> Princess, elevated to heaven,
> Goddess ... thou art great.

These two expansions do not introduce any new motif or add any new part. In one case Part II is added to Part V (the beginning to the conclusion), and in the other Part V has been moved to the beginning. Here it can be seen that the sequence of the five motifs is a circle, that is, that Part V is open toward Parts I and II. The vow of praise is to some extent the link between the two main parts, between the lament and petition on the one hand and the praise to god on the other. The vow of praise promises to the god, to whom the suppliant cries out in his need, the praise of his name.

Here a comparison with the Psalms of the O.T. shows that the above-mentioned two main differences between the psalms of Babylon and those of Israel (I. Babylon, *one* main category, praise and petition; Israel, *two* main categories, Psalm of praise and Psalm of petition. II. Babylon, almost only descriptive praise; Israel, declarative and descriptive praise) have the same root. In the Psalms of Israel we often find the two expansions that have been indicated in the Babylonian psalms.

(a) The expansion at the end. In a large number of LI the vow of praise at the end of the Psalm is followed by yet additional praise of God.

15. K 3258, Zimmern B, p. 20, Gressmann, *op. cit.*, p. 267.
16. Gressmann, *op. cit.*, p. 267.

Ps. 13:6: "I will sing to the LORD, because he has dealt bountifully with me."

Ps. 54:7: "For thou hast delivered me from every trouble . . ." Cf. also 51:11 f.; 71:24; 69:33, etc.

When these clauses are compared with the expansions in the two songs of Ishtar, the difference is obvious; there descriptive praise, here declarative praise

(b) The expansion at the beginning. In exact correspondence to the way the Babylonian psalms begin in verbal agreement with the vow of praise at the end, but with the sense of a proclamation at the beginning, a great many of the Psalms of the O.T. begin with the proclamation, "I will praise . . ." or a similar expression. This proclamation, however, never introduces a descriptive Psalm of praise but always a declarative Psalm of praise. (In late extra-canonical psalms this proclamation is also found in descriptive Psalms of praise.)

This means therefore that the circle of five motifs in one psalm was possible in Babylon because the vow of praise is intended to be descriptive praise (at the end) and introduces it (at the beginning). Thereby the praise of God for a specific, unique deed, which is begun at this place in the Psalms of the O.T., is bypassed. A remnant of declarative praise can often be found in the appositional phrases of the address (e.g., "who hears prayer").[17]

In some instances the address is expanded by so many appositional expressions that it becomes itself a psalm of praise. (See Cumming, op. cit., p. 61. The address can be as long as 23 lines!) The declarative psalm of praise presupposes a lapse of time between the supplication in dire need and the reporting of the marvelous help of God that has been experienced. If praise, as in most of the Babylonian psalms, precedes lament and petition

---

17. Further examples are as follows:
"Who destroy evil" (KM 62, 9. Ea, Marduk, Shamash 1a).
"Who bring deliverance" (KM 62, 9. Ea, Marduk, Shamash 1a).
"Who cut the thread of misfortune" (Marduk, Shamash 1a).
"Who causes her words to be heard" (Tasmetu 2, KM 33, 2).
"Who frees the captives" (Nergal 1, KM 287).
"Who intercedes" (Gula 1, Sarpanitum 1, KM 6, 90; 9, 45).
"Who hears prayer" (Shamash 35, KM 59, 5).

it can only be a general, timeless, descriptive praise. This is the basis of the fact that in Babylon declarative praise is so insignificant in comparison with the descriptive that it almost vanishes entirely.

In this way the real difference in the manner of speaking to God in these two settings now becomes completely clear. In both cultures the one praying stands within the circle of petition and praise; in both the turning point is the vow of praise, which leads from petition into praise. The difference lies in the fact that in the Babylonian psalm the emphasis lies entirely on the praise which prepares the way for the petition, and in the Psalms of the O.T. it lies entirely on the praise that looks back on the wonderful help of God in intervening.

In Babylon the psalms primarily praise the one who exists, the god who exists in his world of gods. In Israel they primarily praise the God who acts marvelously by intervening in the history of his people and in the history of the individual member of his people. The gods praised in Babylon have their history among the gods. In Israel's praise from beginning to end the basic theme is the history of God with his people.

Literature on the Babylonian Psalms

Begrich: "Die Vertrauensäusserungen im israelitischen Klagelied des Einzelnen und in seinen babylonischen Gegenstücken," *ZAW* 46, 1928.

Cumming, C. G.: *The Assyrian and Hebrew Hymns of Praise,* 1934.

Driver: *The Psalms in the Light of Babylonian Research.*

Blackmann: "The Psalms in the Light of Egyptian Research" (in Simpson: *The Psalmists),* Oxford, 1926.

Ebeling, E.: *Quellen zur Kenntnis der babylonischen Religion,* 1918.

Ebeling, E.: *Babylonisch-assyrische Texte,* 1933.

Gressmann, H.: *Altorientalische Texte und Bilder zum A.T.,* 1926/27.

Falckenstein, S.: "Die Haupttypen der sumerischen Gebetsbeschwörung," *LSSt,* NF 2, 1931.

Böllenrücher, J.: *Gebete und Hymnen an Nergal,* Leipzig, 1904.

Hehn, J.: *Hymnen und Gebete an Marduk,* Leipzig, 1905.

Kunstmann, W. G.: "Die babylonische Gebetsbeschwörung," *LSSt,* NF 2, 1932.

Stummer, Fr.: *Sumerisch-akkadische Parallelen zum Aufbau alttestamentlicher Psalmen,* Paderborn, 1922.

Weber, O.: "Dämonenbeschwörungen bei den Babyloniern und Assyrern," *Der Alte Orient* VII, 4.

Zimmern, H.: "Babylonische Hymnen und Gebete," *Der Alte Orient* VII, 3 und XIII, 1, 1905 and 1911.

Bahr, H.: *Die babylonischen Busspsalmen und das A.T.*, Leipzig, 1918.

Widengren, G.: *The Accadian and Hebrew Psalms of Lamentation as Religious Documents*, 1937 (not available to me before completion of this work).

Jastrow, M.: *Die Religion Babyloniens und Assyriens*, 3 vols., Giessen, 1905-12.

EXCURSUS: THE PRAISE OF GOD IN THE EGYPTIAN PSALMS

I have taken as my sources here A. Erman, *Die Literatur der alten Ägypter*, Leipzig, 1923, and G. Roeder, *Urkunden zur Religion des alten Ägypten*, Jena, 1915, and in addition, A. M. Blackman, "The Psalms in the Light of Egyptian Research," in Simpson, *The Psalmists*, 1926, and Gressmann, *AOT*.

It will not be possible here to give a comprehensive presentation, but the most important similarities and differences will be pointed out.

The most striking difference between the Egyptian and the Babylonian psalms lies in the astonishing predominance of praise and confidence in those of Egypt. The call to rejoice, but even more the depicting of joy, jubilation, and praise occupy a significant place, while they are rarely encountered in the Babylonian psalms. In correspondence to this there is on the other hand very little of the deep anxiety that stands behind a major part of the Babylonian psalms.

Although similarities and points of contact are present, the differences are the expression of different basic attitudes toward the gods.

When the Egyptian psalms speak to the gods there is a preponderance of self-confident assurance, which pushes lament and supplication into the background in favor of a contemplative or pictorial narration that rejoices in the splendor and beauty of the gods. This great self-assurance is striking. In a very detailed self-justification of the dead before the judge of the dead we read (Roeder, *op. cit.*, pp. 274 ff.): "Lo, I come to thee, filled with righteousness . . ." It is seen also in that we never encounter the expressions so frequent in the Babylonian psalms, "whom I know—do not know," but very often encounter the assurance, "I know him," "I know thee." In the journeys of the dead the knowledge of names plays an important role.

We very seldom encounter laments. In Erman's work there is a detailed lament only in the prayer to Amon, p. 381, over a "year of misery." But this too is more objective description than a true cry of dire need. The distinction of the prayers of the poor from all others is particularly striking. (See Roeder, *op. cit.,* pp. 52-58 f., "Memorials of the Poor.") It is almost only here that we meet true confession of sin, and genuine, strong lamentation. The speaking to God is here much more immediate. The mythical-cultic element almost disappears. Especial reference should be made to the "Prayer of the Penitent Sinner" (Roeder, *op. cit.,* p. 57). Also, Erman, *op. cit.,* p. 380, the lament of a poor man from whom the court demands too much. Both laments, however, occur in prayers which resemble the "heard petitions" of the Psalter. The first is quite certain of being heard, and the major part of the second prayer consists of praise and expressions of confidence. In both the transition is easily recognized. Both times it is introduced, "There one finds, that Amon . . ."

The same feature is noticeable in the prayer of Neb-re, painter in the service of Amon (Erman, *op. cit.,* pp. 383 f. and Gunkel, *Einleitung,* pp. 287 f.). The structure closely approaches that of the declarative praise of the Psalms. After an introductory summary we read as follows:

He wrote hymns to his name,
For his might is so great,
And wrote laments before him,
Before the whole land,
For the sake of Nacht-Amon the painter,
Who was sick and near death,
Who had incurred the wrath of Amon
Because of his cow (?).

At the point where the report of his plight has its proper place, the one praying steps out of his prayer and reports only that during the illness of his son he wrote songs of praise and of lament (or petition?). The one praying is thus not the one who is sick or who has been healed. We find here the sentence so frequent in the psalms, "Thou Amon art he who rescues the one who is in the world of the dead." However, this does not come in the report, but in the introductory confession of confidence. Thus here the reality of the plight has moved in a remarkable way into the background. An immediate, loud, distraught cry to God is nowhere to be found.

This agrees with the observation made concerning the petitions. Petitions for salvation out of a presently threatening need are inconspicuous. There is one petition for a just judgment (p. 379): "Amon, incline thine ear to one who stands alone in judgment, to one who is poor, but whose foe is wealthy." And once, "Come to me, save me in this year of misery!" There is one prayer of confession, p. 379, that sounds, however, more like mere excuses.

The majority of the petitions are for something constant, something which does not arise from acute need:

"That thou wouldest care for me," p. 379.
"That thou wouldest grant me skill in my office," p. 377.
"Send me to Hermopolis, where one can live in comfort!", p. 377.
Petition for the promotion of the teacher, p. 379.

In all these petitions lament is naturally missing. Especially typical is the prayer to Thoth, p. 377, which begins with the petition for transfer to Hermopolis. In the middle of the text these words appear: "Come, save me." This petition for salvation has already become quite stereotyped and can be spoken where there is no question of salvation in the strict sense.

It is quite clear that the petition for salvation was originally in two parts, (a) come to me! and (b) save me! So also pp. 381, 379, 377 (only in the middle of the song).

The confession of confidence and the certainty of being heard are encountered frequently and are expressed forcefully, pp. 377, 379. "Come to me, Re Harakhte . . . ," pp. 380, 381, 383. But it has already been pointed out that this point must not be seen in isolation. The counterbalance to these words of confidence and the certainty of a hearing, *the vow of praise,* is absent. Little can be seen here of the strict way in which in the Babylonian psalms the vow of praise must of necessity follow the petition. Only once does it clearly stand at the end of a petition, but it is there in the form of a petition (p. 377): "Come to me and care for me, I am indeed . . . Let me speak of thy mighty deeds, in whatever land I am; then the people will say, What God does is great. . . ."

In the prayer to Amon, p. 381, it is merely hinted at. There is, however, a clear and detailed witness to it in the memorial of the painter Neb-re, pp. 383 f., and it is by this that we learn of the vow of praise as a fixed form. This makes all the more notable the fact that it is usually missing in prayers.

Praise

1. The relation of praise and petition to each other: In the Babylonian psalms, it is almost always the rule that praise precedes and prepares the way for petition. The same thing is found in the Egyptian psalms, where, while it is not so regular, it still predominates. Thus it is in all three songs to the crowns on p. 35 (even though the relationship of petition to praise is different in each of the three songs). In addition, pp. 184, 185?, 186, 362, 374, 375 (in Songs to the Sun and to Osiris), 379 (in prayers of petition to Re and in prayers to Amon), 381 (in the song to Amon the petition is in the form of an expression of confidence). Two extremes can be seen. In the songs to the morning sun, p. 184, the petition is merely appended at the conclusion, and it is quite indefinite: "Illumine me that I may see thy beauty!" The emphasis is entirely on praise. The song to the sun god, p. 374, is just the opposite. Here the powerful praise of the sun god very clearly has the significance of

preparing for very concrete petitions. "Give thou it (my office) to me again! Lo, I see another occupy it." Here the Egyptian psalm agrees with the Babylonian as over against the biblical. Nowhere in the O.T. is the praise of God used in this manner as the means to an end. A distinction to the Babylonian psalms is that often a word of praise follows the petition (e.g., p. 36, the three songs to the crown, and p. 377, prayer to Thoth).

2. There is, however, a large group of psalms that consist only of an address of praise—praise and the depiction of majesty (Cumming: ascription of praise).

(a) Most of these songs are reminiscent of the epiphany psalms. An actual epiphany is found in the song, pp. 30-32, "The Dead Man Devours the Gods." The appearance of god, its consequences, and its effect are described. The expression here, ". . . when they see him, as he appears," corresponds to the Babylonian "when thou comest forth." The motif is taken up once again at the end, "He it is that rises and rises . . ." In between, the song contains only praise and ascriptions of praise, such as, "His majesty is in heaven, his might is on the horizon," and "He it is who devours men and lives on gods."

Likewise the second crown song, p. 35. "Praise to thee, thou eye of Horus . . . when thou arisest in the Eastern horizon"; p. 183 to Min-Horus, "Praise to thee, Min, in thine appearing . . ."; p. 184 to the morning sun, "Praise to thee who now arisest, and who illuminest the two lands when thou comest forth"; p. 185, to the evening sun, "Praise to thee, when thou goest down, Atum, Harakhte. . . ."

In addition, see also the songs on pp. 187-192, 354, 357, 362, 374, 375.

Now, however, an important change becomes noticeable within these epiphany songs, which must be followed through in a wider area. The early epiphany formula ran, "When thou arisest," "When he appears." Later this form changes to a simple description in a relative clause, e.g., p. 357, the fourth song of the great hymn to Amon. "Thou only king . . . among the gods . . . who arisest in the Eastern horizon and settest on the Western horizon . . . ," or in a main clause, p. 362, a prayer for the king in Tel-Amarna, "Thou arisest in beauty, thou ascendest the horizon of heaven to bring life to all that thou hast made . . . ," and p. 374, to the sun god, "Thou awakest in beauty, thou Horus, who journiest over the heaven."

Here a tendency becomes clear which attracts attention in the comparison of all the Egyptian psalms of praise to those of Babylon, and even more in comparison to the Hebrew. This is quite clearly the descriptive praise of an onlooker.

In addition there is a type of praise that clearly passes into mythical tales: pp. 187-192, a song of praise for Osiris, and pp. 363-373, the "1000 Songs," poems to Thebes and its god. This type is found frequently in the Babylonian psalms.

The other type, however, predominates, that of describing what is observed: p. 375, "Thou splendid and bright . . . thou beautiful sun with glowing light . . . and how mysterious is he . . . thou splendid sun with white light"; p. 374, "Thou awakest in beauty . . . thou child of flame with sparkling beams"; p. 184, "Enlighten me, that I may see thy beauty!"; p. 185, "Thou art beautiful, O Re, all the days!"; p. 186, ". . . how he shines in his crown! . . ."; pp. 193-196, "Thou makest green, thou makest green, O Nile, thou makest green!"; p. 354, "Thy beauty conquers hearts . . ."; p. 357, "The gods shout for joy at thy beauty . . ."; p. 362, "He shouts for joy when he sees thy beauty."

This tendency finds even stronger expression in that a depiction of praise is almost always added to this depiction of glory.

There is also a call to praise, and many songs begin, "Praise to thee!" This corresponds approximately to the Hebrew bārūk! In the Babylonian there is nothing to correspond to this. Examples are: p. 35, second and third crown song, pp. 183, 184, 185, 187, 192, 193, 352, 353, 354 (here also at the end in accordance with the practice of forming a framework), and 378.

This "Praise to thee!" is thus an introductory call to praise in the same place where in the Hebrew descriptive Psalms of praise the call to praise stands in the imperative. Even in the Egyptian there is occasionally an imperative. For example, p. 186, ad-

dressed to the gods: "O ye gods, come and see . . . how splendid
he is in his crown . . . Shout for joy . . . Honor him, magnify
him, offer him praise!"

It may also be addressed to men. At the end of the song of
praise to the Nile, pp. 193-196: "All ye men, exalt the nine gods
and be in awe . . ." Also at the beginning of the declarative
psalm of praise of the painter Neb-re, p. 383: "Let sons and
daughters tell it, great and small; tell it generation after generation, those who have not yet arisen, tell it to the fish in the water
and the birds . . . tell it to him who knows it and to him who
knows it not. Beware of him!" Only the introduction, "Praise to
thee!", had become a fixed form, but alongside it the depicting
of praise had taken a large place. Corresponding to the change
in the epiphany formula there is probably here an earlier form
in which honoring and shouting for joy (especially of the gods,
then of the creation, then of men) were a result of the epiphany.
The first effect of the epiphany is fear and trembling. On p. 30:
". . . the bones of the earth god tremble . . . when they see him
as he appears . . ." Compare above, "Beware of him!" But this
is rare. For the most part only jubilation and praise are depicted.
On p. 35, in the second crown song: ". . . over whose beauty the
nine gods shout for joy, when he arises in the Eastern horizon."
Later the shouting for joy, the praise, the rejoicing, were only
described. This depicting of the honoring and the rejoicing at
the appearance of the gods or over their deeds, such as victory,
creation, preservation, is almost never lacking. On p. 184, the
song to the morning sun reads: "All the Nine praise thee . . . all
mankind rejoices in him, the souls of Heliopolis rejoice in him,
the buffoons honor him. Praise to thee! all that is wild cries together."

Further depictions of praise are found on pp. 185-186. In the
song of praise to Osiris the introductory praise is so permeated
with the depiction of praise that they occur in alternate lines,
but the depiction of praise outweighs actual praise. On p. 192,
song of praise for Osiris, the motif is expanded remarkably,
"Thousands praise thee." The number becomes important!

In several places, e.g., p. 354, the third song to Amon, it is quite clear how gradually in the depiction of praise, love takes the place of praise. "Love for thee is spread through the two lands." "Thou art loved in the southern heaven and lovely in the northern heaven." Page 356: "Beloved in Karnak . . ." Page 357: "Praise to thee, Amon Re, from Karnak, whose rising is beloved by his city." This song too is full of depiction of praise and love. Likewise the Song IV, p. 374, to the sun god. Here we encounter a profound difference from the O.T.: the dead praise god! "Those who sleep all praise together thy beauty, when thy light shines before their face . . ." It corresponds to the tone of these psalms, in which the bright side of being stands so much in the foreground, that the other side—death, anxiety, evil powers, doubt—has almost disappeared.

The elevated meaning and wide distribution of the depictions of praise is characteristic of the Egyptian psalms. In the Babylonian psalms it is also encountered, but not so often and not so widespread, and it is usually strictly an effect of the epiphany. The contrast to the Psalms of the O.T. is much sharper here. In them the depiction of praise is encountered only seldom, and only in late Psalms. While the vocabulary of praise in the Egyptian psalms is overwhelmingly indicative, and thus depicts, that of the O.T. in all its fullness is almost only imperative. In the Egyptian psalms the laud and praise of the gods is constantly described as occurring in a contemplative attitude. In the Psalms of the O.T. we have almost always calls to praise. There it is a fact, but here a demand; there it is something given to God, but here something owed to God; there God is the one who receives and has received the praise, while in Israel God is the one whose deeds are an ever new call to praise.

In the praise of God in the Egyptian psalms taken as a whole, a contemplative attitude is prevalent. There is also some declarative praise, but it occurs very seldom. Descriptive praise here is not, like that of the Old Testament, the development of the concept of the majesty and goodness of God, nor is it to the same degree as in the psalms of Babylon a listing of predicates and clauses of praise. In Egypt descriptive praise had before it as in a picture the god, his appearance, his history, and it was then his beauty that was praised. In this praise it is not so much a question of God's being for us as it is of God's being for himself in his world of gods and in his own history.

PART THREE

The Praise of God
in the Categories of the Psalms

THE PSALM OF PETITION OR LAMENT OF THE PEOPLE (LP)

The structure is as follows:

    I. Address
      Introductory Petition
    II. Lament
    III. Confession of Trust
    IV. Petition (Double Wish)[1]
    V. Vow of Praise

These five elements are basic to the structure of the lament of the people. The introductory petition is not an essential part, but it is encountered precisely in the early Psalms and most probably belonged to the original structure of this category of Psalm. The double wish is rare. It probably belongs properly to the lament of the individual and was secondarily included in the lament of the people. The following expansions were likely late:

At the beginning: praise of God by way of introduction.

In the middle: after the petition an expression of the certainty of being heard, and expansions of a reflective nature.

At the end: concluding petition or praise of God.

---

1. That is, a wish or a petition that simultaneously is expressed in two directions. May God do thus to our enemies; may God do thus to us. An example is found in Ps. 80:17-18. Cf. the table.

Structure of the Laments of the People

		79	74	80
Address and introductory cry for help		O God	O God Why? Remember Direct thy steps	Give ear, O Shepherd of Israel
Reference to God's earlier saving deeds		(thy inheritance)	Remember thy congregation which thou hast gotten ... redeemed ... where thou hast dwelt	thou who leadest Joseph like a flock
Lament	the foes	the heathen have come into thy inheritance	The foes have roared in the midst of thy holy place	our enemies laugh all ... feed on it
	we	We have become a taunt to our neighbors	We do not see ... no longer any prophet None ... who knows	Thou dost make us the scorn of our neighbors
	thou	How long, O LORD? Wilt thou be angry forever?	why dost thou cast us off forever? How long?	Thou hast fed them with the bread of tears how long?

Confession of Trust		we thy people, the flock of thy pasture	Yet God is my King from of old ... thou hast ...	Thou didst bring a vine out of Egypt
	hear!	Do not remember against us / let thy compassion come	Do not forget	Turn again / Look down from heaven
Petition	save!	Help us / deliver us	Do not deliver / Arise	have regard for this vine / Restore us
	punish!	Pour out thy anger / Let the avenging ... be known	Do not forget the clamor of thy foes	———
Motifs		Why should the nations say / the groans of the prisoners / we are brought very low	Is the enemy to revile thy name? / the life of thy poor, thy covenant	The stock which thy right hand planted
Double wish		12-13	———	17-18
Vows of Praise		we ... will give thanks to thee for ever ... we will recount thy praise	let the poor and needy praise thy name	give us life, and we will call on thy name

There are also some variations in structure:

1. The most constant of all parts is the petition. It is never missing.

2. A tendency for the petition to expand and for the lament to disappear, or to have something substituted for it, is distinctly noticeable. The end result of this tendency can be for the whole Psalm to become petition.

3. In late Psalms direct praise of God often takes the place of the vow of praise.

4. In some Psalms the confession of trust (or the assurance of a hearing) is so dominant that it is possible to speak of a "Psalm of trust for the people." Examples are Pss. 123; 126; The Song of Zion, Ps. 46; perhaps Ps. 90; Ps. Sol. 7.

What is the relationship of the LP to the praise of God? Three motifs of this type of Psalm are to be kept in mind.

1. *The community which is supplicating God makes reference to his saving deeds in the past.* For the most part this occurs at the beginning of the Psalm after the introductory call for help, e.g., Pss. 44:1-3; 85:1-3. These are not really "confessions of trust" although they are very similar, but they are one of the motifs which should move God to intervene. Many of these Psalms are dominated by the tension, "Of old thou hast done thus—and now?"[2]

This act of referring God to his earlier saving deeds takes place in the second person: "Thou hast done . . ." That is the structure of declarative praise. While God is being referred to his earlier saving actions, he is being praised for these actions. Thus in a large group of LP we find declarative praise which serves as one of the motifs which should move God to intervene in the present desperate situation. This is the case in Pss. 44:1-3; 85:1-3; 74:1b-2; 80:8-11; Isa. 63:7-9, 11b-14; Ps. 106:8-11, 43-46. Ps. 83:9-11 might be included here; however, this motif does not form a constituent part of the Psalm but occurs in the petition:

---

2. The same feature may be seen in prose prayers, e.g., Josh. 7:7-9; Judg. 15:18.

"Do to them as thou didst to Midian, as to Sisera and Jabin . . ."
The same is true of Ecclus. 33:4a.[3]
The significance of this part of the LP is shown quite clearly
in Ps. 80 in the figure of the vine:

> Vs. 8, "Thou didst bring a vine out of Egypt . . ."
> Vs. 12, "Why then hast thou broken down its walls . . . ?"

Ps. 89:19-37 (and 3-4) belongs here also. In this Psalm God's
promise to David has taken the place of his saving deeds of old.
This portion has undergone an interesting transformation in Ps.
74:13-17, where the summarizing sentence in vs. 12, which speaks
of God's saving actions, is expanded in 13-17 by praise of God
the creator. God's activity in creation, however, is depicted as
entirely analogous to his intervention in history:

> Vs. 13, "Thou didst divide the sea by thy might . . ."
> This passage has an exact parallel in Isa. 51:9-16, a passage
> based on an LP.[4]

After the introductory call for help in Isa. 51:9: "Awake,
awake, put on strength . . . ," there follows in 9b-10 the reminder:
"Was it not thou that didst cut Rahab in pieces . . .
That didst make the depths of the sea a way . . ."
Here God's creative activity and his saving activity are regarded
as identical to such a degree that the one passes into the other
without a noticeable break. Thus this passage actually stands in
the middle between those passages in which God is reminded of
his former saving action and Ps. 74:13-17, where at this place in
the structure of the Psalm praise of God the creator is now
found.

Both passages, however, show that this portion of the Psalm,
which is essentially declarative praise, approaches descriptive
praise. To be sure, it is not praise that is called forth by a newly
experienced activity of God, but praise that looks back into the

---

3. Cf. the *Iliad*, I, 451 ff.: "As thou hast heard my former prayer, honored me, and
smitten the people of the Achaeans, now also fulfill this wish!" Also, Heiler, *op. cit.*,
pp. 89 f.
4. Begrich, *op. cit.*, p. 169. He sees in this an imitation of the LI, "but still with
the content of an LP."

distant past, when God—once long ago—did such great things. On this basis it is understandable that in late Psalms descriptive praise is found in the introduction of the LP: Pss. 106:1-3; 89: 5-18 (unless this is a secondary composition) and in Ps. Sol. 5:1-2a; 17:1-4; 9:1-7. Also Add. Dan. 1:3-5 (praise of the righteous God).

In a few Psalms the introductory petition is missing and the remembrance of God's saving acts is so strong that the Psalm is introduced like declarative praise:

> Ps. 89:1, "I will sing of thy steadfast love, O LORD, for ever."

The same is true of Isa. 63:7. This fact provides a simple explanation for the gradual mixture of style.[5]

This motif of the LP, then, could simply be a development of the divine predicates, which were reminders of God's actions, as for instance in Ps. 80:1; Gen. 48:15!

2. *The confession of trust.* Its place is between the lament and the petition: Pss. 74:12; 115:9-11; 85:6; 60:4-5a; 106:43-46; Isa. 64:8; Jer. 14:9b; Lam. 5:19. It is also encountered, however, following the petition or bound up with the petition, and this is always the case in the late Psalms (in some of which the lament has been omitted entirely), e.g., Isa. 63:16; 64:4b; Jer. 14:22; Add. Dan. 1:17c. The structure of Isa. 63:7—64:3 is questionable. A confession of sin precedes both of the other passages. In Ps. Sol. 7:4-5, where the confession of trust follows the petition, lament is completely lacking. There is a strange usage of the confession of trust in appositional phrases in the address at the beginning of some Psalms, Ps. 80:1; Jer. 14:8a; Ps. 85:4, or together with the vow of praise, Ps. 79:13a. Once it is even combined with the reference to God's former saving deeds, Ps. 44:4-8, and once it stands in its stead, Ps. 115:3.[6]

---

5. For this motif, cf. Wendel, *op. cit.,* p. 89. He finds the same motif in the prayer wishes (*Texts,* pp. 10 f.) in the divine predicates. "A divine predicate, such as 'God of Abraham' is intended to . . . obligate the deity. Such an expression was to work as a conjuration: 'Arise, Yahweh, who then didst show thyself so mighty.' "
6. It is completely lacking only in Ps. 83, in which lament and petition have only one subject, the foes.
The subject in these sentences can be God (usually addressed in the second person), or the people.

In these sentences Israel expresses its relation to God, from whom it expects acts of assistance. Most of the passages say that. But also the sentences in which Israel looks to God as shepherd, king, and father express this directly. For here the analogy of the relationships of this world tells what God is for his people.

The sentences that contain the vocabulary of trust say the same indirectly. It is to be noted that these are less common. A certain amount of reflection lies behind this vocabulary. The sentences which praise God's majesty or his compassion are also rare; they are similar to descriptive praise, while the main groups stand closer to declarative praise.

It was only in the latest period that the confession of trust passed into praise of the righteous God, as in Lam. 1:18, and throughout the Psalms of Solomon. This is connected with the fact that in the late Psalms of lament the lamentation is no longer so free and natural as in the earlier ones, but is more and more restricted by the recognition of one's own guilt on the one hand, and by the praise of the righteous God on the other.[7]

A clear boundary between confession of confidence and the praise of God cannot be drawn here. Most of these sentences, taken in themselves, are praise of the God who acts on behalf of his people. *In the confession of trust the lament of the peo-*

Examples of God addressed in the second person: Ps. 80:1; Jer. 14:8a; Pss. 85:6; 60:4-5a; Isa. 63:16; 64:4b; Jer. 14:9b; 14:22; Lam. 5:19; Ps. Sol. 5:5b; 7:4-5.

Of God addressed in the third person: Pss. 74:12; 115:3 (115:9-11); Lam. 1:18a. Of the people: Pss. 79:13a; 115:9-11; Add. Dan. 1:17c.

God is the one who acts (for his people): Pss. 74:12; 115:3; Isa. 64:4b; Jer. 14:22. God is savior, redeemer, helper: Ps. 44:7; Jer. 14:8; Pss. 115:9-11; 85:4, 6; 60:4-5a; Isa. 63:16.

God is in our midst: Jer. 14:9b; is our God: Ps. Sol. 5:5.

God is the shepherd; his people, his flock: Pss. 80:1; 79:13a (74:1c).

God is Israel's king: Pss. 74:12; 44:4.

God is Israel's father: Isa. 63:16; 64:7 (cf. Heiler, *op. cit.*, p. 91, in primitive prayers).

God is hope; Israel trusts, hopes in him: Ps. 115:9-11; Isa. 64:3b; Jer. 14:22; Add. Dan. 1:17.

Israel rejoices in him: Ps. 85:6.

God is enthroned, reigns: Ps. 80:1; 115:3; Lam. 5:19.

God gives his people victory: Ps. 44:4.

God is merciful: Ps. Sol. 7:5.

God is righteous: Lam. 1:18; Ps. Sol. 8:23-26; 9:2b-5; 2:15-18 (praise!).

7. This process is an essential one for an understanding of the prehistory of the N.T. doctrine of justification.

ple is open toward praise. In Ps. 74 the confession of trust (12) introduces a P (13-17); and in Ps. 44, vss. 4-8 taken in themselves are an independent PP.

There is a difference here, however, from the "reference to God's former saving action." In the latter, reference is made to definite facts or data that lie in the past, while here the confidence in the previously experienced activity of God for his people is expressed in the present in faith and praise. The structure of those sentences was: "thou hast done . . . ," and the structure of these is: "thou doest . . ."

3. *Vow of praise and oracle of salvation.* In the LI the petition is followed by the vow of praise, which then often passes over into praise of God. Here therefore within a Psalm, lamentation is often turned into praise. In the canonical Psalms there are no LP that end in distinct praise of God, but some later ones do end this way.[8]

Moreover, the vow of praise is seldom met with in the LP. In the strict sense a vow was probably originally a matter for the individual, and thus the vow of praise has its proper place in the supplications and praise of the individual. In the Babylonian psalms too we never find a vow of praise in the plural.[9] It is therefore all the more to be noted that in the biblical Psalms such a vow is found several times. In Ps. 79:13 it stands in close connection with the confession of trust, and in Ps. 44:8 it forms the end of an expansion of the motif of vss. 1-3 into a PP in vss. 4-8.

In Pss. 106:47b; 80:18, and Ps. Sol. 8:33b it is connected with the petition in a final or a consecutive construction. In both passages an action is praised: "We shall not be moved. . . ." Likewise in the implied vows in Hos. 6:2 and Ps. 74:21b there is a jussive, and the clause sounds like an LI. Ps. 115 can be mentioned here only with reservations. It is a mixture of categories and the vow of praise in vss. 16-18 is characteristic of the LI. In some Psalms another look into the future stands in the

8. Ps. Sol. 8:34; Ecclus. 36.
9. Stummer, *op. cit.,* p. 117.

place of the vow of praise. The foes shall be brought to recognize (through God's intervention against them) that God is the Lord, e.g., Ps. 83:16b, 18; Ecclus. 36:5; 36:22b; Add. Dan. 22. Behind this Psalm ending there probably stands the expression so often used by Ezekiel, e.g., Ezek. 6:14; 7:27.[10] It should be noted that the LP and the LI have in common the fact that in some way we are always pointed beyond mere lament and petition. They differ, however, in that this pointing beyond the present crisis does not have in the LP so definite a form as that of the vow of praise in the LI. This vow is occasionally met with, but not so frequently and not in so standardized a form. We cannot speak of it as a definite conclusion for a Psalm in the same way that we can in connection with the LI. In several Psalms the formulation of the vow of praise (e.g., Pss. 115:6-8; 74:21b) displays a similarity to the LI. In Pss. 79:13; 44:8; 106:47b, the wording is the same as that in the LI. Only Ps. 80:18 (cf. Ps. Sol. 8:33b) is different. According to Wendel, in the free prayers of the laity the only vow is that of an individual. All these factors then indicate that the vow of praise is by nature a part of the LI and was then borrowed as a motif for use in the LP.

The vow in Ps. 80, however, shows a striking relationship to the promise of the people at the assembly in Shechem, Josh. 24:16-18: vs. 18, "Therefore we also will serve the LORD, for he is our God" (and vs. 21); vs. 24, "The LORD our God we will serve, and his voice we will obey." It occurs here in another context, as answer to a question calling for a decision. We might inquire, however, whether this promise of the people at Shechem was an absolutely unique occurrence, or whether there is behind it a vow of the people that had its own fixed place in the cult.[11] Reference should be made here to Hos. 14:3, which contains a formal renunciation of other gods.

These Psalms end with a petition: Pss. 74; 84(?); 80(?); 89; Isa. 64:4-11; Jer. 14:1-10; Lam. 5, or with the confession of trust:

---

10. Or a similar clause found in Isa. 45:14; 45:6.
11. Pedersen makes a similar reference in *Israel*, III-IV, p. 661.

Jer. 14:13—15:4; Pss. 44(?); 80(?); 60; Isa. 63—64:3; Isa. 51:9-16.[12]

Where the vow of praise is lacking, the LP end either with a petition or with the confession of trust. Now, however, there is in some LP an entirely new and different part, which depicts God's answer to the supplications of his people. The answer can be affirmative or negative. That an unfavorable answer of God to the supplication of the people actually was conceivable is shown by Jer. 14:10 and 15:1-4, and also by Hos. 6:1-6. The transitional verse, Hos. 5:15, shows that this is intended to be an LP. It begins with the decision to repent, which is followed by a very detailed confession of trust. (This hints at a vow of praise.) Verses 4-6 give God's answer. Instead of the proclamation of salvation which the people awaited, "I will do unto you . . . ," there is the question, "What shall I do with you . . . ?" And this is based on the inconstancy of Israel. There follows in vs. 5 the (prophetic) proclamation of judgment with the reason for it in vs. 6.[13]

In all other passages God's answer is affirmative. The fact that an answer from God followed the LP can be seen more clearly in the prophetic books than in the LP contained in the Psalter. In addition to Jer. 14:15, there is in Jeremiah one other passage where an LP is clearly cited, Jer. 3:21 ff. In vs. 21 the lament of the people is given; in vss. 22b-25 we have the turning of the people to Yahweh with a confession of sins and an expression of trust. 4:1-2 is God's answer, a conditional proclamation of salvation. Between the portrayal of the lament and the turning to God there has been inserted a (prophetic) call to repentance.

Hos. 14 is very similar to this passage in Jeremiah. It seems

---

12. The question mark with Ps. 44 and Ps. 80 means that it is not possible to make a clear decision here. The final *sentence* in 44 is a petition, but the last words are, "for the sake of thy steadfast love." In Ps. 80 the final sentence is usually translated, "that we may be helped," or "that we may be saved." Luther translated, "so genesen wir" and the Zürich Bible, "so wird uns geholfen." According to Delitzsch in his commentary on this passage, both translations are possible. As for content, the passages which approach in form the vow of praise also belong in this group of Psalm endings, Ps. 83:18; Ecclus. 36:5, 22b; Add. Dan. 1:22. Behind the final or consecutive clause, "that they may know . . ." stands the belief that God is surely Lord.

13. Cf. H. Schmidt, "Hosea 6:1-6," *Sellin-Festschrift,* 1927, pp. 111 ff.

that a liturgy of penitence is the basis of both passages. In Hos. 14 the exhortation to petition for forgiveness of sin and for help, and also the indication of a vow of praise (vs. 3) have been inserted into the call to repent (vs. 2). Verse 4 quotes the renunciation of the foreign gods. Now follows in vss. 6-9 God's answer, which is here an unconditioned and very full proclamation of salvation, almost approaching the apocalyptic pictures of salvation.

In Ps. 85, as in the two just-mentioned passages, the petition is followed by a proclamation of salvation, introduced in vs. 8 as follows:

Let me hear what God the LORD will speak,
for he will speak peace to his people . . .

The sentences which follow depict rather than proclaim. In part they have many similarities with Hos. 14:6-9, and both actually speak more of the God who blesses than of him who intervenes to help.

The proclamation is very different in Ps. 60:6-9. Here God announces his victory over the nations who are Israel's foes (not at the End!). Isa. 33:10-13 is quite similar, " 'Now I will arise,' says the LORD . . .'" (cf. Ps. 12:5). Gunkel refers to this connection between lament of the people and oracle of salvation on pp. 137 f., where he has collected a large number of examples. This approach was taken up by Begrich, "Das priesterliche Heilsorakel," *ZAW* 52, 1934, pp. 81-92. There, however, he dealt with it mainly as the answer to the lament of the individual. The answer of God to the lament of the people should be made the subject of a separate study.[14]

For our present investigation it is significant that the oracle of salvation often proclaims the coming intervention of God. (Begrich, *op. cit.*, p. 8, "The message of Yahweh [is] addressed to the one seeking help, and speaks of his intervention.")
Isa. 33:10-13:
" 'Now I will arise,' says the LORD . . ." (cf. Ps. 12:5).
Ps. 60:6-9:

14. Cf. Begrich, "Deuterojesaja-Studien," *BWANT* 4. F. H. 25, 1938: "Das Heils- oder Erhörungsorakel," pp. 6-19.

"With exultation I will divide up Shechem."
Isa. 49:22:
"Behold, I will lift up my hand to the nations, and raise my signal to the peoples."[15]
Isa. 59:15b f.: "The LORD saw it . . . He saw that there was no man . . . then his own arm brought him victory . . . He put on righteousness as a breastplate, and a helmet of salvation upon his head . . . he will come like a rushing stream . . . And he will come to Zion as Redeemer."
Jer. 51:36: "Therefore thus says the LORD: 'Behold I will plead your cause and take vengeance for you.' "
Mic. 7:11-13: "A day for the building of your walls!"
Hab. 3:3-15: "God came from Teman . . . He stood and measured the earth . . . Thou didst bestride the earth in fury . . . Thou wentest forth for the salvation of thy people."
Joel 2:1 ff.: "Blow the trumpet in Zion . . . Let all the inhabitants of the land tremble, for the day of the LORD is coming, it is near."

No fixed form is discernible. They have in common only the following features:

(a) They are oracles of salvation or occupy the place of such oracles.

(b) They all speak in some manner of God's intervention for the salvation of his people.

Two groups can be distinguished as follows:

1. Oracles of salvation as a word of Yahweh. He himself proclaims his intervention, as, for example, in Isa. 33:10-13. It is in this form that Second Isaiah took up the oracle of salvation.

2. This intervention of God is depicted in the third person. Isa. 59:13 ff.; Hab. 3:3-15; Joel 2:1 ff. belong to this group. These represent already a further development of the oracles of salvation. One of them is an epiphany, and the others are reminiscent of that form.

---

15. Begrich designates 24 passages as oracles of salvation or of God's hearing (*op. cit.*, p. 6). Every one of these contains the above-mentioned part in which God proclaims that he will intervene.

The variety of form of these oracles indicates a particular difficulty which should lead us to exercise the greatest caution. It is no accident that oracles of salvation are hardly ever found in the Psalter, but occur frequently, almost regularly, as answers to the laments of the people in the prophetic books. It is also no accident that the oracle of salvation is the most important literary form in Second Isaiah.

The answer to the lament of the people is communicated as God's answer by the priest or by the prophet. If it is combined with the lament of the people, we no longer have a Psalm in the strict sense, but a liturgy. In the designation "prophetic liturgy" the two component parts are clearly expressed.[16]

THE PSALM OF PETITION OR LAMENT OF THE INDIVIDUAL (LI)

The Parts:

I. Address, with an introductory cry for help and/or of turning to God.

II. Lament. (It has three subjects: Thou, O God . . . ; I . . . ; the foes . . .)

III. Confession of trust. (Contrasted to the lament by the *waw* adversative.)

IV. Petition: (a) for God to be favorable (look . . . incline thyself . . . hear . . .); (b) for God to intervene (help . . . save . . .).
Motifs designed to move God to intervene.

V. Assurance of being heard.

VI. Double wish (wish or petition that God will intervene against . . . and for . . .).

VII. Vow of praise.

VIII. Praise of God (only where the petition has been answered!).

The following are the constituent parts of the LI: address, lament, confession of trust, or assurance of being heard, petition, vow of praise. This is the basic scheme, but it never becomes stereotyped. The possibilities of variation are unusually numerous.

16. Cf. Gunkel, *op. cit.*, pp. 136 ff., 329, 410 f.

When we consider the relationship of the praise of God to the petition of the individual, two questions arise: 1. What is the significance of the vow of praise in and for the Psalm of petition? 2. What is the significance of the oracle of salvation in and for the Psalm of petition?

Let us look at the second question first. Begrich's work "Das priesterliche Heilsorakel"[17] cast new light on the lament of the individual. The conclusions of this work are so clear and convincing that most of them have won general acceptance. Accordingly, as far as the lament of the individual is concerned we must reckon in every case with the possibility that the content is not only the lament and petition of the one who comes before God, that is, that he not only "pours out his heart" before Yahweh, but in some instances it is to be assumed that an oracle of salvation was given in the *midst* of the Psalm and that the Psalm also includes the words that follow the giving of the oracle. This conclusion had already been drawn for some Psalms, in which this can be seen with especial clarity. This explains the "abrupt change in mood" (Gunkel, *op. cit.,* p. 243) from lament to jubilation within a Psalm. But the consequences for the category as a whole have not yet been drawn. A group of Psalms within the category may then be distinguished. These are Psalms in which the oracle of salvation is to be assumed *in the middle,* and which contain not only what the petitioner says *before* the oracle, but also what he says after the oracle has been given. Thus these Psalms do not merely have something cheerful or trustful added, but the whole Psalm takes on a different character. Within these Psalms something decisive has occurred, something which changes what is being said here. This change will be pointed out in the Psalms involved.

Gunkel rightly said that the oracle of salvation as such is not a sufficient explanation of these Psalms (*op. cit.,* p. 247). In addition a real change must have taken place in the one speaking. It is therefore not the fact of the oracle as such that created this special type of Psalms of petition, but the word which in

17. *ZAW* 52, 1934, p. 43, note. Cf. Gunkel, *Einleitung,* pp. 245 ff. Fr. Küchler, "Das priesterliche Orakel in Israel und Juda," *Baudissin-Festschrift,* Giessen, 1918, p. 285.

Structure of the Psalm of Petition or Lament of the Individual

	142	102	27B
Address (Turning to God) Introductory cry for help	O LORD (first in vs. 5) I cry with my voice to the LORD	O LORD Hear my prayer Let my cry come to thee	O LORD Thy face, Lord, do I seek Hear!
Foes	They have hidden a trap for me	All the day my enemies taunt me	For false witnesses have risen against me
Lament — I	I look to the right There is none who takes notice of me	3-7, 9, 11 My days are like an evening shadow	———
Lament — Thou	———	Because of thy indignation For thou hast taken me up and thrown me away	(in anger)
Confession of trust	3a, 5 Thou art my refuge	12 ff. But thou, O LORD, art enthroned for ever	Thou who hast been my help O God of my salvation For my father and my mother . . . but the LORD

	Hear!	Give heed to my cry	(1-2)	Hide not thy face
Petition	Save!	Deliver me from my persecutors	Take me not hence in the midst of my days	Give me not up to the will of my adversaries
Motifs		For I am brought very low / For they are too strong for me	25-28 Thou dost endure	Because of my enemies
Vow of praise		That I may give thanks to thy name	—	—
Assurance of being heard		The righteous will surround me; for thou wilt deal	28? The children of thy servants shall dwell secure	I believe that I shall see the goodness of the LORD in the land of the living!

Structure of the Psalm of Petition or Lament of the Individual
(Petition has been heard)

		13	6	22
Address (Turning to God) Introductory cry for help		LORD	O LORD, rebuke me not Be gracious to me	My God, why?
Lament	Foes	How long shall my enemy be exalted over me?	———	(12-18) Surround me
	I	How long must I bear pain?	For I am languishing My bones are troubled (and 6-7)	(6-8) But I am a worm, and no man
	Thou	Wilt thou forget me for ever?	But thou, O LORD—how long?	(1-2) Why hast thou Thou dost lay me in the dust of death
Confession of trust		But I have trusted in thy steadfast love	For the sake of thy steadfast love	(3) Yet thou art holy (4-5) In thee our fathers trusted (9-10) Upon thee was I cast from my birth

Petition	Hear!	Consider and answer me	Turn	(11, 19) Be not far off
	Save!	Lighten my eyes	Save my life	19b-21 Hasten to my aid / Deliver my soul / Save me
	Punish!	—	—	—
Motifs		Lest my enemy say	For in death there is no remembrance of thee	There is none to help
Double wish		(4-5?)	(9-10)	—
Vow of praise		I will sing to the LORD	—	I will tell of thy name to my brethren (23 ff.)
(Declarative) Praise of God		Because he has dealt bountifully with me	Depart from me / For the LORD has heard	(24) For he has not despised / (31) He has wrought it

these oracles came from God to the one petitioning and lamenting. There is much evidence of this in the Psalms themselves, as for instance, Ps. 28:6, "He has heard the voice of my supplications." This word changes the one speaking. The one who speaks now has been transformed by God's having heard his supplication. Often even the moment of this change has been captured by a "now," or "but now," e.g., Pss. 27:6; 12:5 (God speaks); 20:6, "Now I know that the LORD will help" (cf. Ps. 119:67). Or God himself intervenes, Ps. 12:5.[18]

Usually the change is not so obvious. But there is an unequivocal mark that in the past has not been given sufficient attention. At the place where the change occurs, almost all of these Psalms contain a *waw* adversative, "But thou O God . . . ," or "But I . . ."

"But" (Waw *Adversative) in the Lament of the Individual*

But thou . . .   But I . . .

I. *In the lamentation*
Ps. 6:3: "But thou, O LORD—how long?"

Ps. 38:13: "But I am like a deaf man"
Ps. 70:5: "But I am poor and needy"
In a protestation of innocence:
Ps. 26:11: "But as for me, I walk in my integrity"

II. *In the petition*
Ps. 22:19: "But thou, O LORD, be not far off!"
Ps. 59:5: Thou, LORD God of hosts . . . awake"

Ps. 69:13: "But as for me, my prayer is to thee"
Ps. 55:16: "But I call upon God"

III. *As confession of trust* (after the lamentation) *or as assurance of being heard* (after the petition)

Ps. 22:3: "Yet thou art holy"
Ps. 102:12: "But thou, O LORD, art enthroned for ever"

Ps. 13:5: "But I have trusted in thy steadfast love"
Ps. 31:14: "But I trust in thee"

18. Compare the situation of the oracle in 1 Sam. 1 where this change is clearly expressed.

26: "But thou dost endure"
27: "But thou art the same"
Ps. 86:15: "But thou, O LORD, art
a God merciful and gracious"
Ps. 3:3: "But thou, O LORD, art a
shield"
Ps. 55:23: "But thou, O God, wilt
cast them down"
Ps. 59:8: "But thou, O LORD, dost
laugh at them" (cf. Ps. 2:4)
Ps. 109:28: "Let them curse, but
do thou bless"
Ps. 64:7: "But God will shoot his
arrow at them"
Isa. 38:17b: "But thou hast held
back my life from the pit of
destruction"

Ps. 52:8: "But I am like a green
olive tree . . . I trust in the
steadfast love of God"
Ps. 73:23: "Nevertheless I am continually with thee"
Ps. 27:6: "And now my head shall
be lifted up"
Ps. 27:13: "[But] I believe that"
Ps. 35:9: "Then my soul shall rejoice in the LORD"
Ps. 71:14: "But I will hope continually"
Ps. 109:28: "[But] may thy servant
be glad"
("Behold" instead of "but")
Ps. 54:4: "Behold, God is my
helper"

The Waw Adversative in the Petition of the Individual

GRAMMATICAL OBSERVATION

It is necessary to imagine a conjunction that has not yet been differentiated into a copulative and an adversative.[19]

The *we'attah* can usually be translated in either of two ways: "and now" or "but now." Even where the *waw* is clearly adversative and is to be translated as "but," there remains a connection, even though only one of contrast. The contrast is actually made, not by the *waw*, but by the structure of the sentence. The *waw* always stands with the subject at the beginning of the sentence, as in Ps. 13:5: "But I—in thy steadfast love I have trusted" (order of the words in the Hebrew). This same contrast can occasionally take place without the *waw*. Ps. 17:15: "As for me, I shall behold thy face in righteousness." The contrast is therefore more deeply embedded in the structure of the sentence than by a conjunction only.

The *waw* adversative combined with the subject at the beginning of the clause indicates that here something else begins.

19. The German word "aber" once had this complex meaning. This is still shown by the words "abermals," and "tausend und abertausend." This was pointed out by Prof. Köhler.

This is especially clear when these clauses with "but" follow the lament. They indicate a transition from lamentation to another mode of speech, the confession of trust or the assurance of being heard.[20]

The attached table not only shows how numerous these clauses are, but also their vitality. No two of these sentences use the same words, and they never have a pre-determined form. The vitality of this form seems to me especially clear in the fact that expressions with the same meaning can occur in sentences whose subject is God as well as in sentences whose subject is "I." The transition which is expressed in all these sentences is one that occurs in a happening between God and man, and both are affected by it. It should be added that this transition is not schematically bound to any place in the Psalms. Its most frequent place is in connection with the "assurance of being heard," after the petition and before the vow of praise. But it can also stand earlier with the "confession of trust" between lament and petition. Often, to be sure, these two patterns coincide (as in Ps. 13:5). In addition, this clause with "but" is found a few times within the petition, and even in the midst of the lament. (See the table.) Here it cannot be said that it already indicates a transition, but it does likely already represent a contrast. In it we are already looking beyond the lament or the petition. The expression "but thou" is especially impressive in connection with the cry "How long?" in Ps. 6:3.

The clauses with "but thou . . ." The following observations should be taken in conjunction with Begrich's recognition of the significance of the oracle of salvation for the petition of the individual. The expression "but thou" usually marks the place at which in Ps. 12:5 the word from God stands, the place therefore at which the oracle of salvation occurs. We might even say it designates the oracle of salvation. If, however, it were necessary to think of each of these Psalms as standing in direct ritual connection with the oracle, this rite would have to have been defined by a much more fixed form. Yet even the "but clauses"

20. This is already found in prose prayers, as, e.g., Gen. 32:12.

in petitions and laments can scarcely be tied in with such a rite.
In Ps. 22, for instance, the "but" is already clearly present in
vs. 3 (after the first cry of dire need) and recurs in vs. 19 after
the detailed lamentation. The actual turning point, however,
comes between vs. 21 and vs. 22. In some Psalms (13; 22; 6; 28)
it can readily be assumed that the oracle of salvation is actually
to be pictured in the middle of the Psalm, but for others this is
scarcely conceivable. The strongest argument is that it is not
possible to make a clear and certain distinction between petitions that are "open" and those that have been heard. The rite
of the oracle of salvation gives expression to the fact that God
answers the one who cries to him. We must assume that what
actually happened in the rite was not unconditionally bound to
it and that it can be observed in the Psalms without being immediately accompanied by the rite (so also Gunkel).

It seems to me that a certain correspondence to these clauses
with *but* can be found in two Egyptian petitions of the individual.[21] They are completely absent, as far as I can tell, in the
Babylonian psalms. There we find in a few passages the "confession of trust," and some Egyptian psalms contain an "assurance of being heard," but the transition within the prayer
which is indicated by the clauses with *but* occurs uniquely in
the Psalms of Israel. In them there is the strongest witness to
the reality of the help that is experienced, the condescending
of God to the one who cries out to him.

The same sentence, which in Ps. 6:8 is the basis of the cry to
the foes, "Depart!", is found again in Ps. 28:6, except that instead of that imperative we have here the shout of praise,
"Blessed!" This "Blessed" therefore occupies here and in Ps.
31:21 the place of the "but." *These passages substantiate the
fact that the "but" designates the transition from petition to
praise within the Psalm of petition.* If this form of the *waw*
adversative within the petition of the individual is peculiar to
the Psalms of Israel, that means that here in the face of the still
existing predicament the praise of God can be boldly sung in

21. See above p. 44. They are similar to the heard petitions of the Psalter.

the certainty that Yahweh in his heights (Ps. 22:3) has heard the one praying in the depths (28:6).[22]

The clauses with "but I . . ." The most frequent expression is, "But I have trusted thee" or similar words, e.g., Ps. 13:5; 31:14; 52:8; 27:13; 141:8; 38:15; 73:23.[23]

These clauses with "but I" are all confessions of trust. In each case they have in the whole of the Psalm exactly the same significance as the clauses with "but thou." There is no essential difference between the two groups. The sentence in Ps. 3:3, "But thou, O LORD, art a shield about me," does not say in its context anything different from Ps. 31:14, "But I trust in thee, O LORD." In Ps. 38:15 the two expressions stand together. Praise of God and confession of trust are very intimately related to each other in the clauses with "but."

The fact that confession of trust, certainty of being heard, and praise of God cannot be clearly distinguished here but merge with one another corresponds to the fact which has been mentioned earlier: no hard and fast boundary can be drawn in the category of petitions of the individual between petitions that have been heard and those that remain "open." It is an essential element in these Psalms that this boundary remain open. Now a further observation must be added.

In the investigation of all the LI of the Old Testament I found to my astonishment that there are no Psalms which do not progress beyond petition and lament! Ps. 143, which contains only lament and petition in its structure, still expresses clearly a confession of trust in the second half of each verse from vss. 8-10. There is a whole group of Psalms which contain neither the assurance of being heard, nor the vow of praise, nor a word of praise at the end, but not one of these Psalms, which consist essentially of only lament and petition, is entirely

---

22. In the N.T., John 11:41 is to be understood in precisely this way.
23. In Ps. 71:14 the "waiting" has taken the form of a vow of praise; similarly the words of rejoicing in Ps. 35:9; in Ps. 109:28 the "but" of the double wish is bound with the vocabulary of praise. A variation of the vow of praise is seen in "I shall behold thy face," Ps. 17:15. Instead of by "but," the caesura is marked by a new start which is contrasted with the previous one: "I know . . . ," Ps. 140:12; 56:9, or "I say . . . ," Ps. 140:6; 142:6; and once, "My heart is steadfast . . . ," Ps. 57:7.

without a glance beyond the present situation, even if only a half verse, which expresses a confession of trust. Between this type and, for instance, Ps. 22, which ends with a full, broad Psalm of praise, there are all the transitional steps imaginable.

In my opinion, this fact that in the Psalms of the O.T. there is no, or almost no, such thing as "mere" lament and petition, shows conclusively the polarity between praise and petition in the Psalms. The cry to God is here never one-dimensional, without tension. It is always somewhere in the middle between petition and praise. By nature it cannot be *mere* petition or lament, but is always underway from supplication to praise.

The Vow of Praise

The vow of praise is a constant component of the Psalms of petition (cf. the tables).[24] The position of the vow is at the end of the petition. That is, the petition passes over into the vow of praise. In the Psalms of petition of the individual the order of motifs seldom corresponds exactly to the schema. We have here such a large number of variations as almost to defy analysis, even when new motifs are scarcely added. It is thus all the more striking that almost without exception the vow of praise maintains its fixed place at the end of the petition. This shows the power and consistency of this motif.

The same holds true for the structure of the motif itself. It is almost always a voluntative with the subject "I" and the object "God," thus a single, invariable clause. The possibilities for variation are to be sought in the vocabulary. The typical

---

24. Where it is lacking, it is either present in a different form, "I shall behold thy face in righteousness; when I awake, I shall be satisfied with beholding thy form," Ps. 17:15 (as also in the Babylonian psalms); "I will rejoice," Ps. 31:7, or it has been transformed into a report, Ps. 73:28, or an exhortation, Pss. 27:14; 31:24, or into a future condition, 43:4. Traces of it are there in Pss. 6:5; 88:10-12, where it is said as a motif to gain the desired result that in Sheol God can no longer be praised. Cf. Isa. 38:18 f. Its place can also be taken by another consequence of God's intervention, Ps. 58:11. Or, in some cases its absence is motivated by the structure of the Psalm, especially there where praise itself has already taken the place of the vow of praise, "Blessed be the LORD," Pss. 28:6; 31:23 f. We find declarative praise in Pss. 6:8-9; 10:17; and descriptive praise in Pss. 10:16-18; 12:6; 102:24b-27. It is completely absent in Pss. 143; 141; 38; 25 (alphabetic Psalm); 58, and the above-mentioned Psalms in which another form is substituted for it. It is omitted from the Psalms of trust, but even in them there are still clear traces of the vow of praise, Pss. 73:28; 23:6b.

verb for this vow of praise is *hōdāh*. Only in exceptions which are mostly late does there appear in its stead or alongside of it one of the other expressions for praise. On the other hand there is often an accompanying word, especially, "I will sing."

More precise designations provide other possibilities for variations. A survey of all the voluntative expressions (inclusive of those at the beginning of Psalms) gives the following results:

1. The original form of the vow of praise contained only *one* verb. Where more are to be found, it is to be assumed that the Psalm is later. Those Psalms in which the voluntative form is particularly numerous are certainly late, as, e.g., Ps. 71.

2. The only specific designation that is certainly original is that of the place, "before the congregation," etc. This is often found in the Babylonian psalms. The specific designations of the extent of time, such as "for ever," are certainly late.

3. It can be assumed with assurance that the oldest form of the vow of praise is the simple voluntative with God as the object, and followed by a statement of the reason for the vow. An example is Ps. 13:6: "I will sing to the LORD, because he has dealt bountifully with me."

What is the significance of the vow of praise? We should first of all recall that this vow is common to both the Psalms of the Old Testament and those of Babylon. Moreover, it is also to be found in those of Egypt (see above, pp. 38-39, 46).

It is certain that the vow of praise originally was connected with a vow to offer sacrifice. In the Psalms, the vows of praise show this by a polemical addition such as that in Ps. 51:16 ff. and Ps. 69:31. In addition, both could be included in one vow, as Ps. 27:6 and Ps. 54:6. Ps. 66:13-16 shows sacrifice and praise side by side in the fulfillment of a vow. In the Babylonian sources that have been preserved the vows of praise far outnumber those of sacrifice.

Moreover, the vow of praise is encountered even in primitive prayers. A Khoikhoi prayer (Heiler, *Das Gebet*, p. 159) reads, "Thou, O Tsuiga . . . thou art our father . . . Let our herds live, let us live . . . O that we might praise thee. . . ."

The attempt to interpret the vow of praise as a spiritualizing of an original vow of sacrifice does not correspond to the facts. The vow of praise has not simply taken the place of one of sacrifice. In any case, that is not the whole story. Praise is not a substitute for sacrifice, but had its own original meaning alongside of sacrifice. Sacrifice is food for the god; praise, however, belongs to the life of the god as much as does food. This is to be thought of in much the same way as the fact that man cannot exist without food, but also not without some recognition, some "honor." Thus both parallel each other back into very early times.

But just what meaning does the vow have? Why does a vow belong at the end of a petition? For us "vow" contains an element of the solemn, of the extraordinary, which conceals from us the real meaning of the word. There is really no difference at all between "to promise" and "to vow." The form could equally well be called a "promise of praise." It is a witness to an understanding of existence in which man does not yet stand alone, or need God only for his religious requirements. The vow of praise is the link between petition and praise. It closes the circle from petition to praise. It is one of the sure signs that the petition does not arise out of itself or out of some lack in the one petitioning, but out of the polarity of petition and praise.

The vow of praise does not correspond to thanks but to the praise of God. This is expressed especially in the specific statements such as the following:

Ps. 22:22: "I will tell of thy name to my brethren; in the midst of the congregation I will praise thee."
Ps. 22:25: "in the great congregation; . . . before those who fear him."
Ps. 26:12b: "in the great congregation."
Ps. 27:5b: "under the cover of his tent."
Ps. 57:9: "among the peoples; . . . among the nations."
Ps. 71:18: "till I proclaim thy might to all the generations to come."

To praise is to speak, to tell, to proclaim, to magnify his glory. It is telling abroad God's great deeds, just as it is said at the beginning of the proclamation of the apostles of Jesus Christ, Acts 2:11. *The concept and the reality of proclamation have one of their roots in the forensic element of the praise of God, as it is expressed particularly in the vow of praise.*

Because the petition for continuity more and more took the place of the cry out of dire need, the vow of praise lost its importance and finally disappeared entirely. It was no longer regarded as necessary. This can be seen in the Babylonian prayer literature and even more clearly in that of Egypt, where the petition for continuity is absolutely dominant and, correspondingly, the vow of praise is seldom encountered. It is probably generally true that in the late period of a religion, prayers expressing continuity outnumber those which arise from the cry of dire momentary need, and finally largely or entirely displace them. This process can also be observed in the petitionary Psalms of the O.T. But just at the point where this almost necessary development is recognized we are astonished to see to what extent, even down to the latest period, the petition in the midst of tribulation, the cry from the depths, is dominant in the Psalms. For this reason the vow of praise is appropriate and remained alive throughout the period in which Psalms were written. The fitting place for the vow of praise was alongside the cry of need. A feeling that this is so has remained everywhere down to the present. Whoever truly cries to God out of the depths, and in this cry thinks not of his need but of God (cf. the dual nature of the petition, "Hear!" and "Save!") knows that the moment of making a vow, a promise, is a part of this cry. I *know* then that the matter is not finished when I have pled and God has heard, but that something else must still come. I know that I owe something to God. It is totally false to belittle this as a bargain, as a *do ut des.* On the contrary, it is only through the promise that I bind to my petition that the petition gains its weight and value. I know that with the promise that I add to my petition I have entered into a relationship with God.[25]

25. The Roman Catholic practice of vows contains a reminder of the original reality of vows. Luther's vow at Stotternheim, "Help, holy St. Anna, and I will

The Transition to Declarative Praise

The fact that lamentation and petition can change into praise in the same Psalm has as a consequence a development which is peculiar to the Israelite Psalms, i.e., that praise is already heard in the conclusion of lament and petition, and that it forms the basis for the vow of praise.[26]

> Ps. 13:6: "I will sing to the LORD, because he has dealt bountifully with me" (cf. 22:31).
> Ps. 3:7: "For thou dost smite."
> Ps. 10:17: "Thou wilt hear" (or, hast heard).
> Ps. 6:8: "Depart ... for the LORD has heard."
> Ps. 54:7: "For thou hast delivered me from every trouble."
> Ps. 56:13: "For thou hast delivered my soul from death."
> Ps. 31:7: "I will rejoice . . . because thou hast seen my affliction."
> Ps. 28:6: "Blessed be the LORD! for he has heard the voice of my supplications."
> Ps. 31:21: "For he has wondrously shown his steadfast love to me."
> Ps. 22:24: "For he has not despised or abhorred."

In order for the contrast which governs each of these Psalms to become clear it would be necessary to hear all these statements in the direct context of the loudest lament or most urgent entreaty of the same Psalm. It should be noted that the grief over which the suppliant is lamenting, and for the removal of which he pleads with God, still remains. During the praying of these Psalms no miracle has occurred, but something else has occurred. God has heard and inclined himself to the one praying; God has had mercy on him. (See the passages cited.)

---

become a monk," is a typical example of the way in which this outlook was so dominant then.

It is characteristic, however, that in the Roman Church the vow of praise has been almost entirely displaced by the vow of works. Franz Werfel's novel *The Song of Bernadette* is excellent evidence of the vitality of this vow even in the present day.

26. A corresponding reason following the vow of praise is never found in the LP.

And in this the decisive event has taken place. That which is yet to come, the turning point in the situation, must of necessity follow. Therefore it can now already be regarded as realized.

This transition is the real theme of the Psalms which are being discussed here. *They are no longer mere petition, but petition that has been heard. They are no longer mere lament, but lament that has been turned to praise.*

There is a difficulty, in that, as has been mentioned, this group of Psalms cannot be exactly delimited. In addition to those already listed (Pss. 3; 6; 10; 13; 22; 28; 31A; 31B; 54; 56) I should like to include here Isa. 38:10-20;[27] Pss. 27A; 64. Those which stand in the middle between open and heard petition are Pss. 12; 5; 86; 102; 69; 71; 7; 35A. The transition from the LI to the Psalms of confidence is seen in Pss. 73; 130; 123, and the transition to a didactic Psalm similar to Ps. 1, in Ps. 52.

This fluidity of transition, however, is one of the essential elements in these Psalms. They are all on the way from petition or supplication and lament to praise. It is not possible to determine the points at which they stand on this road. Even the Psalms that are open petition, petition before the turning point in the situation, and end with the vow of praise or a petition, as Pss. 141; 142; 55; 9:13-14; 61; etc., do not *only* stand on that side of the turning point but already anticipate it in the certainty of being heard or in a confession of confidence.

Thus it is that the picture of the Psalter which we find in contemporary research is changed at one point. Scholars have spoken of the absolute preponderance of Psalms of petition, and Gunkel explained this through the frailty of the human heart, which is quick enough to ask, but which readily forgets to thank. When the category which has up till now been called "Song of Thanks of the Individual" is compared with the songs of lament of the individual that judgment is correct. But this comparison is unjustifiable. A major portion of the LI consists of heard

27. The so-called "Psalm of Thanks of Hezekiah" has quite clearly the structure of these heard petitions, and not that of the declarative Psalm of praise or Psalm of thanks!

petitions. Within these Psalms lamentation has been turned into praise. They already contain the "thanks." All these Psalms, in which lament and petition end in a statement that is already declarative praise are rather witnesses to the power of the praise of God, which can well up from the depths. It is no longer possible to speak of an absolute predominance of petition and lament. Rather, precisely this group of heard petitions becomes a powerful witness to the experience of God's intervention, intervention that is able to awaken in the one lamenting, while his sorrow is materially unchanged, the jubilant praise of the God who has heard the suppliant and come down to him.

THE DECLARATIVE PSALM OF PRAISE OF THE PEOPLE (PP)

This category[28] is the most difficult of all. What is presented here can be only tentative. We found a firm connection between the lament and the praise of the individual in the final part of the LI (assurance of being heard), where lamentation was already turned into praise, "for God has heard," "for he has done . . ." There is no such connection between the lamentation and the praise of the people. The corresponding part is found only in very late Psalms (Ps. Sol. 7:6-10; 9:9-11). Perhaps this lack can be explained in that the supplication of the people in a time of national calamity, especially of defeat and its consequences, *could not* be turned so quickly into praise as the supplication of the individual out of his personal need.

Although the predominance of lament over praise in the Psalms of the individual found a simple explanation in the fact that a great many of the LI are petitions that have already been heard and therefore contain the praise of the one who is sure of deliverance, the same cannot be said of the Psalms of the people. This is all the more significant in that there are very few Psalms of praise of the people, as separate Psalms only 124 and 129, which belong to the little collection of the *Ma'alot* Psalms (Psalms of ascent), 120-134. How is this to be explained? It is all but impossible that there can have been as little declara-

28. Gunkel, *Einleitung*, "Danklied Israels," pp. 315 ff.

tive praise of the people, of jubilant, joyous relating of what
God had done for his people, as appears from the Psalter as it
has come down to us. Why, here we are dealing with the fundamental relationship of Israel to her God! What can be the basis
of the fact that the category of the Psalms which has precisely
this as its own theme is represented with such striking rarity in
the Psalter?

One reason is probably that the Psalter as we now have it is
a postexilic collection. The time in which Israel experienced
God's wonderful intervention in *history* lies in the distant
past. To be sure, the remembrance of those saving deeds of God
remained constantly alive. The praise of God, however, which
was uttered directly under the influence of God's saving deed
which had just occurred, was preserved, insofar as it was handed
on at all, only a few places in the Psalter.

There is, though, in the Psalter a strong, indirect witness to
the immediate praise of God for his deeds on behalf of his people, though this praise was not transmitted: those parts of the
LI which look back on the earlier saving activity of God. (See
above, p. 55.) They contain echoes of that praise that was once
awakened in direct response to what God had done.

Another reason could be the fact that this declarative praise
of the people stood in the middle between the conventional expression of the Psalms (poetry) and a simple report. There are
many indications of this, and they will be considered presently.

There is, however, in addition to this first difficulty of the
extremely limited number of Psalms that have been preserved,
a second. These few Psalms belong to different groups. They
belong first of all to the two groups which Gunkel distinguished
in his *Einleitung* as "Song of Thanks of Israel" (pp. 315 ff.) and
"Song of Victory" (pp. 311 ff.). They have in common that
almost every word is filled with the joy which has been released.
God has helped us—we are saved! The following three features
recur in each of the songs:

1. God has acted; let him be praised!

2. Praise is a direct response to the act which has just occurred.

3. Praise is expressed joyously.

Moreover the occasion for praising God is essentially the same in both groups: God has delivered his people in a marvelous manner from the threats of their foes.[29]

The only difference between the two groups is that in the Psalms of praise of the people there is no allusion to a battle that preceded the deliverance, while the report of battle and victory is a component part of the song of victory. Thus there is an appreciable difference between Ps. 124, a detailed song of praise of the people, and Judg. 5, a detailed song of victory. This difference disappears, however, in those songs of both groups which consist of only one or two sentences, that is, where God's saving act or the victory is only alluded to but not recounted. This can be seen on the one hand in Exod. 15:21 and on the other hand in Judg. 16:23 f. In these very brief songs that distinction is no longer of any significance.

To these two groups must be added the epiphanies, that is, Psalms or parts of Psalms in which God's coming to the aid of his people is depicted. It is a question, however, whether they represent originally independent Psalms or whether they were from the beginning a part of a Psalm, a motif. Such an epiphany is found as a part of a Psalm in the song of victory, Judg. 5 (vss. 4-5), and in Ps. 18 (vss. 7-18), which resembles a song of victory, and in addition in many other Psalms and in passages in the prophetic literature. Ps. 114[30] and Ps. 29 are the only epiphanies which are independent Psalms (but these are greatly modified).

Pss. 124; 129; Exod. 15:21; Ps. 66:8-12; Isa. 26:13-19; Ps. Sol. 13:1-4, fall in this category. Motifs or allusions are found in Deut. 32:43; Pss. 44:4-8; 66:6; 81:6-7; 85:1-3; 93:3-4; 126:2-3;

---

29. Gunkel, *op. cit.*, p. 316, "The most frequent occasions of thank festivals in Israel are political in nature."

30. This is questionable. LXX reads 114 and 115 as a single Psalm. Ps. 77:13-20 is combined with an LI.

144:9-10; Isa. 25:1-5 (a mixed form of PI and PP); Isa. 25:9; 2 Macc. 15:34; Judg. 13:17; Luke 1:68-75.

Ps. 124 and Ps. 129 have essentially the same structure and display great similarity in other respects. The main part is the report of deliverance (here they agree even in the metaphor used!): Pss. 124:6, 7; 129:4.

In both Psalms this is preceded only by an allusion that glances back at the time of need. Both are introduced by a jussive after the initial clause, "Let Israel now say." Ps. 118 begins in the same manner. In Ps. 124:7a the report of deliverance is followed by a short sentence which tells the consequence of God's act for the one freed, and this is expanded by a picture; in Ps. 129:5-8 it is followed by the consequences of God's act for the foes.[31]

If the repetitions and expansions through figures of speech are omitted in Ps. 124, the following two sentences remain (1a+3a+6):

> "If it had not been the LORD who was on our side, then they would have swallowed us up alive." "Blessed be the LORD, who has not given us as prey to their teeth!"

In Ps. 129 it is even clearer that these two sentences are the core of the Psalm. Here vss. 1-2 are a summarizing introduction (as in the PI!), and the body of the Psalm (vss. 3-4) then consists of only the two sentences:

> "The plowers plowed upon my back; they made long their furrows. The LORD is righteous; he has cut the cords of the wicked."

In my opinion these two Psalms demonstrate the simplest and most original way of praising God. Yahweh has acted. He has broken the bonds with which his people were bound. For this reason praise is uttered. It consisted of a simple declarative sentence, to which may be added the shout of praise, *"bārūk yahweh!"*

---

31. Ps. 129:8b is probably an addition. **Ps.** 124:8, a confession of confidence, is only loosely connected to the Psalm, even if it originally was a part of it.

The Psalm of Praise of the People

	Exodus 18:10	Exodus 15:21	Ps. 126:3, 4	Ps. 144:9, 10
Shout of praise	Blessed be the LORD	Sing to the LORD	(2, 3) We are glad	I will sing a new song to thee, O God.
Report of God's act	Who has delivered you out of the hand of the Egyptians	He has triumphed gloriously; the horse and his rider he has thrown into the sea	The LORD has done great things for us	Who givest victory to kings, who rescuest David thy servant

	Ps. 124	Ps. 129	Ps. Sol. 13:1-4
Exhortation	Let Israel now say	Let Israel now say	———
Introductory summary	If it had not been the LORD who was on our side	Sorely have they afflicted me . . . yet they have not prevailed	(1, 2) The Lord's right hand has preserved us

Looking back on the time of need	When men rose up against us . . . then they would . . . then over us would have gone	The plowers plowed upon my back	(3) Wild beasts have fallen upon them
Praise	Blessed be the LORD	The LORD is righteous	
Report of God's acts	Who has not given us as prey to their teeth! We have escaped!	He has cut the cords of the wicked	But out of all that the Lord has freed us!
	(8) Confession of confidence	(5-8) Wishes against Zion's foes	

The sentences to which the 124th Psalm were reduced no longer give an unconditional impression of a fixed mode of speech. They sound more like a prose report. Here it can be seen that the PP is still very near to the simple report. Only the sentence Ps. 124:6 (the σκόπος of this Psalm) resembles in its structure and in its meaning a sentence which is often encountered in the historical books, e.g.: Exod. 18:10, "Blessed be the LORD, who has delivered you out of the hand of the Egyptians." But it may also occur without the *bārūk:*

> 2 Sam. 5:20, "And he [David] said, 'The LORD has broken through my enemies before me, like a bursting flood.' "[32]

These sentences show the same three elements which are in general determinative for declarative praise:

1. The praise of Yahweh for a deed that he has done.
2. The nature of these sentences as *immediate* response to God's intervention.
3. The essentially joyful nature of this praise.[33]

In their structure (shout of praise and the reason for it: God has acted) *as well as in these three elements the bārūk sentences in the historical books correspond to the declarative Psalms of praise.* In the declarative Psalms of praise these simple sentences which were born in the moment when help was experienced have become songs.[34]

This connection between the Psalms and the historical reports is further strengthened by the fact that of all the vocabulary of praise only this form of the verb *bārak* (with God as object) is encountered in both places. No other form of any of the vocabulary of praise is encountered in both the historical books and the Psalms.

Here we can recognize the point at which the praise of God in its simplest form is to be found in the midst of the history of

32. Similarly, Gen. 14:19 f.; 1 Sam. 25:32 f., 39; 2 Sam. 18:28; Gen. 24:27; 1 Kings 1:48; 5:21; 10:9; Ruth 2:19 f.; 4:14 f. For the formula, see R. Kittel, *PRE³* XVIII, p. 154.
33. Similarly, Wendel, *Laiengebet,* pp. 170 ff.
34. *Ibid.,* p. 188. Structure: I, Praise; II, Recounting of Praise. "The Hymns show, principally, the same structure."

God's people as reported in the historical books. We can recognize in these sentences the most original and immediate form of the praise of God, the simple and joyous response to a definite act of God which has just been experienced. For this form of the praise of God we can say in any case that its origin is *not* the cult. This praise of God accompanies God's great deeds as their necessary echo:

> Ps. 106:8, 11-12, "Yet he saved them for his name's sake, that he might make known his mighty power." "And the waters covered their adversaries; not one of them was left. Then they believed his words; they sang his praise."

There was no need here for any intermediate step, any arrangement, any particular representation. God's great deeds awaken praise, and this can be expressed in *one* sentence.[35]

There are then many ways in which this one sentence can be varied, repeated, adorned, or developed. Still, the essence of the matter remains contained in the one sentence, as can be seen in Ps. 124 and Ps. 129. The nearer this praise is to God's deed, the shorter and simpler it will be.

The road by which praise moved from this simplest stage to the great descriptive Psalms of praise (hymns) can be seen in miniature with singular clarity in the history of those *bārūk* sentences of which we have spoken above. In the original stage they agree with the sentences in the Psalms.[36] Two passages from Solomon's prayer at the dedication of the temple, 1 Kings 8:14 f. and 55 f., illustrate the second stage. Here the *bārūk* does not follow directly on God's actions, but is rather reserved for the feast day, the great day of the dedication of the temple. One of the three elements, the "today," is here in the background. As a consequence of this, the praise is directed not only to a specific act of God, but to an act that extends over a longer period of time. "Blessed be the LORD who has given rest to his people Israel, according to all that he promised" (1 Kings 8:56). The final

---

35. Köberle, "Die Motive des Glaubens an die Gebetserhörung im A.T.," Leipzig, 1901. He regards the deliverance from Egypt as the most important of these motifs, pp. 15, 20, 23.

36. Thus Pss. 124:6; 68:19; 28:6; 66:20; 18:46; 144:1.

stage can be seen in the doxologies that conclude the books of the Psalter.[37]

Here there is no concrete occasion for praise. The cry of praise, *bārūk*, has been entirely removed from the historical scene and is a timeless liturgy. In the place of the very simple language of the *bārūk* sentences there now appears in Ps. 72:18 f., for example, a developed, liturgically full, and solemn language, and these sentences become like the heavy, golden implements of an altar.

The fact that the *bārūk* sentences of the earlier stage resemble the central part of the declarative Psalms of praise points to the possibility that there were Psalms of praise of the people which were contained in one sentence. Such a Psalm has been preserved in what is apparently the oldest Psalm of Israel, the so-called Song of Miriam, Exod. 15:21:

> "Sing to the LORD, for he has triumphed gloriously;*
> the horse and his rider he has thrown into the sea."[38]

This sentence is a typical declarative Psalm of praise with the cry of praise and the reason for it, God's deed. Here we do not find the looking back to the time of need as a separate part of the Psalm, and it is only hinted at in the second sentence, which is an explication of God's act. Exod. 15:21 contains the three elements (see above) which constitute the essence of declarative praise. The twofold nature of the sentence is to be observed. The second part reports the saving deed itself, and the first part gives the action of God which led to it. This corresponds to the double request, for God to turn to the one praying ("Arise!") and for God's intervention. The former is expressed in a singular manner in Exod. 15:21; the verb is not used in connection with God elsewhere in the O.T. (although its derivatives are), and it is to be understood in a sense similar to that of *qūm*, which is often applied to God both in laments and in praise.

---

37. Pss. 41:13; 72:18 f.; 89:52; 106:48 (=41:13).

* Westermann translates here "denn hoch hat er sich erhoben," "for he has arisen on high."

38. LXX reads, "Let us sing," probably correctly.

A sentence from a Psalm of the time of the exile, Ps. 126:3, is similar to the Song of Miriam, "The LORD has done great things for us; we are glad." This sentence shows that the basic character and the simple structure of the declarative Psalm of praise were preserved down to that period.[39]

THE SONGS OF VICTORY

Judg. 5; 16:23 f.; Pss. 118:15 f.; (149?); Judith 16.
Motifs of the songs of victory are found in Pss. 68; 18; 149; Exod. 15; Deut. 32.

As far as the songs which consist of a single sentence are concerned it is hardly possible to stress any difference between this group and the former one. Exod. 15:21 is certainly no song of victory, because no battle took place, but it can scarcely be separated from those short songs of victory, which are to be recognized as such by the situation in which they arose.

Thus there has been transmitted to us in its original form what is probably a very old song of the Philistines which they sang when they had overcome Samson:

Judg. 16:23 f., "Our god has given Samson our enemy into our hand."

In verse 24 the song is given once again, now expanded by a twofold designation of "our enemy," which in content corresponds to the element of "looking back to the time of need":

"... the ravager of our country,
who has slain many of us."

This small variation gives an indication of the way in which a song which originally consisted of a single sentence, or rather a mere shout of joy, could gradually grow into a song. It shows

---

39. There are two indications that this declarative praise of God was really much more frequent and varied than the sources would now lead us to believe. The first of these is the constant feature of the historical books, where after a marvelous, saving act of God a memorial is set up (e.g., 1 Sam. 14:35, and Josh. 4:20-23). This memorial was intended to bear witness to God's saving action. The other indication is the personal names, of which a great many have the significance of declarative praise, not only of the individual, but also of the people. Cf. Noth, *Die israelitischen Personennamen*, Stuttgart, 1928; Greiff, *Das Gebet im A.T.*, Münster, 1915, p. 93.

also that looking back to the time of dire need is not necessarily a part of it, but is rather the first expansion which the simple sentence underwent.

The Song of Deborah, the only extensive song of victory from pre-exilic times that has been transmitted fully, shows by its structure that it is similar to the Psalms of praise of the people, or that it is a type of Psalm of praise of the people.

Judg. 5: 2-3: Exhortation to praise Yahweh.
        4-5: Portrayal of the epiphany of God.
        6-8: Looking back at the time of need.
        9-11: New introduction (a call to praise God).
        12-30: Account of the victory.
        31: God's foes—God's friends.

The Song of Deborah, moreover, contains many of the traits that are associated with the "Holy War."[40]

Israel's songs of victory from the early period were likely connected closely with the wars of Yahweh. The early end of this institution must be the reason that so few of them have been preserved.[41] It is to be assumed that the "Book of the Wars of Yahweh" also contained Israelite songs of victory. On the basis of the material that has been transmitted, it seems reasonable to conclude that praise of Yahweh for the victory was an essential part of the wars of Yahweh. Just as the Song of Deborah is a part, namely the conclusion of one of the wars of Yahweh, so the Song of the Philistines, Judg. 16:23 f., has come down to us as a part of the celebration in a service of worship after the overcoming of the foe. The expression of this short song, "Our god has given into our hand . . . ," has been shown by von Rad to be a statement connected with the holy war (*op. cit.*, pp. 7 f.). The same seems to be the case with the statement of Saul that concludes the battle in 1 Sam. 11:13, ". . . for today the LORD has wrought deliverance in Israel." Praise of God for victory is also preserved in a very late passage, 2 Chron. 20:26.[42]

40. Cf. von Rad, *Der Heilige Krieg im alten Israel*, Zürich, 1951, pp. 18 ff.
41. *Ibid.*, p. 33.
42. Cf. *ibid.*, p. 80 f.

The sentence in 1 Sam. 11:13 is very close to Ps. 118:15 f. where we have echoes of a song of victory:

Hark, glad songs of victory in the tents of the righteous:
"The right hand of the LORD does valiantly,
    the right hand of the LORD is exalted,
    the right hand of the LORD does valiantly!"

Allusions to the song of victory are found frequently. Ps. 68, above all, is permeated by the motifs of these songs: vss. 1-4 (cf. Judg. 5:31!); 8-9 (epiphany of God); 11-14; 17-18; 20; 22-23; 35. In Ps. 18, an epiphany of God has been inserted into a PI (vss. 7-15), and vss. 32-48 are probably a sharply modified portion of a song of victory. In Deut. 32, vss. 40-43 are reminiscent of a song of victory, as are vss. 65-66 in Ps. 78. It can also be said of Ps. 149 that it contains echoes of a song of victory in vss. 4-9.[43]

The original form of the song of victory, looking back to the time of need, the report of the victory, and the praise of God, can no longer be recognized here. On the other hand, Judith 16:2-21 shows the revival of the song of victory in very late times with the old structure. There is, however, a very distinctive difference between it and Judg. 5; in Judith there is no battle! Judith alone did the deed (vss. 7-11) that put the foes to flight (vss. 12-13), and the only task the men had was to kill the fleeing enemies (vs. 14). Here too there is a feature of the epiphany (vs. 18). The conclusion, vss. 19-21, corresponds to Judg. 5:31.

Gunkel (*op. cit.,* p. 341) draws attention to the fact that when there were again victories in Israel in very late times, "hymns" replaced songs of victory, and he refers to 1 Macc. 13:48-51 and 2 Macc. 3:30. The same could be said of 2 Chron. 20:26. In the later history of Israel the song of victory could live on only as an eschatological song that anticipated the coming victory of Yahweh. But no distinctive development took place here. It was also a set motif in some of the Zion Psalms, in which a victory of Yahweh over his foes before his city Zion was celebrated.

43. Gunkel regarded this Psalm as an eschatological hymn that had been written for the future victory feast (see his commentary on this passage).

This is seen above all in Ps. 48:2-8; in Pss. 46:4-7; 76:3-6, and perhaps also in Ps. 68.

These motifs of the eschatological songs of victory are very close to the enthronement Psalms. Both are Psalms of expectation. God's entry into his kingship, however, is not connected with a victory of God, but with a day of judgment of the nations.

THE EPIPHANY OF GOD

Judg. 5:4-5; Ps. 18:7-15; Hab. 3:3-15; Pss. 68:7 f., 33; 77:16-19; 97:2-5; 114; 29; 50:1-3; Deut. 33; Isa. 30:27-33; 59:15b-20; 63:1-6; Mic. 1:3-4; Nah. 1:3b-6; Zech. 9:14; Judith 16:18.

It is striking that in the few songs of victory that have been preserved there is often connected a portrayal or at least an allusion to the epiphany of God. Judg. 5:4-5; Pss. 68:7-8, 33; 18:7-15; Judith 16:18 (cf. Zech. 9:15 following vs. 14). That which unites them is God's intervention to help his people. When he intervenes in this way, God appears from afar (epiphany), and he fulfills his purpose by gaining victory for his people (song of victory). Thus in Judg. 5 there follows on the epiphany (vss. 4-5) the report of victory. It is therefore reasonable to assume that the epiphanies were originally parts of Psalms, and do not represent independent Psalms.[44]

Judg. 5:4-5 begins, "LORD, when thou didst go forth from Seir" (or, "When thou goest out"). Thus also Ps. 68:7. Similar are Hab. 3; Deut. 33; Isa. 30; Mic. 1:5; Nah. 1:3. The beginning of the epiphany resembles unmistakably the epiphany of a god in the Babylonian and Egyptian psalms. For example:

The great hymn to Shamash, VR 50 and 51, Stummer, *op. cit.*, p. 40, Zimmern A, p. 15:

"Shamash, when thou goest forth from thy great mountain,
The great gods come before thee to judgment. . . ."
Hymn K 256 (also IV R 17), Stummer, *op. cit.*, p. 41:

---

44. Further evidence is the fact that they can be occasionally heard in the laments of the people; see above, p. 63.

The Epiphany of God

	Hab. 3:3-15	Judg. 5:4-5	Ps. 18:7-15
God comes from . . .	God came from Teman and the Holy One from Mount Paran	LORD, when thou didst go forth from Seir, when thou didst march from the region of Edom	He bowed the heavens, and came down; thick darkness was under his feet
The earth quakes	He stood and measured the earth; he looked and shook the nations	The earth trembled	Then the earth reeled and rocked
Mountains quake	Then the eternal mountains were scattered, the everlasting hills sank low	The mountains quaked before the LORD	The foundations also of the mountains trembled
Upon horses and chariots	Was thy wrath against the rivers? When thou didst ride upon thy horses, upon thy chariot of victory	——	He rode on a cherub and flew . . . upon the wings of the wind

Streams of water	Thou didst cleave the earth with rivers. The mountains saw thee, and writhed; the raging waters swept on; the deep gave forth its voice	The heavens dropped, yea, the clouds dropped water	Then the channels of the sea were seen
Thunder			The LORD also thundered in the heavens
Darkness	The sun and moon stood still in their habitation	——	He made darkness his covering around him, his canopy thick clouds dark with water
Arrows	At the light of thine arrows as they sped . . . flash . . . spear	——	He sent out his arrows . . . lightnings . . . blast
Before Yahweh (his wrath)	Thou didst bestride the earth in fury, thou didst trample the nations in anger. Thou didst trample the sea with thy horses	Before the LORD, before the LORD, the God of Israel	At thy rebuke, O LORD, at the blast of the breath of thy nostrils
God comes to help his people	Thou wentest forth for the salvation of thy people	(vs. 11) The triumphs of the LORD, the triumphs of his peasantry in Israel	He reached from on high, he took me, he drew me out of many waters.

"Great Lord, when thou goest forth in the bright heavens
. . .

Openest the great door of the bright heavens,
Then (Anu and) Enlil worship thee with joy . . ."

Stummer pointed out the similarity of this hymn's opening lines
to Judg. 5:4-5 (*op. cit.*, pp. 44 ff.). In another connection Gunkel
compared Ps. 68 and a hymn to Adad in Ungnad, *Die Religion
der Babylonier und Assyrer*, Jena, 1921, p. 194:

"When the Lord roars, the heavens tremble before him;
When Adad is angry, the earth quakes before him;
Great mountains break down before him . . ."

The clearly mythological language of the descriptions of epiphanies in the Psalms is to be explained on the basis of this background of other ancient religions. A whole list of parallels in individual features could be added.[45] Stummer, however, pointed
out[46] the characteristic difference between these and the biblical
epiphanies, that is, the Bible borrowed the schema, but the relation to the calendar has disappeared. In this connection it must
be said that in the place of a cosmic-mythical occurrence in the
Babylonian epiphanies there is in the O.T. a historical one:
Yahweh appears in order to help his people and to destroy his
foes. In one passage, however, this historicizing of a mythical
motif is carried one step further. In Ps. 114:1 the exodus of Israel
from Egypt has taken the place of God's appearing.[47] Ps. 114 is
the only one in which the epiphany constitutes the entire Psalm.[48]
It gives a late variation of the epiphany. Only with certain
reservations can Ps. 29 be included here. Here the epiphany
has been greatly modified in the direction of praise of the mighty

45. These are mentioned in part in the commentaries.
46. *Op. cit.*, p. 46.
47. Perhaps this alteration of the beginning of the Psalm can still be recognized.
Verse 2 begins, "Judah became his sanctuary." The suffix of the third person in the
two halves of vs. 2 (read, *memshalto*) can only refer to Yahweh. The subject of vs. 1,
however, is Israel. Verse 2 therefore presupposes a beginning of the Psalm in which
Yahweh was the subject! A similar change is to be assumed for Ps. 97, where the
original beginning of the epiphany was replaced by "The LORD reigns."
48. But LXX reads 114 and 115 as one Psalm.

voice of God, in a way that is similar to the hymn of the storm god Adad.[49]

In the other passages the epiphanies of God are encountered in a variety of contexts. The actual connection, however, remains always the same, whether explicit or implicit: God appears in order to help his people. The vitality of this motif which appears in the poetic literature of the O.T. in such varied places and at such different times is anchored in neither history nor cult, but in the experience of this help. And moreover in most of the epiphanies this event is related to the events that occurred at the beginning of Israel's history,[50] above all to the events at the Red Sea. This tight interweaving of the accounts of epiphanies with the initial events as well as the relatively independent appearance of the epiphanies in so many contexts can be explained most simply by the fact that the account of the epiphany was originally historicized in connection with those occurrences.[51]

That first occasion on which God came to the aid of his people was experienced anew in God's saving deeds. In this way it became a part of the songs of victory, and is heard again in a variety of contexts where God's helping and saving acts for his people are told or sung. In correspondence with later theology there also developed out of Yahweh's coming from a place in the desert a coming "from far" (Isa. 30:27), or "from the heavens" (Ps. 18:9), "out of his place" (Mic. 1:3), "out of Zion" (Ps. 50:2).

How greatly the epiphanies could be altered in this process is shown by the framework in Hab. 3 and Deut. 33. In the latter passage the epiphany is the framework of the blessing of Moses (vss. 2, 26 f.), and in Hab. 3 it is in the framework of the prophet's vision (vss. 2, 16).

In Isa. 30:27-33 and Mic. 1:3 ff. the epiphany is connected with the prophetic proclamation of doom. In Mic. 1:3 ff. the God who punishes strides forth against the capital city of his people (vss.

49. Jastrow, *Religion*, I, pp. 482 f. Cf. F. M. Cross, "Notes on a Canaanite Psalm in the O.T.," *BASOR* 117 (1950), pp. 19-21.

50. E.g., Judg. 5:4-5; Pss. 18:15; 77:15 f., 19 f., etc.

51. In this I am building on a surmise of Gunkel's in reference to Ps. 77:17-20: "May we assume that there was an old poem that expanded the saga of the Red Sea with such mythological features, and that this account contains echoes of it?"

6, 9), and in Isa. 30 God comes in order to intervene for his people against Assyria.

And finally in Zech. 9:14-17 and Isa. 59:15b-20 and 63:1-6 the epiphany is transformed into apocalypse. This line of development could be followed out even further.

The structure and motifs of the epiphany

A comparison of all the passages shows that *one* form is the basis of the many variants. There are only a few sentences that are met with only once, and several expressions are found in all the passages. The following three features are most frequently encountered, and they clearly represent the outline of the epiphany:

1. God's coming from, or his going forth from . . .
2. Cosmic disturbances which accompany this coming of God.
3. God's (wrathful) intervention for or against . . .

The difficulty of this outline lies in the fact that the third part is almost always demanded by the context and is to be deduced from it, but that it is hardly ever met with as a part of the epiphany. Thus for example in Judg. 5 and Ps. 18 the epiphany is separated from the account of victory, and in Deut. 33 the epiphany is the framework which contains the varied deeds of God for the various tribes. Even in Mic. 1:3 ff. God's intervention does not belong to the epiphany, but to the prophetic proclamation of doom which follows it. It is a part of the epiphany itself only in Hab. 3 and Isa. 30. On the other hand there are few epiphanies which do not contain allusions to the events of the early days. These facts strengthen the above surmise concerning the origin of the epiphany.

The explanation given here of the accounts of epiphanies in the Psalms differs radically from the cultic explanation of these passages as it has now been particularly developed by Weiser in the *Bertholet-Festschrift* (1950).[52]

52. "Zur Frage nach den Beziehungen der Psalmen zum Kult. Die Darstellung der Theophanie in den Psalmen und im Festkult," pp. 513-531.

1. Weiser rightly opposes the position that these passages are only poetic decorations, "stylized, obsolete traditional material." "For the poets of the Psalms the theophany must have still had living reality."

In his explanation Weiser proceeded from the thesis that "As far as the history of tradition is concerned the representations of the theophany have as their model the Sinai theophany." The careful comparison of Exod. 19 and Exod. 34 on the one hand with the epiphanies listed at the beginning of this section on the other hand gives the following results. The third of the three structural features which are encountered in almost all epiphanies is completely lacking in Exod. 19 and 34. Here God appears to a mediator in order to speak with him. What he says concerns of course the entire people, but the people take part in it only from afar. This self-revelation of God in Exod. 19 and 34 displays the basic features of a cultic occurrence:

> the locality: a specific place (the sacred boundary), 19:12, 13;
> the time: a specified day (with preparations for sanctification), 19:11;
> the personnel: Moses as the mediator of God's activity toward the people.

These cultic features are totally lacking in the epiphanies. They are in the nature of an event in history. We have then to distinguish between two types of divine appearances which are different from the very first.

In Exod. 19 and 34 God appears in order to reveal himself, and to communicate with his people through a mediator. This is a theophany.

In Judg. 5, etc., God appears in order to aid his people. This is an epiphany. (I am proposing this distinction of terminology on practical grounds.)

There are two groups of theophanies that may be distinguished from each other. In addition to the Sinai theophany there are later appearances of God to a prophet: 1 Kings 19; Isa. 6; Ezek. 1, 2. The significance of the divine appearance in these passages is to give a commission to the prophet (1 Kings 19:15) or to issue a call to prophetic service (Isa. 6; Ezek. 1, 2). They have the following points in common with the Sinai theophany:

I. God appears to one individual.
II. He appears in order to say something.

They are different in that the goal of God's appearing is in the latter cases the giving of a commission to a prophet (or the calling of a prophet), and thus they do not have the nature of a cultic occurrence.[53]

2. The distinction between two basic forms of God's appearing is therefore based on the different goals that these appearances have. But the actual events of God's appearing are different in the two instances.

(a) In Exod. 19 the report tells that God descended onto a mountain; in Judg. 5, etc., the report tells of God's breaking forth and coming out from a specific place.

(b) In Exod. 19 the fixed point, whose name we are told, is the *goal* of God's coming. In Judg. 5 the fixed point, whose name is given, is the *starting point* from which God comes.

(c) God himself determines the place at which he appears in Exod. 19, but in Judg. 5, the place where he appears is the scene of his people's distress.

3. The phenomena that accompany the two types of divine appearances are all that remains to them in common. But even here the agreement is by no means complete. In the epiphanies the accompanying phenomenon of Exod. 19 which is most often found is the quaking of the mountains. In Exod. 19, however, it is *the* mountain which quakes, and in the epiphanies we find only the plural (often with the parallelism of mountains and hills). The smoke, which is so important in the manifestation of God at Sinai, is found only once in the epiphanies, in Ps. 18. And here the conception is different from that in Exod. 19.

Of the various accompanying phenomena only the clouds cor-

---

53. Strictly speaking this is true only for 1 Kings 19 and Isa. 6. In Ezek. 1, 2, there are features which are unmistakably cultic.

respond exactly in the two types of passages. In Exod. 19 the quaking of the earth (the most frequent feature of the epiphanies) and the pouring of water from the clouds are both missing. In the account of the Yahwist[54] there is no shooting of arrows (lightning) and no divine thunder or voice. The Elohist speaks of lightning and of the blasts of a trumpet.

The total comparison shows that even with reference to the accompanying phenomena the differences are more pronounced than the similarities. Specifically, it appears that for the theophany in Exod. 19 the volcanic activity (fire, smoke, quaking of *one* mountain) are typical, and for the epiphanies, the meteorological activity (thunder, lightning, rain). In addition, however, we find the quaking of the earth and the shaking, or shattering, or melting of the mountains caused by the approach of Yahweh.

If this comparison of the two types of the manifestations of God is accurate, it will not be possible to call Exod. 19 the prototype of the epiphanies in the Psalter. This then casts doubt on the conclusion which Weiser drew from that thesis, namely that the theophany tradition had its origin in the cult of the festivals and that it went back to the Sinai theophany, which was "re-presented" and actualized in it. What Weiser said (*op. cit.*, p. 519) by way of summary concerning the significance of these theophanies, that God himself was hidden in the dark clouds and revealed himself in his word, fits only Exod. 19 and the prophetic revelations, and there is no single case where it applies to the epiphanies. Thus these epiphanies in the Psalms cannot bear witness to a "sacral act of sacramental effect," which presented a "cultic recapitulation of the ancient event" (that is, the theophany at Sinai).

The epiphanies belong to the context of the declarative praise of Israel. In them the God is praised who intervened in the decisive hour to help his people and to save them from their foes. They can be traced back to Israel's original experience of God's saving intervention at the Red Sea. This is shown by the allusions to this event in Hab. 3; Ps. 77; Nah. 1; Pss. 18; 114.

54. Following Beer's division of sources.

THE DECLARATIVE PSALM OF PRAISE OF THE INDIVIDUAL[55]

The structure can be seen in the chart. The Psalm of lament and the Psalm of praise of the individual are connected by three features.

I. In the "petition that has been heard" the vow of praise was followed by a section, usually consisting of only a single sentence, which corresponded in content and form to the main part of the declarative Psalm of praise: Pss. 13:5; 3:7; 10:17; 6:8; 54:7; 56:13; 31:7; 28:6; 31:21; 22:24, 31; Isa. 38:17b. All these statements are reports of deliverance. Ps. 56:13 reads, "For thou hast delivered my soul from death." *The petition that has been heard leads to declarative praise.*[56]

Here it at once becomes clear that (declarative) praise results from God's actions. God's intervention is the source of declarative praise. This declaration of praise reports what God has done. This is true both of the heard petition and of the declarative Psalm of praise.

II. The most frequent introduction in the declarative Psalms of praise is the voluntative, as in Ps. 30:1, "I will extol thee," perhaps also in Ps. 18:1 (cj.), in Ps. 138:1, 2a, "I give thee thanks, O LORD," in Ecclus. 51, and in Ps. 34:1, "I will bless the LORD at all times." In Ps. 107:8, 15, 21, 31, verbs in the jussive have the same force as the voluntative. This whole Psalm is no longer properly declarative praise, but a liturgical exhortation to such praise. The set formula, "O give thanks to the LORD, for he is good," has been placed at the beginning of the Psalm as an introduction to the liturgy.[57]

Precisely in this connection it becomes clear that the call to praise in the imperative is not the original introduction of the Psalm of declarative praise. Only once does an imperative serve

---

55. Pss. 116; 30; 40:1-12; 18; 107; 66:13-20; 118; 138; 34; 52; Jonah 2:2-9; Lam. 3:52-58; Job 33:26-28; Ecclus. 51; Ps. Sol. 15:1-6; 16:1-15 (Add. Dan. 1:65); Od. Sol. 25; 29 (9:2-11 is a mixed form). A unique development of the PI is found in Dan. 2:20-23 where declarative praise is introduced by descriptive praise.
56. So also Gunkel, *op. cit.*, p. 265.
57. Properly it is the introduction of the descriptive Psalm of praise, vss. 33-43, which concludes the whole Psalm.

Declarative Psalm of Praise (Psalm of Thanks) of the Individual

	Ps. 66:13-20	Ps. 30	Ps. 40	Ps. 18
Proclamation	(13-15) of sacrifice (16) of praise	I will extol thee, O LORD	(6-10)	I love thee (I will extol thee?), O LORD
Introductory summary	I cried aloud to him, and he was extolled with my tongue	For thou hast drawn me up	(11)	(3?)
Looking back at the time of need	If I had cherished iniquity in my heart	(6, 7) I said in my prosperity . . . Thou didst hide thy face		(4, 5) The cords of death encompassed me
Report of deliverance — I cried	(I cried aloud to him)	To thee, O LORD, I cried . . . Hear, O LORD	I waited patiently for the LORD	In my distress I called upon the LORD
Report of deliverance — He heard	But truly God has listened		He inclined to me and heard my cry	(6b) He heard (7-15, Epiphany)
Report of deliverance — He drew me out	(What he has done for me)	Thou hast turned for me my mourning into dancing	He drew me up . . . and set my feet	16-19 He reached from on high, he took me

Renewed vow of praise	Blessed be God	That my soul may praise thee and not be silent. O LORD my God, I will give thanks to thee for ever	He put a new song in my mouth, a song of praise to our God	(49) For this I will extol thee, O LORD, among the nations
Praise (descriptive)	He has not rejected my prayer or removed his steadfast love from me	(The expansion in vss. 4-5)	(5) Thou hast multiplied . . . thy wondrous deeds and thy thoughts toward us	(27) Thou dost deliver . . . thou dost bring down (30 f.) This God—his way is perfect

as introduction of the PI, and this is in a declarative Psalm of praise that has become a liturgy, Ps. 118.[58]

The first part of Ps. 92, vss. 1-3, is a reflection on praise, and the introduction proper in vs. 4 is then also a voluntative. The same is true of Ps. 66, which begins with an exhortation to hear, as is usual in the wisdom literature.[59] Ps. 40A and Ps. Sol. 15 and 16 are without any introduction. Thus it can be said that the introduction of the declarative Psalms of praise is usually a voluntative. We saw that in its literary aspect the vow of praise is a conclusion, but in its content an announcement of the praise that was promised in the vow.[60] In the vow of praise, the Psalm of petition and lamentation is open toward praise. The voluntative, then, in the beginning of the declarative Psalm of praise, is simply taking up where the vow of praise left off. That which was promised there is now to take place.[61]

The change that was necessitated by the fact that the vow of praise at the end of the petition became the beginning of declarative praise was very slight. The vow of praise was made in the face of immediate, pressing need. Even when the one praying poured out his heart in the temple and received the answer through a saving word from God, he was alone in all this action. In the vow he promises to praise God, to make his name great. But this can happen only in a group of people (cf. the forensic aspects of the vow). The vow of praise therefore means in simple words that he will tell others what God has done for him. It is in this and not in the vocabulary of praise, not even in a simple

58. The same is true of the small declarative Psalm of praise, Add. Dan. 1:65, which is added to a descriptive Psalm of praise:
"Praise the Lord, O Hananiah, Azariah, and Mishael,
Sing his praise and magnify him forever,
For he has delivered us from the grave
And saved us from the power of death."
59. Similar to this is the exhortation to take heed to what was said at the end of Ps. 107 (vs. 43).
60. See above, pp. 38-39.
61. We have established that the same was true of the Babylonian psalms of praise. There, however, it is striking that the vow of praise soon lost its character of announcement of praise, and is to be found in many cases where it is followed directly by petition and lament. This must be connected with the fact that this announcement properly belongs to declarative praise. In Babylon, however, declarative praise of the individual did not develop into a separate category. We are aware of only the one example at the end of the lament of an old man. See above.

expression of thanks, that he praises God, that he extols him.

The only difference when the vow of praise is announced is that he *is* now in a group to whom he can tell what has happened to him. When this announcement comes at the beginning there are never specifications of a forensic nature. This would no longer have any meaning, because the forum, the group, the congregation is there. This is shown in Ps. 66:16. The use of the third person is grounded in this forensic nature of the praise of God. God is praised by the others who hear what he has done. But this does not mean that speaking of God in the third person is thereby any less praise that is directed to God.

III. The introductory summary. On several occasions in petitions that have been heard the vow of praise is based on a brief report, cf. especially Ps. 13:6. The declarative Psalm of praise of the individual (see the table) is the only Psalm category that regularly has after the introduction a short summary that corresponds exactly to the vow of praise and the reason it gives for praise:

> Ps. 116:1, "I love the LORD, because he has heard my voice and my supplications."
> Ps. 138:3, "On the day I called, thou didst answer me."

If the vow of praise of Ps. 56 is placed alongside the proclamation of Ps. 30, it can be seen how closely they correspond to each other:

> Ps. 56:12 f., "I will render thank offerings to thee. For thou hast delivered my soul from death."
> Ps. 30:1, 3, "I will extol thee, O LORD . . . thou hast brought up my soul from Sheol."

This third combining of petition and praise means that the two categories correspond in having a section that could exist in itself as a Psalm. It has exactly the same structure as Exod. 15:21!

What is the meaning of this short summary at the beginning

of the declarative Psalm of praise? The Psalms of praise of the people give a clue. We found in both Ps. 124 and Ps. 129 that they basically consist of a single sentence, or one compound sentence. The expansions through which this sentence became a song are recognizable as such at first glance. The Song of Miriam, Exod. 15:21, consists of only one sentence, and this is the case even with Ps. 93, if the introduction and conclusion are left out of account. The category of the declarative Psalm of praise clearly has the tendency to be concentrated in a single sentence. The content of this sentence is always the same (although it never becomes stereotyped, as should be noted especially here): God has intervened; he has saved. This, however, is never said as a statement of fact, but always as a confession. That is to say, the one who utters this sentence backs it up with his own existence; he is committed to the fact that this has happened to him. The principal word in the vocabulary of praise is *hōdāh*. The form of this word, "I will praise" (which is its most frequent form) means also "I will confess."

All true, living confession, however, occurs in *one* sentence.[62] The tendency of the declarative Psalm of praise to concentrate itself into *one* sentence, or the comprehension of the declarative Psalm of praise in a single sentence, is due to its being confession. In it God is lauded, praised, exalted by my acknowledging, confessing before men that he has helped me. As confession this praise of God must be capable of being comprehended in *one* sentence.

62. This is shown also by the history of the confessions of the church. The original confession of Christendom is the single sentence Κύριος Ἰησοῦς, (in various formulations, cf. esp. Phil. 2:11). The Apostles' Creed is a development of this sentence, which was then more and more expanded in the confessions of the great councils.
The confessions of the Reformation period show this clearly once again. Luther's Smalcald Articles are in their structure clearly the development of *one* sentence (that of the *articulus stantis et cadentis ecclesiae*). The Augsburg Confession of Melanchthon is a summary of separate confessional sentences, but in it the one sentence of justification (Art. IV) is clearly the most prominent. That which then follows, the Apology and later the Formula of Concord, is no longer properly confession but explanation of confession. The moment of existence in which a confession can be made in one sentence was no longer present. In the Barmen Declaration this moment was again present, and all its statements are only the development of the first thesis, "Jesus Christ, as the holy Scriptures of the Old and New Testaments bear witness to him, is the *one* Word of God which we must hear, which we are to trust and obey in life and in death."

The fact that the Psalms of this category are still aware of the simplicity of true praise of God may be taken as a sign of the power of such simple confessional praise. Still more, however, must it be taken as a direct testimony to God's marvelous activity for mankind, testimony which preserved this simplicity despite the opposing tendency of all cultic activity. It is this simplicity which is seen in the words of the song of Exod. 15:21 and in the confession which defies reality in Ps. 126:3 and Job 1:21. However different these sentences and their circumstances may be, they still contain the same declaration, "Yahweh has acted." This means for the category of the declarative Psalms of praise of the individual that they are and intend to be nothing but the development of this one sentence. There is in the entire O.T. no finer and clearer example of such speaking that has no purpose except the explication of *one* sentence which precedes it. This is the reason that this group of Psalms has the strictest structure of all Psalm categories. There are in all 15 or 18 (Ps. 107 properly consists of four Psalms) songs which have this same structure. At least ten of them agree in the three parts and the four motifs of the main part, and almost all of them also agree in the order of the parts. This group enables us best to understand and demonstrate that the speech of the Psalms is determined from within. In spite of this regularity, the manner of speaking never becomes stereotyped. These Psalms show how a confession can speak with many voices and also with one.

The Main Section

In the Psalm of praise the various parts develop so obviously that there is no need to explain this further: the looking back to the time of need and the report proper of deliverance with its threefold message, "I cried to God—he heard—he delivered me." This then climaxes in a vow of praise that is usually followed by (in most cases descriptive) praise.

A few comments must be made on details.

1. The lament of the people and of the individual show the dual nature of the petitions "Hear!" and "Save!" The influence

of this duality was felt in the heard petitions, where praise resulted from the certainty of being heard. The report of God's intervention in declarative praise is likewise in two parts: he heard (inclined to me), and he delivered. Here that which we found to be the meaning of this duality of petition is confirmed. Neither in those petitions nor in this praise is it a question of only the momentary need and its being met. Suffering is understood in terms of God's being distant, asleep, or silent. Thus in the petition as in the praise it is really a question concerning God. It is a very serious matter that *God* should again be favorable to man. The Psalm of praise rejoices because *God* has heard and answered.

2. In the looking back to the time of need (this corresponds to the lament in the Psalms of petition) two features attract particular attention. This need may be described as being bound (Pss. 116:3; 18:4-5), but it is much more frequently described as being under the power of death.[63]

The typical speech of all these Psalms (including Jonah 2) makes it clear that the one speaking does not at all intend to speak of what actually happened to him. The Psalmist does not intend to relate what happened to him, but to testify what God has done for him. For the congregation before whom he praised God with this confession the important thing was not the "individual features" but the testimony of the witness. The one confessing in this manner did not intend to give a picture, but to call to them, "O magnify the LORD with me, and let us exalt his name together!" (Ps. 34:3).

3. Two statements seem to me to make it clear what it was that was decisive for the singers of these Psalms of praise.

(a) Ps. 40:2 f., "He drew me up from the desolate pit . . . He put a new song in my mouth, a song of praise to our God."

Here God's mighty deeds and the praise which grew out of them are viewed as one. It is a "new" song, not because of a new melody or new thoughts, but because God's miracle was new.

---

63. Cf. here Christoph Barth, *Die Errettung vom Tode,* Dissertation, Zollikon, 1947, I gratefully agree with all the essentials of this work.

(b) Ps: 30:11, "Thou hast turned for me my mourning into dancing."

The meaning of this sentence is similar to that of Ps. 40:3, but it speaks even more clearly of the transformation that has occurred in that the deliverance and the rejoicing that it produced are here totally united. In both passages praise is so closely and firmly related to God's saving intervention that it can even be designated as belonging itself to God's act of deliverance. These passages show better than any explanation the real Sitz-im-Leben of the praise of God in Israel (see above, p. 24).

4. What is the meaning of the vow of praise at the end of declarative praise, when it really belongs at the conclusion of petition? Psalm 116:12-14 gives a clue: "What shall I render to the LORD for all his bounty to me? I will lift up the cup of salvation . . ." This word is spoken at the end of declarative praise. And thus an "I will" stands at the end of almost each of these Psalms. Here again the inadequacy of the word "thank" is evident. What could be the significance of a vow of thanks at the end of a Psalm of thanks? If, however, these Psalms are a mode of praise, then the vow of praise at the end of declarative praise takes on special meaning in relation to the vow at the end of petition. That which the one praying promised at the end of petition, and proclaimed in the introduction of declarative praise, has now occurred. *But not a single one of these Psalms ends with the final part of the report, "and he drew me out."* That praise which arises out of the moment of deliverance does not come to an end when the deliverance has been reported once. Psalm 30:11 f., "Thou hast loosed my sackcloth and girded me with gladness, that my soul may praise thee and not be silent." In this sentence the meaning of the vow of praise at the end of the report of deliverance is clearly expressed: praise cannot be silent, but must be continually expressed. The same thing is said in a different manner in Ps. 118:17, "I shall not die, but I shall live, and recount the deeds of the LORD." The life which was restored by deliverance out of *sheōl* finds its meaning in praise.

Similarly Ps. 92:14 f., "They [the righteous] are ever full of sap and green, to show that the LORD is upright." Cf. Isa. 38:18 f.

5. A further distinction from the vow of praise at the end of the petition points in the same direction. While there the foundation of the vow of praise is in most passages the specific saving action, praise which summarizes, brings together, and describes always follows the vow of praise at the end of declarative praise, except in Ps. 66. Ps. 40:5 shows particularly well how this develops out of declarative praise: "Thou hast multiplied, O LORD my God, thy wondrous deeds." Here we can sense how declarative praise passes into descriptive praise. Similarly, Ps. 116:15, "Precious in the sight of the LORD is the death of his saints." This statement is still focused on specific deliverance, but it looks beyond one saving deed to the total activity of God.

Already at the end of the petitions that had been heard, statements which described the totality of God's actions, in Pss. 10:16, 18; 12:6; 102:24b-27 were made alongside the statement, "Yahweh has acted." They are the rule at the end of Psalms of declarative praise:

> Jonah 2:9c, "Deliverance belongs to the LORD."
> Ps. 18:25 f., "With the loyal thou dost show thyself loyal."
> 30, "This God—his way is perfect; the promise of the LORD proves true."
> "He is a shield for all those who take refuge in him."
> 31, "For who is God, but the LORD?"
> 118:15 f., "The right hand of the LORD does valiantly, the right hand of the LORD is exalted."
> 138:5, "For great is the glory of the LORD."
> 8, "Thy steadfast love, O LORD, endures for ever."
> 34:7, "The angel of the LORD encamps around those who fear him, and delivers them."
> 34:22, "The LORD redeems the life of his servants; none of those who take refuge in him will be condemned."
> 92:15, "To show that the LORD is upright."
> Job 33:26, "He recounts to men his salvation."

Ps. Sol. 15:1-3, "For thou art the hope and confidence of the poor."

Ps. Sol. 16:13-15, "For when thou dost not give strength."

6. An apparent variation in the sequence of parts is found in Ps. 30:4, 5:

> "Sing praises to the LORD, O you his saints . . .
> For his anger is but for a moment,
>   and his favor is for a lifetime.
> Weeping may tarry for the night,
>   but joy comes with the morning."

These lines are to be compared with the previously cited passages Ps. 40:5 and Ps. 116:15. There is agreement as to the experience of the ones singing. But now it is said, "What happened to me is in accord with the manner in which Yahweh acts." This passage follows the introductory summary, and thus corresponds in content to the lines of descriptive praise which follow the report of deliverance. Here an imperative call to praise forms a new introduction for the statement. Ps. 30:1-5 is an illustration of the fact that declarative praise is introduced by a voluntative, and descriptive praise by an imperative.

7. The praise of the one who confesses before the congregation what God has done for him is always uttered with joy. We have here not a "cultic festive joy," as most interpreters say, but the joy of the one who has been saved. It is the joy of the one whom God has drawn up out of the dark depths, the joy of the one who has been freed from the "bands of death," the joy of the one in whose mouth God has placed a new song of praise to our God, of him whose sorrow God has turned into joy.

Ps. 92:4a, "For thou, O LORD, hast made me glad by thy work."

Ps. 107:29, "He made the storm be still. . . . Then they were glad." It is the joy of the sign of relief expressed in the cry *bārūk!* (see above), Ps. 66:19 f.: "But truly God has listened . . . Blessed be God, because he has not rejected my prayer or removed his steadfast love from me!"

THE FURTHER SIGNIFICANCE OF THE CATEGORY

1. Oriental parallels:

An Egyptian psalm: Roeder, *op. cit.*, pp. 52 ff., Erman, *op. cit.*, pp. 383 f., Gunkel, *op. cit.*, pp. 287 f.

Praise of Amon

Structure (following the numbers of the strophes in Gunkel):

1: Superscription: "Praise of Amon Re, the Lord of Karnak . . ."

2: Proclamation: "I write for him . . . I praise him . . . I proclaim his might . . ."

3: Exhortation to praise: "Beware of him—proclaim . . ."

4-5: Summation: "When I call upon thee, thou dost come to me to save me . . . It is thou who dost save the one who is in the underworld . . ."

6-7: Looking back to the time of trouble (indirect): "Neb-re, the painter of Amon . . . wrote songs of lament for him . . . on behalf of Nacht-Amon, who was sick and near death . . ."

8-9: Report of deliverance and praise of the deliverer.

10: Fulfillment of the vow of praise.

A Babylonian psalm: "Hiobpsalm," *ZiA*, p. 30 (Looking back to the time of need—I cried—he delivered).

Declarative praise of the people: *ZiA*, p. 7 (Hehn, no. 4).

Announcement: "I will glorify his deity, proclaim his might . . ."

Summary: "He . . . inclined his ear, showed grace."

There follows the report of deliverance: overthrow of the enemy, the Elamites.

2. In the Psalms of the O.T. it is still clearly recognizable that the declarative praise of the individual, like that of the people, is the development of *one* sentence. Among primitive peoples, declarative praise often consists of only this one sentence. Heiler (*op. cit.*, p. 95) gives the following examples:

Among the pygmies: "Waka, thou hast given me this buffalo, this honey!"

Konde: "Thou hast delivered me, O God!"

Jagga: "Thou, O God, hast enriched me with cattle, hast led me . . . !"

Ewe: "Thou hast delivered me out of this quarrel!"

Everywhere it is essentially the same sentence, with the same basic structure, "Thou, O God, hast done . . . ," which also forms the basis of the declarative praise of the O.T.

These examples, which could be multiplied, show that declarative praise is a basic mode of addressing God. They show also that this declarative praise is always present *before* that which is called "cult." In all these examples praise grows directly out of everyday experiences.

Heiler gives another example (*op. cit.*, p. 45) which leads a step further. "When the Herero encounter an unexpected good fortune, they stand still in astonishment, look up to heaven, and call out, 'Ndjambi Karunga!' " (the name of the god of heaven). This is thus an address of praise, which according to its significance is declarative praise. Here we have evidence of a very early stage, in which declarative and descriptive praise had not been yet distinguished. In this very simple calling on God[64] the meaning cannot be disputed from the context; this calling on God is declarative praise. Declarative praise is primary in relationship to descriptive praise.

3. It is not surprising that such a thing as declarative praise exists in many forms and in many places. Wherever a man encounters God's activity something like this must occur. It is astonishing, rather, that this category, insofar as I can see, is developed so richly and fully only in Israel. Nor is it here found isolated in the Psalms. The basic structure of this declarative praise: "Thou, O God, hast done . . ." occurs often and in many forms in the O.T. Here it will suffice to refer to only three examples, where a clear similarity is recognizable: Deut. 26:5-10, in the historical account of Ps. 106, and in the framework of the book of Judges.[65]

64. We still know this. Both the complaining petition and jubilant and thankful praise can be expressed by us too in moments when we are in the depths or the heights merely by calling out the name.

65. Von Rad (in *Das formgeschichtliche Problem des Hexateuch*, Stuttgart, 1938) designated Deut. 26:5-10 as a "small, historical Credo" and saw in it a primitive form of the transmission of the Pentateuch. If this "Credo" corresponds to the structure of the declarative Psalm of praise (cf. the table!), then we have here a connection that can hardly be disputed between the declarative Psalms of praise and the transmission of history in Israel at its roots.

	Deut. 26:5-10	Ps. 106	Judg. 2, 3
Looking back to the time of need	5, 6	6, 7	2:13-15; 3:7, 8
Then we cried	7a		
He heard their cry	7b	(44-46)	16a; 9a
He drew them out	10	8-11 (43a-46)	16b-18; 9b-11
Vow of praise and praise	8, 9	12	

The declarative Psalm of praise is found also in the N.T. The examples Luke 1:68-75 (declarative praise of the people) and 2:29-32 (1:46-55) (of the individual) show that declarative praise was again awakened when God performed the decisive, final deed of salvation for his people in the sending of his Son.[66]

But here a change occurs in declarative praise. The forensic element and the accompanying words of the vow of praise showed that confessional praise is at the same time proclamation: "I will tell of thy name to my brethren," Ps. 22:22. In declarative praise the one who has been saved declares God's great deeds. The messengers of Jesus Christ do the same thing, Acts 2:11. The difference is merely that God's saving, helping activity has now attained its τέλος in the sending of his Son. He has "fulfilled" the history of his people. In his resurrection the "pangs of death" (LXX) have been loosed, and it was to these that the one freed looked back in the declarative Psalms of praise.[67]

In the proclamation of the church of Jesus Christ the proclamation of declarative praise is continued and fulfilled. Thus it should not be surprising that the letter to the Romans, in which the message of the N.T. is summarized, has the structure of a declarative Psalm of praise.

In the history of the church of Jesus Christ the declarative Psalm of praise occurs once again in all clarity, in Luther's Reformation hymn.* The same resemblance is seen in the

66. Cf. Gunkel, *Harnack-Festschrift*, pp. 43 ff.
67. Acts 2:24 quotes the declarative Psalm of praise 18:5 = 116:3!
* "Dear Christians, One and All, Rejoice," No. 387 in *The Lutheran Hymnal*, Saint Louis: Concordia Publishing House, 1941.

fourth verse of the hymn "Sei Lob und Ehr' dem höchsten Gut
. . ." (Joh. Jak. Schütz) more briefly and almost in the exact
words of the Psalms, "I cried to the Lord in my need . . ."

	Romans	Dear Christians, One and All . . .
Proclamation	Rom. 1:14 f.	1: With holy rapture singing . . .
Summary	1:16 f.	Proclaim the wonders God hath done
Report of Deliverance		
1. Looking back to the time of need	1:18—3:20	2-3: Fast bound in Satan's chains I lay, Death brooded darkly o'er me . . .
2. I cried to Yahweh		4-5: But God beheld my wretched state Before the world's foundation . . .
3. He heard	3:21—8:39	6-9: The Son obeyed His Father's will . . . He came to be my Brother . . .
4. He drew me out		Life shall from death the victory win . . .
Vow of praise	12-15 "a living sacrifice" "your spiritual worship"	10: What I have done and taught, teach thou . . . So shall my kingdom flourish now and God be praised forever
Praise	16:25-27	

THE DESCRIPTIVE PSALM OF PRAISE

1. *The Connections Between Declarative and Descriptive Praise.*

1. It has been shown how the declarative Psalm of praise,

following the vow of praise, passes over into the descriptive Psalm of praise. Just as the conclusion of the petition that has been heard (vow of praise and summarizing report of deliverance) is a small but complete declarative Psalm of praise, so the conclusion of the declarative Psalm of praise is a descriptive Psalm of praise.

2. We found, in any case, clear traces of the introduction which is peculiar to descriptive praise: the call to praise in the imperative (esp. Ps. 30:4).

3. In addition there is in the content a yet firmer connection between the declarative and the descriptive Psalms of praise in a summarizing sentence which often occurs at the end of these songs:

> Ps. 18:27, "For thou dost deliver . . . dost bring down."
> Ps. 138:6, "The LORD is high, he regards the lowly."
> Ps. 107:33-41, God humbles and exalts.
> Ps. 118:22-23, "The stone which the builders rejected has become the head of the corner."
> Job 5:11-14; Tobit 13:2.

In all these sentences the declaration of these Psalms is changed into description. For it was the theme of the declarative Psalms of praise that God looked down from his heights and rescued from the depths the one who called to him.

Strictly speaking this is said only in Ps. 138:6 and Ps. 118:22 f. The other passages add a complement, an expansion to this statement: there is a humbling that corresponds to this exaltation. What is the reason for this addition? In the Psalm of petition of the individual we found at the end, before the vow of praise, the formula of the double wish. Deliverance has here a twofold meaning for the one saved. In order that he may be freed, God's enemies must be destroyed or put to silence. Here the double praise of God, which looks in two directions, corresponds to this double wish. In Jonah 2:8-9 the double wish is included in the PI, and in Ps. 129:5-8 in the PP; in Ps. 34:10 and Ps. 107:42 it is included as a part of the expression of praise.

Ps. 34:10, "The young lions suffer want and hunger; but those who seek the LORD lack no good thing."[68] (Cf. Luke 1:53!)

  Ps. 107:42, "The upright see it and are glad; and all wickedness stops its mouth."

  Jonah 2:8 f., "Those who pay regard to vain idols forsake their true loyalty. But I with the voice of thanksgiving will sacrifice to thee."

It is certain, however, that originally there was nothing but the simple sentence which looked only at the miracle of exaltation. This sentence is the basic theme of the descriptive Psalm of praise. This is shown with special clarity in Ps. 113.

  1-3, Call to praise
  4-5, God is exalted (read 6b after 5a)
  5b and 6a, He who is enthroned on high—he who looks into the depth
  7-9, God exalts the lowly
  5b and 6a constitute the midpoint of the Psalm; 5b summarizes 4-5, and 6a is developed in 7-9.

The Psalm has a very simple and clear structure. The language is obviously different from that of the declarative Psalms of praise. It is speech directed toward God in the sense that it looks away from the unique occurrence of a specific deliverance and speaks of God's majesty and grace in a summarizing, recapitulating, and descriptive manner. But in Israel this recapitulating praise which brings together descriptions never lost its connection with the unique, concrete intervention which was experienced in the history of the people or of the individual. In Ps. 113 a single sentence stands at the midpoint, vss. 5b and 6a. Here there is brought together in a general statement that which was reported as a specific experience of deliverance. This is what the one who cried out of the depths was pleading for: Look! Come down! Hear! This is what the one delivered told to others:

68. The author reads "the rich" for "the young lions," following the LXX.

Ps. 40:1, "He inclined to me and heard my cry."

Just as there the action which had been experienced by the one giving praise was at first summarized in *one* sentence, so here it is stated in *one* sentence who the God is or what he is like, whom we are called to praise in the Psalm.[69]

Verses 7-9 explain what it means for those who are in the depths when God looks down to them from the heights. It means a reversal of fortune, a "joyous change." This change is described in a twofold action: God elevates the poor man out of the depths and gives him a new, good place. The "drawing up" is the fourth motif of the "report of deliverance" in the declarative Psalms of praise. There is added an element which was not mentioned or was only implied in the declarative Psalms of praise, the new, transformed situation of good fortune, of salvation for the one who has been delivered; this is the "life" for which he prayed. The laments almost always dwelt on the shame which the isolation of grief brought with it. Suffering was consistently viewed in its social aspects. Everyone forsook the sufferer; they fled from him as from a leper; they pointed their fingers at him and said that God had forsaken him. This was the depth of suffering and the real sharpness of the trial. In Ps. 113 this suffering is transformed: the one who is saved regains his honor in the sight of others. There is included in the raising of the poor from the dust that which we would term the real deliverance, whether that is the healing of sickness, or justification before one's enemies, or deliverance from the danger of death. These, however, are not described, but only the social significance of the deliverance.

In vs. 8 and vs. 9 two important examples of the restoration of honor are described: the example of the childless woman, which is found so often in the O.T., and the restoration of the honor of a man in his clan.

The fact that Ps. 113 has as its center and then develops a single sentence which describes and summarizes what is reported in the declarative Psalms of praise can be demonstrated once

69. Cf. Isa. 63. See above, pp. 47 ff.

more by the singular structure of the Psalm. The declarative
sentence in vss. 4-5 tells of the glory of God, but it is the participles in 5b and 6a, and not this sentence, which form the central part of the Psalm. These participles, which make the declaration more specific, speak of precisely the other element: that he
descends from that height to our depths. The only significance
which the majesty of God has for the one giving praise here is
that it comes down to where we are.

In this basic form of the descriptive Psalm of praise we can
see the line along which the O.T. moves in all decisive passages
when it speaks of God. God is the one whom Israel encountered
in its history, and whom it experienced as the one who from his
heights intervenes in the depths of tribulation.[70]

The close relationship of Ps. 113 to the declarative Psalms
of praise can be noted in yet another of its distinctive modes of
expression. The Psalm does not contain a single noun descriptive
of God. Such nouns, which we usually call the attributes of God,
are otherwise quite characteristic of descriptive praise. That
which is described in Ps. 113:6-8 is called in precisely comparable
contexts (cf. the table) at the same position in the Psalm *hesed*
(i.e., "grace"). Here reference should be made to the results of
the work of N. Glueck, *Das Wort hesed in alttestamentlichen
Sprachgebrauch als menschliche und göttliche gemeinschaftsgemässe Verhaltungsweise.*[71] Here it is shown that on the basis
of the usage in the O.T. our category of "attribute" is not
relevant. A specific mode of relationship always precedes the occurrence of *hesed*. "Only those who stand in a specific relationship to one another receive and express *hesed*" (*op. cit.,* p. 3).
"*Hesed* is a mode of relationship that corresponds to the relationship of law and duty" (*ibid.,* p. 20). "The *hesed* of God is
to be understood only as the way in which God stands in a com-
munal relationship to those who belong to him. . . . God's *hesed*

70. It is thus not accidental that this same declaration is found also in the sermon
in Deuteronomy: Deut. 10:14, "Behold, to the LORD your God belong heaven and
the heaven of heavens, the earth with all that is in it"; 15, "yet the LORD set his
heart in love upon your fathers and chose their descendents after them, you above all
peoples."
71. Giessen, 1927.

is the consequence of his covenant, or of his promise, or of his oath" (*ibid.*, p. 65)[72]

Hesed is thus a way in which God is related in a community. Precisely in this is it grace in the proper sense of the word. The O.T. does not know any grace except this. God's grace is both a free expression and a relationship determined by a community. It never becomes God's "duty," but it also never was and never is merely arbitrary. Freedom and restriction are one in God's grace.

Psalm 113 describes God's *hesed*. It is the other side of his majesty; it is the looking into the depths by the one who is enthroned in the heights. That is the constantly recurring declaration of the descriptive Psalms of praise.[73]

This can be made clear by reference to Ps. 107. This is a liturgical combination of four PI. It is no longer the individual who speaks, but individuals are called upon to praise God for the deliverance which they have experienced. The first of these reports concludes with the words: "Let them thank the LORD for his steadfast love [*hesed*], for his wonderful works to the sons of men" (vss. 8, 15, 21, 31). This sentence recurs after each of the reports. In this occurrence those whom Yahweh has saved encounter God's *hesed*. All four accounts are concerned with everyday occurrences, everyday reality in all its manifold fullness. The merchant or the wanderer on his way through the wilderness, the prisoner who is paying for his crime, the sick, the seafarers, have all experienced God's *hesed* in their own particular existence. They cry to him from *their* depths and he looks down into *their* depths. In this they experience God's *hesed*. That is to say, God's *hesed* is expressed each time he looks down into the depths of a specific need (that of the people or that of an individual); it is the mode of relationship to God which is experienced when one is "drawn out." The fact that

72. There is a more recent investigation of the concept *hesed* in N. H. Snaith, *The Distinctive Ideas of the O.T.*, London, 1944, pp. 94-130.
73. It will perhaps become clearer that the Psalms say this again and again by comparison with a sentence from a novel of the period after the First World War, *Mich Hungert* by Georg Fink, Berlin, 1926, on the next to last page: "No God descends into the abysses of his creation."

the one delivered experiences God's grace is substantiated by Ps. 116:5, "Gracious [*hannun*] is the LORD, and righteous; our God is merciful." Ps. 18:50, "and shows steadfast love [*hesed*] to his anointed." Ps. 66:20, "Blessed be God, because he has not . . . removed his steadfast love [*hesed*] from me!" Pss. 118:1 (=107:1); 138:2; 92:2. Cf. Ps. 40:10 f.

It is thus the intention of all these Psalms to tell of God's grace (even those which do not contain the word, as Ps. 30). Everywhere we encounter Yahweh's true grace in a unique intervention, and, as has been shown in relation to Ps. 107, it means deliverance in time of need. There is nothing else that can be meant by the *hesed* of God which is praised in the descriptive Psalms of praise. Ps. 107:1 and Ps. 118:1 mean the same thing as the sentence in Ps. 136:1. Even in the descriptive Psalms of praise God is not praised as "God in himself," as one transcendentally present, as a "being" with "attributes," but as the same God whose actions were reported in the declarative Psalms of praise. The fact that all these Psalms speak only in praise and in calling to such praise and never in a manner of attempting to establish the fact that something is there agrees with this view. Praise is response to God's actions. God's majesty and goodness can be spoken of only in such a response. This can be shown by the structure of the descriptive Psalm of praise.

2. The Structure of the Descriptive Psalm of Praise

The descriptive Psalms of praise do not have the same unity of structure as the declarative. Nevertheless they are clearly distinguished from the sections of praise in the Babylonian and the Egyptian psalms in that they (1) have a fixed, well-defined basic structure, and (2) do not consist of a summation of predicates and declarations of praise, but like Ps. 113, whether more or less clearly, are the development and expansion of a single declaration, the one which so clearly forms the center of Ps. 113.

The first group consists of Pss. 113; 117; 33; 36; 105; 135; 136; 147; 146; 111; 89:5-18; Neh. 9:6-31; 1 Sam. 2:1-10; Nah. 1:2-11 (without an imperative); cf. Jer. 32:17-23.

1. All these Psalms begin with an imperative call to praise. This confirms that the imperative call to praise is an integral part of descriptive praise. In Ps. 65 its place has been taken by a reflection on praise (as Ps. 92, cf. 33:1; 147). In Ps. 146, where the transition to a didactic Psalm can be noted, the call to praise is issued in the proper place. The most frequent verb is *hillēl:* Pss. 113; 117; 135; 147; 146; noun form in Ps. 65. *Hōdāh* occurs only in Ps. 136, and accompanying words of praise are found in Ps. 147 (3 terms); Ps. 33 (6); Ps. 105 (9!).[74]

2. In most of the Psalms there follows the reason for praise, which is also an introductory summary, corresponding to the declarative Psalms of praise. This introductory summary, even though it is not found in all the Psalms, is the surest sign that what is said in these Psalms is not synthetic but analytic, that is, we do not have sentences heaped on one another, but *one* sentence is developed.

Ps. 117[75] consists of only the one sentence which gives the reason for the imperative of the first verse, "For great is [=he has made] his steadfast love toward us; and the faithfulness of the LORD endures for ever." The first part of the sentence clearly contains the two motifs of Ps. 113, Yahweh's might over us, and the reality of the steadfast love and faithfulness which are ever available for us through his power. These two statements, which praise God's majesty and his condescension to us, run through all these Psalms without exception. They are, however, not always summarized in advance. This is the case in the following Psalms:

Ps. 136:1, "For he is good, for his steadfast love endures for ever."

2 f., "God of gods, . . . Lord of lords."

Ps. 135:3 f., "For the LORD is good; . . . the LORD has chosen Jacob for himself."

74. In Neh. 9:5 ff. the original situation of this imperative call to praise is related. Originally it was not a part of the Psalm, but preceded it: "Then the Levites . . . said, 'Stand up and bless the LORD your God . . .'" There follows a long Psalm of praise which extends to the end of the chapter.

75. This is probably the conclusion of a small collection of Psalms.

5, "The LORD is great."
Ps. 33:5, "He loves righteousness and justice; the earth is
full of the steadfast love of the LORD."

In the following Psalms there is no clear division in the transition to the main part of the Psalm:

Ps. 105:7, "His judgments are in all the earth."
8, "He is mindful of his covenant for ever."
Ps. 147:2-3, the one who heals; 3-4, the Creator, the Lord.
Ps. 146, an entirely different introduction, with a transition
to exhortation and instruction, vss. 3-5.

There is also in addition to this another pair of terms: God
exalts and brings low. Ps. 147:6; 1 Sam. 2:4-8 (compare the passages in the declarative Psalms of praise, above, pp. 41-42).[76]

This sentence, "God exalts and brings low," as a summary of
descriptive praise, shows from another side that in such praise
it is not an existent, available God who is praised, but the One
who intervenes in history. Israel's historical experience stands
behind this sentence. It demonstrates once again a connection
between the historical writings and the Psalms. In the former
it is a constant motif that an insignificant person is chosen by
Yahweh and thereby exalted, that Yahweh does not perform his
mighty deeds for his people through the great, the famous, the
daring, but through small, limited, despised men. *This* is the
God who is praised here. This sentence, however, includes the
whole nation as well as the individual; the God who is praised
is the one who can reverse the destiny of his people, who has
destroyed and will destroy great and powerful nations. This
sentence can also be heard behind the strong hope of Israel in
the hardest times, for Israel knows that God exalts and brings
low. But that it also held good for the individual and was so
understood by him is shown especially by 1 Sam. 2. Here is the
strongest expression of exalting and bringing low: vs. 6, "The

76. Outside of this group there are also Tobit 13:2; Ecclus. 10:14-17; Luke 1:51-53;
Pss. 107:39-41; 68:6; 75:7 (Deut. 32:43); 1 Chron. 29:12b (only exaltation); Ps.
Sol. 2:31.

LORD kills and brings to life; he brings down to Sheol and raises up." Its reappearance in Luke 1 indicates how strong this motif was.

This motif alone is enough to show that even in descriptive praise we are dealing with a God who comes down into our history, and not with one who is contemplated in a speculative manner. 1 Sam. 2:6 shows clearly that behind this motif there stands the confession of praise of the one who has been saved, as found in the declarative Psalm of praise.

3. This double sentence of God's actions from the heights into the depths, or of his majesty and his grace is now further developed and supplemented. This can be shown first of all in Ps. 33:

> vss. 1-3, A call to praise in the imperative.
> 4 then, "The word of the LORD is upright; and all his work is done in faithfulness" (=vss. 5-19).
> 5, "He loves righteousness and justice; the earth is full of the steadfast love of the LORD."
> 5a   6-9, the Creator: "By the word of the LORD the heavens were made."
>   10-12, The Lord of history: "The Lord brings the counsel of the nations to nought."
> 5b   13-19, "The LORD looks down from heaven . . . on those who fear him."
>   16-17, Human power is of no avail!
>   20-21, Confession of confidence: "He is our help."
>   22, *Petition:* "Let thy steadfast love, O LORD, be upon us."

The structure of this Psalm shows with all clarity that it is really the development of the two sentences, vs. 4 and vs. 5.[77]

The greatness of Yahweh and his majesty are not expressed in any specific term. Thus the account of creation in vss. 6-9

---

77. Gunkel on the structure of this Psalm: "Where so much value is given to the number of the lines (alphabetical principle: the number of verses corresponds to the number of letters) it is understandable that the order of thoughts is not particularly strict and that the separate groups of thoughts stand in comparative independence of one another . . . Therefore the exegetes disagree about the divisions of the Psalm."

proclaims his greatness all the more clearly, and at its end all the world is called to fear him whose word established the world. The development of the one part of the theme sentence in the descriptive Psalm of praise has the meaning of exalting. Here the basic statement is developed *in order that* Yahweh may be feared. This speaking of God the Creator is completely directed toward God, and does not intend to unfold the greatness of Yahweh in the sense of an explanation that is directed to man. It arises, not from any theoretical interest, but from the will to praise him. Creation is here the secondary theme. It is the creation that is spoken of for the sake of the Creator, and not the Creator for the sake of the creation.[78]

4. The praise of the Creator in the other Psalms of the category.

Ps. 136:5, "who by understanding made the heavens, for his steadfast love endures for ever."

6, "who spread out the earth upon the waters, for his steadfast love endures for ever."

7-9, "who made the great lights . . . sun . . . moon . . . for his steadfast love endures for ever."

78. At this point the work of von Rad, "Das theologische Problem des alttestamentlichen Schöpfungsglaubens," *Werden und Wesen des A.T.*, Berlin, 1936, pp. 138 ff., can be substantiated and carried a step further. What von Rad says of Second Isaiah, "The creation faith is never the main theme of a passage—it is never adduced for its own sake," p. 140, holds also for the descriptive Psalms of praise. In the structure of these Psalms we can see the preliminary step that led to Second Isaiah, where it is only formulated more clearly, but is not new, namely that "the protological is brought together with the soteriological." In these Psalms praise of the Creator is development of the twofold sentence of Yahweh's majesty and grace, in which that which the declarative Psalms report is described and summarized, and this is the soteriological element. Here too the exaltation of Yahweh experienced by the one saved is the basis of the praise of the Creator, even though not explicitly so. It is the development of the praise of the one who exalts and brings low. Von Rad's thesis (p. 143) that the soteriological understanding of the work of creation is the basic expression of the Yahweh religion concerning Yahweh the Creator of the world is further attested by the structure of the descriptive Psalms of praise. The relationship of the descriptive Psalm of praise to the declarative shows that the statements about creation are secondary with respect to those of Yahweh's intervention to save. In them a statement of the declarative Psalm of praise is developed. This does not mean that all declarative Psalms must be older than all descriptive ones. The category of the declarative Psalm of praise must, however, be given precedence over that of the descriptive. The latter can be explained only in terms of the former, and some of the declarative Psalms show how the descriptive Psalm of praise developed out of them. In this connection compare the almost total absence of declarative Psalms of praise in Babylon, see above p. 36.

10, "who smote the first-born of Egypt."[79]

In most of the Psalms of the group the praise of the Creator passes directly into praise of the Lord of history.[80]

God's activity in the creation and direction of his works is the same as his activity in the history of the nations. What is created and what occurs have not yet been separated from one another; the special realm "nature" does not yet exist. Yahweh's lordship is praised in both. Thus historical occurrences can frequently be spoken of in mythical pictures, which generally have also a cosmic significance.[81]

This praise of the Lord of history stands quite properly in the center between the praise of the majesty of God and the praise of his grace. His Lordship over the history of all nations witnesses to his majesty, but usually Yahweh's mighty actions in history which bring help to his people are the ones which are described. This is the significance of the motif, Ps. 33:10 f. "The LORD brings the counsel of the nations to nought." In Ps. 136:10-22 it is only the saving activity of Yahweh that is described. In Ps. 65:7 God's activity in creation and in history are spoken of in the same sentence, "who dost still the roaring of the seas, . . . the tumult of the peoples." Psalm 135:8-12 corresponds to Ps. 136. Psalm 105:7, 1 Sam. 2:10, and Ps. 89:13 f. correspond rather to Ps. 33. In Ps. 147 and Neh. 9 praise of the Lord of history is only indirectly present; Ps. 147:2, 13a, 14a, in the protection of Jerusalem from her foes; in Neh. 9, in the great historical account in vss. 9-31. It is changed distinctively in Ps. 146:3-5.[82]

---

79. Except for Ps. 105 all Psalms of this group contain praise of the Creator: Pss. 65:6-8; 135:6-7; 147:4, 8, 16-18; 146:6; 1 Sam. 2:8c; Ps. 89:9-12; Neh. 9:6b. In addition, Pss. 24:1-2; 90:2-5; Judith 16:15; Job 9:5-10; Pr. Man. 2; Ecclus. 39:16 ff.; Od. Sol. 16:10-19.

80. Cf. H. Schmidt's commentary in HAT, on Ps. 29, p. 54: "It is peculiar to the hymns that in them praise customarily directs its attention to two things, first to God's powerful activity in nature, in creation, and then to his work in the history of his people."

81. In the following passages it is expressed especially clearly that God is praised as both Creator and Lord of history: Isa. 40:12-31; 43:1-7, 14-15, 16-20; 44:24-28; 45:1-7, etc.

82. Praise of the Lord of history is also found in Job 12:14-25. It corresponds to the praise of the Creator in the preceding speech of Job in 9:5-10. The same elements are together in Ps. Sol. 2:29b-31 and 34-37.

5. Praise of the Lord of history can pass immediately into praise of his grace.

> Ps. 33:13, "The LORD looks down from heaven."
> 18, "Behold, the eye of the LORD is on those who fear him."
> 19, "That he may deliver their soul from death."

The same "looking into the depths" occurs, in addition to Ps. 113 and Ps. 33, in other Psalms, widely removed from them in time:

Add. Dan. 1:32, "Blessed art thou, who enthroned on the Cherubim lookest into the depths."

Luke 1:48, "For he has regarded the low estate of his handmaiden."

This remained the living source of praise from the earliest beginnings of Israel's history to the commencement of the new age: the joyous experience that God looks into the depths and saves from the depths. Not only the declarative Psalms of praise, but also the descriptive bear witness to this. Many passages are similar in this respect.

> Ps. 136:23 f., "It is he who remembered us in our low estate ... and rescued us from our foes."
> Ps. 135:14, "For the LORD will vindicate his people, and have compassion on his servants."
> Ps. 105:8-11, "He is mindful of his covenant."
> vss. 12-44, He helped his people. Cf. Neh. 9:9-31.
> Ps. 147:2-3, "The LORD builds up Jerusalem; ... He heals the brokenhearted."
> vs. 6, "The LORD lifts up the downtrodden."
> vss. 15, 19, 20, "He declares his word to Jacob."
> Ps. 65:2, 3b, "O thou who hearest prayer ... thou dost forgive."
> Ps. 146:7, "Who executes judgment for the oppressed; who gives food to the hungry" (cf. vss. 8-9).

Ps. 89:17b, "By thy favor our horn is exalted" (cf. vss. 14-18, 1 Sam. 2:9).[83]

It is to be noted that in this second section, in which Yahweh's grace is described, it is always expressed by the use of verbs (including several very late passages). Where God's grace is praised, there his actions are praised.

6. We noted earlier that there was a tendency to supplement the descriptive Psalms of praise in two places. In one, the statement of exaltation from the depths, which summarizes declarative praise (Ps. 113:7-9), was supplemented by the statement concerning bringing down the high and the mighty. But then the double statement of Yahweh's majesty and grace, which forms the basis of descriptive praise, is also to be understood as such a supplement. In the declarative Psalms of praise it is implicit in the motif, "He drew . . . out of the depths." This can be done only from on high. This fact that Yahweh is on high became as such the theme of the descriptive Psalms of praise. In addition there is also a third supplement: Yahweh's looking down into the depths means not only deliverance, but also *preservation*. In the declarative Psalms of praise, preservation and support (that is, continuity of action) are seldom mentioned. They appear marginally in Ps. 107:9. When a Psalm culminates in a petition, this is a petition for continuous action, Pss. 138:8; 33:22.

In the descriptive Psalms of praise, the praise of the one who upholds and preserves appears alongside the praise of the one who saves. This motif is occasionally encountered in the praise of the Creator, who in certain Psalms is praised also as the Preserver, Ps. 147:8, 9, 13, 14; Neh. 9:6c; Ps. 36:6b-9, and especially Ps. 65:9-13. It becomes the only theme in Ecclus. 39:14b-35.

But the preserving love of God occupies also another place in descriptive praise. In a number of Psalms God's saving action is directly combined with a specific kind of preservation, preservation from hunger. This is seen especially in the following:

83. In addition, Ps. 68:5a, 8, 12; Nah. 1:7-8; Pr. of Man. 6-7; 2 Chron. 6:14 f.; Ezra 3:11; Neh. 1:5; Luke 1:48, 50, 54, 55; 2:14b; Ecclus. 15:19.

Ps. 136:23, "who remembered us in our low estate."
  24, "and rescued us from our foes."
  25, "he who gives food to all flesh."

Ps. 33:19, "that he may deliver their soul from death, and keep them alive in famine."

Ps. 111:5, "He provides food for those who fear him; he is ever mindful of his covenant."

Ps. 145:14 f., "The LORD upholds all who are falling, and raises up all who are bowed down. The eyes of all look to thee, and thou givest them their food in due season." Cf. Ps. 104:10-30.

7. This Psalm category does not have a concluding formula. Most of these Psalms end with the praise of the goodness of God without any set form of ending. Psalm 33 has a confession of confidence in vss. 20 f., but then concludes in vs. 22 with a petition. In some Psalms of this group the imperative at the beginning of the Psalm is repeated: Ps. 136; Ps. 135; Tobit 13:6-8 (imperative, voluntative, and jussive!). In two there is an exhortation at the end, Ps. 65 and Ps. 105. One ends with a word of wisdom, Ps. 111. It is clear, however, that the original structure had an imperative call to praise only at the beginning; the expansion in praise of the statement of God's majesty and goodness followed. These are the two parts of the descriptive Psalm of praise.

This group is clearly recognizable as a further development of the simple form of the category. In the indicative statements, praise proper, it agrees with the preceding group. The further development consists in the insertion of a new imperative between the two basic statements, "Yahweh is exalted—Yahweh is good," and, in a few of the Psalms, in the occurrence of the imperative once again at the end. It is clearly a development that was determined liturgically and designed for liturgical use, and as a result of this the imperatives came to outnumber completely the proper exclamations of praise in these Psalms.

The insertion of the imperatives between the two parts of

3. The Imperative Psalms[84]

	Imperative call to praise	God's majesty	Imperative call to praise	God's goodness
100	Make a joyful noise to the LORD, all the lands!	Know that the LORD is God! It is he that made us	Enter . . . his courts with praise!	For the LORD is good; his steadfast love endures for ever
95	O come, let us sing to the LORD	For the LORD is a great God (4-5, the earth is his)	O come, let us worship and bow down	For he is our God, and we are the people of his pasture (in 7b-11 a prophetic exhortation follows)
148	Praise the LORD from the heavens . . . Praise the LORD from the earth	For he commanded and they were created . . . For his name alone is exalted	(Praise is proper to all his saints)	14, He has raised up a horn for his people
145	I will extol thee, my God and King	(God is great and greatly to be praised, vss. 13-20)	6-7, Men shall proclaim the might of thy terrible acts . . . They shall pour forth the fame of thy abundant goodness	8-9, The LORD is gracious and merciful (13 passim) 21, an exhortation to praise
150	Praise God in . . .	. . . for his mighty deeds . . . according to his exceeding greatness	Praise him with . . . Let everything that breathes praise the LORD!	—

84. Pss. 100; 148; 150; 145; 95A; Add. Dan. 1:29 ff.

the main section confirms the structure which was demonstrated
for the first group. Aside from the increase in the number of
imperatives this group scarcely presents any new elements.
1. Introduction. Imperative in Pss. 100; 148; 150; Add. Dan.
1. In Ps. 95 there is a cohortative instead of the imperative and
in Ps. 145 voluntative and jussive forms alternate throughout the
Psalm. Ps. 150 consists solely of manifold variations of the imperative call to praise.
2. Main section. With the exception of Ps. 150, where the
praise of the grace of God has given way before the impressive
imperatives, all these Psalms contain the praise of God in his
majesty and in his goodness. Ps. 148 departs from this to the
extent that the main section is not divided according to what
is to be praised in God, but according to the subjects who are
called to praise: vss. 1-6, "Praise the LORD from the heaven,"
vss. 7-12, "Praise the LORD from the earth." The two statements
of the main section are scarcely developed in any of these
Psalms. It is characteristic that the Creator is praised, but not the
Lord of history. The fact that in the second part static declarations take the place of active ones corresponds to this. The more
strongly liturgical the style becomes, the more static the praise is!

It can be stated with certainty that this group, in relation to
the first group, constitutes a further development. The opposite
relation seems to me to be impossible. The direction of this
development is shown clearly by what is probably the latest
Psalm of the group, Add. Dan. 1:29 ff. The imperative conclusions of the Psalms (especially Ps. 103), the imperative framework, and the conclusions of the books of the Psalter all point
in the same direction.[85]

85. Gunkel held that the imperative call to praise, the "Hallelujah," was the
"basic unit of hymn singing" (*Einleitung*, p. 37 f. and the article "Halleluja"
in *RGG²*. So also Hempel, *Literaturgeschichte*, p. 19). Nöldeke expressly opposed
this in the *Baudissin-Festschrift*, pp. 375-380, as Delitzsch had done much earlier
in his commentary on Ps. 104:35 (p. 689). So also Greiff, *Das Gebet im A.T.*,
1915, p. 76. On the basis of a total investigation of the verbs and forms of
the praise of God it can be concluded with certainty that Gunkel's thesis cannot be
maintained. Nor is it correct that "originally at the end of a song of praise all the
people joined in" (p. 37), for it is an exhortation to praise and therefore belongs
before the song of praise proper (this is shown, e.g., by Neh. 9:5 ff.). This exhortation to praise was then united to the song of praise itself and thus became the in-

4. Conclusion of Groups 2 and 3

All the sentences in which God is here praised have their individual parallels in the Babylonian, Egyptian, and many other psalms. If the essential element in the Psalms were the "thoughts about God" which are expressed here, then in this category a clear and significant difference could scarcely be shown between biblical Psalms and the others. As far as the thought is concerned it would not be particularly difficult to reduce descriptive praise in the Babylonian psalms, for instance, to this twofold denominator of majesty and grace. And further, it is of the nature of descriptive praise that it does not have the strict structure of declarative praise. Here as elsewhere descriptive praise flows and overflows. Expression is here restricted the least.

When this has been granted, we then see in the proper light what it means that in this category of the Psalms of the O.T. a structure can nevertheless be recognized, a structure in which the following traits are evident:

1. All these Psalms still show that they do not speak by way of summary but by unfolding. There is not a one of the descriptive Psalms of praise which is a summation of predications of praise (which are as good as nonexistent) or of declarations of praise. *All* descriptive Psalms of praise are—more or less clearly —governed by the tension of the relation to each other of the two statements that God is enthroned in majesty, and *yet* is the one who is moved with compassion.[86]

Through this dominant motif it becomes clear that descriptive praise lives on declarative praise. In this one statement, which stands in the middle of these Psalms, that which is reported in the declarative Psalms of praise is described by way of summary.[87]

---

troduction of the descriptive Psalm of praise. Through the tendency to construct a framework it then also became a concluding formula. Only in the final stage did it become fully separated from the Psalm and become the independent "Hallelujah," existing in and for itself.

86. It is possible that this basic structure of descriptive praise is repeated in the prologue of John's Gospel in the relationship of its two parts, vss. 1-13 and 14-18, to each other. In any case, vs. 14 corresponds exactly to the motif of praise that God looks out of his heights into our depths in order to help those in the depths.

87. Corresponding to this, in John 1:14-16 descriptive praise is combined with the

2. The "exegetical speaking" of the descriptive Psalm of praise becomes evident in a large number of Psalms, in that the one twofold statement is developed in specific declarations which agree in a whole group of Psalms even in their order, and whose individual motifs are repeated in many others. God's greatness, his exaltation, his majesty are seen in creation and in his Lordship in history.

God's grace is at work when he looks into the depths, saves, redeems, and heals, and "exalts the horn of his people." But it is also at work there where he sustains his creation and gives bread to the hungry.

3. In the structure of these Psalms a tendency to praise God's deity in its fullness can be noticed. That is the tendency which forms the basis for this category. It is demonstrated in a threefold expansion: 1. the one who looks into the depths is the one who is enthroned in the heights, 2. the one who delivers from the depths is the one who casts into the depths, 3. the Creator is the Sustainer, the Savior is the Preserver.

The same tendency lies at the basis of all teaching about God, of all dogmatics: the tendency to describe God in the fullness of his being. The category of descriptive praise gives a twofold indication of this.

Praise of God in the fullness of his "being for us" occurs in the development of *one* sentence. This *one* sentence is confession, confession of the one who testifies before the congregation that God has delivered him from the depths. It never lost its connection with declarative, witnessing praise. Only in the late history of the category (see below) was this connection lost.

The description of God's being for us in its fullness remains here still surrounded by praise of God. It cannot be and does not intend to be anything else except praise. It is and knows itself to be an *answer* to the call to praise, with which it is introduced. Here there occurs that to which the one saved calls in Ps. 34:3, "O magnify the LORD with me."

---

declarative: "We have beheld his glory . . . and from his fulness have we all received."

Here the relationship of descriptive to declarative praise may perhaps help us to understand the relationship of proclamation and teaching in the church. Proclamation corresponds to declarative, teaching to descriptive, praise. As in the Psalms descriptive praise lives on declarative (or confessing) praise—the teaching of the church is dependent on proclamation. Just as descriptive praise is development and expansion of the *one* statement in which the one who experienced God's help confesses God's actions before the congregation, so can all teaching, all "dogmatics" of the church be only development of the confession of Jesus as the Christ. Then, however, the teaching of the church can be neither "summa" nor σύστημα (= a compiled whole), but only an explanatory development of the *one* sentence which is not a dogma, but a confession of praise directed toward God. It seems to me that the limit of the "objectivity" of all theological expression lies here. Theology, that is, speaking about God, statements about God, can exist only when surrounded by praise of God. Strictly speaking, God can never become an object. In theology knowledge must never divorce itself from acknowledgment.

5. The Late History of the Category

In the late history of the category we see a remarkable differentiation. On the one side there is a powerful increase of calls to praise, which overrun the Psalm itself, and on the other side a gradual loosening of the ties between descriptive speaking about God and the framework of praise. And it can be shown that the one cannot live without the other. The two statements which form the major section of the descriptive Psalm of praise begin to separate from each other.

1. The one-sided praise of God's grace. Already in the Psalter, Ps. 103 shows a definite preponderance of the praise of God's grace. But precisely this Psalm shows how strongly influenced the praise of the congregation in Israel was by the polarity which has been demonstrated. The singer of this Psalm *wanted* to sing of the grace of God, and yet for him the other side of

this grace is not only there, but this Psalm concludes with praise of the majesty of God, vs. 19, which is then followed in vss. 20-22 by the final call to praise. Moreover, the two expressions of this praise are at least alluded to, the Creator in vs. 14, and the Lord of history in vs. 7.

In the Psalms and prayers of the work of the Chronicler as a rule both statements are there.[88] Ezra 3:11, however, gives as call to praise only the statement of the reason for it, "For he is good, for his steadfast love endures for ever toward Israel." So also 2 Chron. 5:13; 20:21; Jer. 33:11. This sentence plainly became the quintessence of the praise of God altogether, as is shown by its widespread usage. This too is a sign that the one statement, without the corresponding one of praise of God's majesty, continued on. The book of Micah ends in 7:18-20 with praise of the grace of God. Also Luke 1:46-55 shows an absolute preponderance of praise of the goodness of God, but the other side can still be heard in vs. 49.

The Psalms of Solomon show the separation of the motifs very clearly. Typical is 2:33-37, a Psalm complete in itself with a call to praise at the beginning and at the end (33a, 37), the ground for praise, vs. 33b, "For the Lord's mercy [is shown] at the judgment to those who honor him." This is developed in vss. 34-35. Verse 36 repeats 33b, "for the Lord is gracious to those who patiently call on him." The structure is also very simple: a call to praise (imperative) with a broadly developed ground for praise, the content of which, however, is exclusively God's mercy.

The same Psalm shows how a new category develops out of the descriptive Psalm of praise. The grace of God toward his saints means a distinction in the judgment.

> 2:34, "that he separate the pious from the godless, and punish the godless for ever according to their works."
> 35, "and show mercy to the pious because of the oppres-

---

88. Neh. 1:5; 9:6 ff.; 2 Chron. 6:14 f. (each time the introduction of a petition); 1 Chron. 29:10-12 expresses a great number of statements in praise of God's greatness and might only, but in vss. 13-17 there follows praise of God's goodness (which made the people willing to bring an offering).

sion of the godless and repay the godless what he has done to the pious."

All this is intended to be praise of God (see above, vs. 33b), but we sense clearly how the poet tarries here and the contrast of pious and godless becomes an independent theme. The "double wish" of the petition of the individual clearly stands behind this motif. Another example from the Psalms of Solomon, chapter 3,[89] shows how there was further development in this direction.

Verses 1-2 are a reflection which expands a self-exhortation to praise (cf. Ps. 103). That which follows in vss. 3-12, however, is not praise of God, but a contrast of the righteous and the godless. This is probably still intended to be praise of God, for the separation is based (2:33) on God's mercy. But it can really no longer be said that this is speech addressed to God. Without vss. 1-2 this Psalm is a companion piece to Ps. 1.[90]

A further example for the one-sided nature of praise of God is chapter 5:1-2, "O Lord I give praise . . . for thou art gracious." In vs. 2b a petition is added, which is followed by an alternation of praise and petition. In vss. 9-11 there is praise of the one who sustains, followed again by a petition in vs. 12. Throughout the entire Psalm to vs. 19 the praise remains one-sided.

The other alteration is this: Praise becomes the introduction to a petition, as is general in the Babylonian and Egyptian psalms. A further example of this is Ps. Sol. 18:1-5. Here also there is in vss. 1-4 a long, one-sided praising of God's mercy, preparatory to the petition in vs. 5. So also praise of goodness only is combined with praise of the pious in 10:1-8. The only exception is the concluding doxology in 18:10-12, which probably[91] is a secondary addition here. In it there is one-sided praise of only the Creator: "Great is our God . . . who set the lights in their courses."

89. Gunkel incorrectly separates vss. 1-2 from the rest (*op. cit.*, p. 33). The chapter is a unit.
90. This contrast of righteous and godless is found often in the Ps. Sol.: 4:23-25 (here, like Ps. 1, beginning with "Blessed is . . ."); 6:1-6, only one side, "Blessed is the pious"; 14:1-10 (corresponding to Ps. 1 even in the metaphors!); 15:7-13.
91. So says Kittel on this passage.

In the Ps. Sol. both observations seem to me to stand in relationship to each other, and this is significant for the praise of God as a whole. A displacement can be clearly perceived. The descriptive praise of God loses its polarity (majesty-goodness) and becomes one-sided. Only the goodness of God is praised. The polarity returns, however, in another form, in the contrast of the pious and the godless. To be sure, God's goodness is still praised, but attention is directed much more strongly to the point where now the real tension is seen, that is, no longer in God, but in man, in the contrast of pious and godless. The trace of a deep-going transformation can be seen in this late change in the descriptive Psalms of praise. In the place of God as the sole object in descriptive praise there comes quietly another—the pious man in contrast to the godless man! The loss of the living polarity in the praise of God leads to this gradual shift of attention away from God to the pious man.

2. The one-sided praise of God's majesty. Already in Ps. 150 the ground for the call to praise, which indeed fills the entire Psalm, is only the majesty of God (vs. 2). Alongside this final note of the Psalter we should place the already mentioned concluding doxology of Ps. Sol. 18:10-12. In it also only the greatness of God (specifically, the greatness of the Creator) is praised. 1 Chron. 29:10-12 should also be mentioned. There the praise of God's greatness does not stand entirely by itself, but it is still relatively independent in contrast to what follows.[92]

These are only a few examples of the separation of the praise of God's majesty. It was first completely worked out in the separation of the two developments—as praise of the Creator, and of the Lord of history. These two motifs developed into separate Psalms. Still it is actually only in the creation Psalms that we can speak of the praise of the majesty of God. The historical Psalms consistently unite God's judging and God's saving actions.[93]

92. Jer. 10:6-16 (perhaps without vss. 8-11; cf. Jer. 51:15-19) is almost entirely praise of the majesty of God and praise of the Creator. (An allusion to God's saving action is found in vs. 16.) So also the doxologies in the book of Amos (4:13; 5:8-9; 9:5-6) give together only praise of the Creator, and in one verse (5:9) praise of the Lord of history.
93. Cf. the structure of Ps. 33!

The creation Psalms are the only group of Psalms of praise in the Psalter in which *one* motif developed into an independent Psalm. They are Pss. 8; 19; (29); 104; 139; (148). Each of them is quite distinctive. This group shows that where *one* motif is expanded to form a whole Psalm there is no longer any rigid form.

The clearest similarity to the basic structure of the Psalm of praise is shown by Ps. 8, in which the polarity of God's majesty (vss. 2, 10) and God's grace (vs. 5) still influences the whole of the Psalm. Probably also the bringing together of the two parts of Ps. 19 is intended to move in the direction of this polarity. Ps. 29 also shows the other side in vs. 11.

In the post-canonical Psalms the separating out of one motif goes much further. In Ecclesiasticus there are examples which still show the vitality of that polarity: 15:18-20; 18:1-7. In Ecclus. 39:12-35, God the Creator is praised after an imperative exhortation which is expanded with flowery reflections, vss. 12-15. This song of praise begins and ends,[94] "The works of God are all good." The poet believed he could establish this by observations. Verse 32, "From the beginning I have been convinced, and have thought this out and left it in writing."

Here something else is developed out of praise of the Creator. A turning of attention from God to the creation has been accomplished. That which is praised here is basically no longer creation but nature. It is clear that it is described for its own sake and no longer in its relation to the Creator, in which God alone is to be exalted in such descriptive praise. So then it is also possible for the one praising God to drop out of his role into an easygoing, didactic account, vs. 26, "Basic to all the needs of man's life are water and fire and iron and salt and wheat flour and milk and honey." Then he continues in vs. 28, "There are winds . . ." Alongside this there are other sentences which are moved by God's wonders, such as vss. 19-20, "The works of all flesh are before him, and nothing can be hid from his eyes . . . and nothing is marvelous to him."

94. A double framework! Imperatives in vss. 12-15 and 35; a declaration in vss. 16 and 33.

Also the Odes of Solomon 16 is *only* praise of the Creator, which, even though it contains a very subjective, reflective introduction in vss. 1-5, has in the other verses a manner of speech that is much more disciplined, and much nearer to the O.T., and which remains praise in every line and never turns into verbose description.[95]

Where God the Creator alone is praised, praise can imperceptibly change its object, but will not necessarily do so. It is no longer God who is really being praised, but nature. Ecclesiasticus 39 itself shows that even here a new polarity appears. As among men there are the pious and the godless and there this tension became the theme, so in nature there are adverse happenings and catastrophes in contrast to what is good and wholesome. In vss. 28-31 the poet is concerned specifically with this contrast, and unites it to that of the pious and the godless. All that is adverse exists to punish the godless! In correspondence to this it must be said that all the benefits of nature exist only for the good. For evil men they become harmful, vss. 25, 27.

The other development of the praise of the majesty of God is the praise of God as the Lord of history. A comparison of this motif in the two descriptive Psalms of praise, Ps. 33 and Ps. 136, will show already the expansion and the gradual independence of the motif. In Ps. 33:10-12 (and 16-17) God's activity in history is described only in general and by allusions. In Ps. 136:10-22 a detailed historical report has developed out of it, which recounts the main events from the plagues in Egypt to the conquest of Canaan. It is easy to see that such a historical report could then be separated from the total unit of the descriptive Psalm of praise and become an independent Psalm. Psalm 105 is characteristic of this group. After a long imperative introduction (vss. 1-6) there follows in vss. 7-11, clearly corresponding to the other Psalms of praise, the praise of God as the Lord and Judge (vs. 7), and the praise of the gracious God, the God who entered into a covenant with Israel and who remembers the covenant (vss. 8-11). Then the Psalm tells of God's actions in Israel's history (vss. 12-44).

95. Cf. Ps. Sol. 18:10-12.

The culmination of this historical section is the same as in Ps. 136; the beginning is the life of wandering of the Patriarchs (vs. 12) on the basis of the promise of the land (vs. 11). Psalm 78 also belongs here. The introduction here is not an imperative call to praise; its place has been taken by an introduction in the style of wisdom literature. Still the origin in the descriptive Psalm of praise can be clearly recognized. The theme of the Psalm is "the glorious deeds [tehillōth] of the Lord, and his might, and the wonders which he has wrought" (vs. 4). We are dealing, therefore, with praise of the Lord of history. But here something essentially new has been added to the account: it is continued down to the choosing of David (vss. 67-72). The introduction in Deut. 32 is similar. Here the same theme is announced in vs. 3, "For I will proclaim the name of the Lord. Ascribe greatness to our God!" and descriptive praise follows in vs. 4. Next comes the historical account which is continued here to the rejection of Israel by their God, vss. 19-25. But this rejection is not the final happening. Yahweh will "vindicate his people" (vs. 36) and judge their enemies (vss. 40-42). The whole song concludes with an eschatological song of praise (see below), vs. 43. Deuteronomy 32 is the clearest example of how the historical Psalms pass over into eschatological Psalms. Aside from this there are such historical accounts arising out of the praise of God only in mixed forms. Thus it stands together with declarative praise in Exod. 15. The introduction, vs. 2, is similar to the introduction of Deut. 32. The account of Yahweh's deed at the Sea of Reeds, vss. 4-12, is continued down to the conquest, vss. 13-17.

In the lament of the people, a constant element is the looking back to the earlier saving activities of God. This can be expanded into a historical account. This happens above all in Ps. 106, where, alongside the confession of guilt in vss. 6-7, 13-20a, 24-39, there stands the praise of the God, who in spite of all this has helped Israel in a wonderful manner, vss. 8-12, 21b-22, 43-46. Isaiah 63:7-14 is similar. The introduction again resembles Exod. 15:2, but the historical account is here singularly interwoven with the rueful looking back to God's previous deeds of salvation.

In the following section, vss. 14 ff., there is a pleading for deliverance from present need, as at the conclusion of Ps. 106, vs. 47. The historical report with the same motifs reached its greatest extent, but at the same time passed into an unrestricted report, in Neh. 9:7-31. In one passage this looking back to God's earlier deeds of salvation is attached to a lament of the individual, and here too the historical report can be heard, Ps. 77:15-21. However, the features of the epiphany are predominant here.

A number of the statements of these historical Psalms are encountered in Ps. 81. It begins like the Psalms of praise with an imperative call to praise, vss. 1-4, and in vs. 5 God's saving deed in Egypt is given as the basis for the call to praise. In the following, God speaks and reminds Israel of his activity in history, but also of their disobedience. The Psalm ends in an exhortation to obedience. God's voice speaks similarly of the history of the people in Ps. 89:19-37. It is preceded by a complete Psalm of praise, vss. 5-18, and followed in vss. 38-51 by a lament of the people. We are dealing here, however, with only one point in history, the promise to David, which is contrasted with the present time of need.

6. The Eschatological Song of Praise

Gunkel recognized and demonstrated in detail that in Israel, Psalms and prophecy encountered each other at a definite point and permeated each other. There is much evidence of this, both in the prophetic books and in whole groups of Psalms. That this encounter can only have occurred relatively late is almost self-evident. The two categories of expression, the prophetic oracle on the one hand and the speech of the Psalms, which was directed to God, on the other hand, originally had nothing to do with each other. Each is completely *sui generis*. It is scarcely imaginable that a mixture of the two categories could have taken place in their early period. Besides that, however, this mixing is reflected in the history of prophecy. The first prophet in whose work the prophetic oracle and the type of speech found in the

Psalms come together strongly and unmistakably is Jeremiah. Although since Mowinckel the mixed forms, thus, e.g., the so-called "enthronement Psalms," have been again attributed to early times, this is in contradiction to the simplest basic literary facts.

Gunkel calls the first group of these mixed forms "eschatological hymns" (*Einleitung,* pp. 329, 344). The texts which he lists here include many different types. Precisely in this chapter Gunkel proceeds more strongly than elsewhere from the point of view of content: "What makes these hymns eschatological hymns is their content" (p. 344). If, however, we follow Gunkel's correct determination of form (the imperative introduction, and the narrative main section in the "prophetic perfect") then it is not hard to see that here we have an entirely new form. We recognized that the imperative call to praise introduces descriptive praise (see above, p. 102), but originally never declarative praise (or a narrative main section). In the eschatological songs this imperative introduction has been united to a declarative main section, but it is a report that only apparently looks back at something that has already occurred, while in reality speaking of an event that is being announced as if it had already taken place. The introduction of the descriptive Psalm of praise has been combined with the main section of the Psalm of praise of the people, but in so doing the proclamation in the perfect of a coming event has taken the place of God's deed which has already been done.

This perfect of prophetic proclamation, which speaks of God's coming deed of salvation as accomplished, just as the earlier prophetic proclamation of doom anticipated in the proclamation the coming doom as if it had already occurred, is known to us as one of the basic features of the prophecy of Second Isaiah. It is the "perfect of the pronouncement of salvation."[96]

It can scarcely be accidental that the eschatological song of praise in the form described by Gunkel is found most frequently in Second Isaiah. For example,

96. Cf. Begrich, *Deuterojesajastudien,* p. 9.

Isa. 52:9-10, "Break forth together into singing, you waste
    places of Jerusalem;
    for the LORD has comforted his people, he has redeemed
    Jerusalem.
    The LORD has bared his holy arm before the eyes of all the
    nations;
    And all the ends of the earth shall see the salvation of our
    God."

Other "eschatological songs of praise" (EP) in Second Isaiah
are Isa. 40:9-11; 42:10-13; 44:23; 45:8; 48:20 f.; 49:13; 54:1-2.
A thorough investigation of these texts here would lead too far
afield. The structure is always the same, with minor variations
and expansions (one of these is in Isa. 52:9-10, vs. 10b). It is
enough to say here that this form is firmly anchored in the
prophecy of Second Isaiah, that these eschatological songs of
praise form in several passages the clear conclusion of a larger
context,[97] and that in the introductory imperatives the calls to
joy are preponderant. It can be assumed that in all probability
these songs are a new development made by Second Isaiah. This
would then be the form in which in Second Isaiah Psalms and
prophecy came to be most closely united. These eschatological
songs of praise are to some measure the echo of the community
to the promise of salvation which God had made.

This new form is not confined to Second Isaiah, but can be
found in various other places. Deuteronomy 32:43 has already
been mentioned. There it is the conclusion of a historical Psalm
that looks forward to a coming saving action of God, vss. 26-42
(this section is suggestive of many lines in Second Isaiah!). In
addition we find it in Isa. 12:4-6 (or 6 alone); 26:4-6 (?); in
Jer. 20:13; and 31:7; Ps. 9:12-13 (?); Joel 2:21 (and 23 f. ?); Nah.
2:1 and 3a; Zeph. 3:14-15; Zech. 2:14; 9:9-10.[98]

97. Thus here Isa. 52:9-11 is the conclusion of the composition 51:9–52:12, and
40:9-11 is the conclusion of the prologue.
98. There is also an eschatological song of praise in the supplement to Ps. 69,
vss. 32-36, if at the beginning we read (as suggested in the critical apparatus)
"'Look,' ye needy, and 'rejoice,' you who seek God, let your hearts revive. For the
Lord 'has heard' the needy, and does not despise his own that are in bonds." In
Add. Dan. 1:29-67, vs. 65 has the structure of the EP. Isa. 61:10 must also be

It cannot be asserted with certainty that any of these passages are pre-exilic in origin. In the passages in Jeremiah, Nahum, and Zephaniah we are dealing with later additions, as in Isa. 12. It should not however be asserted as absolutely certain that this eschatological shout of jubilation could not also have been raised before Second Isaiah or at the same period. Still, both historically and theologically and in respect to its occurrence it is firmly anchored in the prophecy of Second Isaiah, in which, even apart from this form, the speech of the Psalms and the words of the prophets came together.

7. Songs of the Enthronement of Yahweh

Alongside the eschatological songs of praise Gunkel places the "Songs of the Enthronement of Yahweh" (op. cit., pp. 329, 345). The problem of these Psalms and the extensive literature concerning them cannot be dealt with thoroughly here. In this connection the work of Kraus, Die Königsherrschaft Gottes im A.T., Tübingen, 1951, should be consulted.[99]

Here I shall only deal with the question of the relation of these Psalms to the previously discussed Psalm categories.

---

reckoned among the eschatological songs of praise. It was intended to be a song of the people, although it is in the singular and has more the character of a PI.

99. In its essentials Kraus's work rests on Gunkel's explanation of the enthronement Psalms and disputes Mowinckel's hypothesis of an early Israelite enthronement festival, to which Mowinckel attributed 46 (!) of the Psalms in the Psalter. He combines Mowinckel's basic material (from the historical accounts in 2 Sam. 6 and 1 Kings 8) with the results of Rost's work on the stories of the ark and deduces on the basis of Ps. 132 a "royal Zion festival," which commemorated every year the two events of 2 Sam. 6 and 7: the choice of Zion and the choice of the house of David. This festival was made meaningless by the exile and then filled with new content by Second Isaiah. Isa. 52:7-10 replaces the choice of the house of David with the proclamation of the dawning of the kingship of God in Jerusalem. The enthronement Psalms are cultic hymns of the thus altered festival.

The essential results of Kraus's work seem to me to prove that Mowinckel's hypothesis, which found such wide acceptance and had such far-reaching consequences, is untenable, and as a result, so is the cultic-mythical interpretation of so many Psalms. Kraus very sharply opposes the more recent representatives of this interpretation, Engnell, Widengren, Bentzen. The main argument against Mowinckel is the demonstration of the dependence of the enthronement Psalms in Second Isaiah.

This critical result is independent of Kraus's assumption of a pre-exilic "royal Zion festival." Here many points must still be dealt with. Basically I can express thankful agreement with his work. Independently of Kraus, whose book I saw only after the conclusion of this work, I myself came to the same conclusion from the point of view of the study of the history of the categories.

The "eschatological song of praise" cited above, Isa. 52:9-10, follows the word of salvation in vss. 7-8. A bearer of glad tidings brings Zion the news that God is (has become) king! This statement corresponds in content to the other portion of the announcement of salvation in the perfect, as in Isa. 43:1. Behind this statement there stands the same event which was the ground for the shout of joy in vss. 9-10 (see above): Yahweh has had mercy on his people (40:2) and by his might destroyed the foe. In and through this he has "become king."[100]

God's kingship is spoken of later in two other eschatological songs of praise: Zeph. 3 and Zech. 9. The same exclamation, "Yahweh has become king," is found in the "enthronement Psalms." It is of decisive importance for the total understanding of these Psalms whether that cry has its origin in the Psalms or in Second Isaiah. It seems to me that the priority of Isa. 52:7-8 can be clearly shown.[101]

I must restrict myself here to presenting the arguments only in the form of theses.

1. In Isa. 52 the exclamation is found in the context where it is a message that has been eagerly awaited and greeted with jubilation, brought by a messenger who comes over the mountains to Jerusalem. In the "enthronement Psalms" the exclamation has become a formula separated from the context.

2. In Isa. 52 Yahweh has become king over and for Israel. In the "enthronement Psalms," as, for example, Ps. 47 shows, he has become king over the nations. The total content of the passages that speak of Yahweh's kingship shows unequivocally that Yahweh was *first* spoken of as King of Israel, and later as king of the nations or king of the entire world.

3. The enthronement Psalms do not constitute a category, nor are the so designated Psalms united by regular marks of a category. Rather, throughout these Psalms we are dealing with mixed forms that are taken from quite varied categories. Also

---

100. Cf. Kraus, *op. cit.*, pp. 99 ff.
101. So also Baudissin, Κυριος, III, pp. 235 f. For postexilic origin see also Eissfeldt, "Jahweh als König," *ZAW* 46, pp. 81-105. And now, above all, Kraus, *op. cit.*, pp. 99-112.

the corresponding Psalms of the enthronement of an earthly king are missing. Neither can they be reconstructed out of the scattered motifs that are preserved.

4. Aside from the fact that all enthronement Psalms are mixed Psalms, in language and composition they show the marks of a later period.

5. The origin of the motif "Yahweh has become king" in the proclamation of Second Isaiah (whereby a connection with the Babylonian cultic cry is quite possible)[102] and the taking over of this motif into a group of Psalms of the postexilic period can be explained without any difficulty. The opposite explanation is not possible without extensive hypotheses, of which the most weighty and at the same time the most questionable is the assumption of an enthronement festival of Yahweh, which in the O.T. material can be based essentially only on these "enthronement Psalms."

6. In Second Isaiah the exclamation has primarily a historical-eschatological significance and not primarily a cultic one. The so-called enthronement Psalms are evidence that the message proclaimed by Second Isaiah, that Yahweh had become king, was carried on despite the contemporary situation which showed the opposite. This prophetic assurance lived on in the songs of the postexilic community as one of the witnesses in the waiting for something to come.

These theses shall be carried further at only one point, in a short explanation of the "enthronement Psalms."

Their basis is the descriptive Psalm of praise.

Psalm 47 begins with an imperative call to praise, vs. 1; in vs. 2, the reason for the call: praise of the majesty of God; vss. 3-4 develop the theme: he is Lord of history. The imperatives recur in vs. 6, and in vs. 8 the reason given is in the perfect: God has become king. This one-time occurrence is foreign to the original descriptive praise, and cannot be explained as a development out of it. It corresponds exactly, however, to the eschatological song of praise, where too a one-time action of

102. So also Kraus, *op. cit.*, pp. 7 f., 107 f.

Yahweh (as here in the prophetic perfect) is the basis for the imperative call to jubilation.

In addition there are a number of features which are alien to descriptive praise, and which all further expand the description of Yahweh's enthronement: the ascent of the king into his castle after the victory (vs. 5; cf. Ps. 68:18 and many oriental parallels), the clapping of hands (cf. 2 Kings 11:12), and above all the presence of the nations (vss. 1 and 9). These passages above all make it clear that Yahweh's enthronement is not a cultic, but a historical-eschatological act.

Psalm 96. The structure is similar: an introductory call to praise in the imperative, vss. 1-3, based on descriptive praise. In vss. 4-6 God's majesty is described: he is the Creator, vs. 5b. Here too the imperatives are resumed in vss. 7-9 with the message that Yahweh has become king, vs. 10. In vss. 11-12 the imperatives are carried forward with jussives which exhort to joy and jubilation. This is based on the announcement that Yahweh comes (perf.!) to judge the earth. The similarity to the eschatological songs of praise is unmistakable here. Similarly, in Deut. 32 the announcement of the Judge of the world (32:41) follows the historical account. This Psalm is even more clearly eschatological than Ps. 47.

Psalm 98 almost seems to be a variant of Ps. 96. The similarity of these two Psalms makes clear that the cry "Yahweh is king" is not a necessary component of these eschatological Psalms, for it is missing in Ps. 98. In the first part, vss. 1-3, the polarity of descriptive praise of God can be seen in this Psalm. After the imperative call to praise there follows praise of the mighty (vss. 1-2) and of the gracious God (vs. 3). In vs. 3b we have the nations present. As in Ps. 47:4-6 there follow imperatives which exhort to jubilation before God the King. As in Ps. 96, this is continued in jussives, vss. 7-8, which are based on God's coming to judge the world, vs. 9.

While the basic form of descriptive praise is clearly recognizable in these three Psalms, in Pss. 93; 97; and 99 we find various mixed forms. All that these three Psalms have in common is that the cry "Yahweh has become king" is found at the beginning of each of them. While in the previous three Psalms it was prefixed to a whole that was ready at hand, it resulted here in formations that are distinctive, but which have scarcely any traits in common and have extremely loose internal structure.

Psalm 97. The proclamation of the king is first, followed by the exhortation to the world to rejoice. Above all in Ps. 47 this exclamation concerning the king is expanded by the features of the act of enthronement; here it is, however, combined with the description of an epiphany of God, vss. 2-5. This combination is surely secondary. The central part of the Psalm, vss. 6-8, speaks of the forum of this event, vs. 6, and of the effect it has on the foes, vs. 7, and on Zion, vs. 8. The conclusion, vss. 9-12, in content corresponds exactly to a descriptive Psalm of praise, only that the imperative call to praise stands at the end. Verses 9-11 praise God in his majesty, vs. 9, and in his goodness, vss. 10-11. The imperative call to praise at the end is quite surprising. In all other instances where it occurs in this position it resumes the call to praise of the introduction. Psalm 97 is the only Psalm in which it is found only at the end. This alone is a sure sign of the late origin of the Psalm.

Psalm 99. The first verse resembles the first verse of Ps. 97. The composition of the rest of this Psalm, however, is hard to understand, and it has probably not been preserved in its original order. Vss. 5-9 form a complete Psalm of praise. It begins, vs. 5, and ends, vs. 9, with an imperative call to praise. It praises God as the Holy One, vss. 5c and 9b (perhaps 5c should be moved to after 9b), and as the one who forgives, vs. 8b. This praise is expanded in vss. 6-8a by a historical motif: three figures out of Israel's history were in relation to God; they called to him, and he answered them. The expansion of the praise of God is an indication of late origin. This Psalm, complete in itself, was secondarily combined with vss. 1-4, whose order can no longer be clearly recognized. Verse 3, in its present form, can scarcely be the sequel to vs. 2, and vs. 4 also cannot be read in its present form as handed down. The separate statements can all be found in other descriptive Psalms of praise. Outside of vs. 1 there is not a sentence that is reminiscent of the enthronement of Yahweh.

Psalm 93. This Psalm is already different from all others in that the imperative (or jussive) call to praise is totally missing. In fact, there is no framework at all. In vs. 1 the exclamation of kingship is followed immediately by praise of the majesty of God. It is, nevertheless, not descriptive praise that describes the being of God. The expression ". . . is robed, he is girded with strength," is rather the continuation of the exclamation in the perfect in vs. 1. (Cf. the petition in Isa. 51:9, "Put on strength, O arm of the Lord.") The praise of the majesty of God is developed in the usual manner. He is the Creator in vss. 1b-2, and the Lord of history in vss. 3-4. But the two cannot be sharply separated here, for vss. 3-4 are a clear allusion to the primeval struggle with chaos. On the other hand, these sentences remind one of the declarative Psalm of the people, Ps. 124. The chaotic forces which rise up correspond to the historical threat to the people of God. Verse 3 is addressed to Yahweh, almost as a lament of those who are threatened by these powers. Verse 4 corresponds then to the account of deliverance. The fact that God is higher than the highest threats of the force that threatens his people means that salvation is certain. The whole, however, is development of the exclamation of kingship, so that the conclusion of vs. 4 is to be understood in an eschatological sense. This Psalm is truly a unit. The connection of vs. 5 to vss. 1-4 is not clear, but it could easily have originally belonged together with them.

In conclusion, thesis 6 above is confirmed in that there is no proper category of the enthronement Psalms. In Pss. 47; 96; 98, a descriptive Psalm of praise is expanded and modified by the exclamation of kingship. In Pss. 97 and 99 this exclamation has become the chief motif of the Psalm, and yet even in these two the basic category of the descriptive Psalm of praise can be clearly recognized. On the other hand, Ps. 93 is purely an expansion of the exclamation of kingship. Here too there are suggestions of the descriptive Psalm of praise, but the style of the declarative Psalm of praise, transformed into eschatology, is dominant.

The significance of these enthronement Psalms lies in that a motif which was prophetic in origin, the eschatological exclamation of kingship, was absorbed into the descriptive praise of the Psalms. In its original occurrence, Isa. 52, this exclamation was the glad tidings proclaimed to exiled Israel, "Your God reigns!" This message was to assure the exiles of their coming deliverance. Since it lived on after the Exile in the worship of the community, the certainty of the coming intervention of God lived in it, Ps. 96:13, "For he comes to judge the earth." In this prophetic anticipation of Yahweh's coming kingship the expansion of the praise of Yahweh as Lord of history took on the characteristic form for Israel, which had become impotent and was subject to the great powers. It is praise of the Lord of history—in expectation.

In relation to this chapter, cf. D. Michel, "Studien zu den sogenannten Thronbesteigungspsalmen," *VT* 6 (1956), pp. 40-68.

Summary and Conclusion

The two modes of calling on God are praise and petition. As the two poles, they determine the nature of all speaking to God. This is true of all calling on God, in which God stands over against man in a personal relationship. The Psalms from Israel's environment are also to be understood as arising in petition and praise or out of petition and praise, insofar as they are intended as speaking to God or before God. The five basic motifs of the Babylonian psalms are to be explained in terms of this polarity:

I. Address, II. Praise, III. Lament, IV. Petition, V. Vow of Praise.

Calling on God in Israel is identical with that in Babylon not only in the polarity of praise and petition, but also in these five basic motifs. The difference is only in the relationship of these parts to one another. The relation of praise and petition in Babylon is essentially determined by the fact that praise is understood as praise of God *before* the petition, and in part as preparatory for the petition. Praise of God in Israel is essentially praise after the petition has been answered. This determines changes in the basic motifs and in their combinations with each other. The most important of these are as follows: (a) In Babylon there is *one* basic category of Psalms, which contains both praise and petition (and lament) at the same time; in Israel there are *two* basic categories: the Psalm of petition (lament) and the Psalm of praise; (b) The nature of praise of

152

the gods in Babylon is almost always that of descriptive praise. In the O.T. there is both declarative and descriptive praise. Moreover, descriptive praise developed from declarative (or confessing) praise and never entirely lost its connection with it. The vow of praise, which forms in Babylon as well as in Israel the link between lament (and petition) and praise, introduces— in the form of an annunciation in the introduction to the Psalm —descriptive praise in Babylon, but in Israel, declarative praise. Descriptive praise came to have a new introduction in Israel, one entirely lacking in the Babylonian psalms: the imperative call to praise. With this introduction, descriptive praise in Israel became a category in itself. In addition to the (open) Psalm of petition, there is also the petition that has been answered. It is not only certain of being answered, but already testifies to it in declarative praise at the end.

The Categories of the Psalms

The "categories" of the Psalms are not first of all literary or cultic in nature. They are this of course, but it is not the essential element. They designate the basic modes of that which occurs when man turns to God with words: plea and praise. As these two basic modes of "prayer" change and expand, the categories also change and expand. They can travel great distances from this original occurrence, but their origin in it can be recognized in all the branchings of the Psalm categories. There is therefore—often in apparent contradiction to the facts—no Psalm category that arose merely out of some thought concept (such as the theme, nature), or merely out of some cultic exclamation (such as "Yahweh has become king"). Even the Psalms of confidence, the didactic Psalms, and the festival liturgies (such as Ps. 132) are derived in the final analysis from those basic occurrences of plea and praise.

In comparison with the Babylonian psalms it has been shown that the Psalms of the O.T. for the most part fall into *two* basic categories, which correspond to the two basic ways of praying. This work has endeavored to show in the Psalms of the O.T.

the vital, tension-filled polarity of plea and praise. Lay prayer in Israel is also governed by this polarity.[103]

"Cultic prayer" in Israel preserved in astounding measure its connection with lay prayer (in great contrast to Egypt!). In Israel all speaking to God moved between these two poles. There is no petition, no pleading from the depths, that did not move at least one step (in looking back to God's earlier saving activity or in confession of confidence) on the road to praise. But there is also no praise that was fully separated from the experience of God's wonderful intervention in time of need, none that had become a mere stereotyped liturgy.

In view of this polarity, the center of the praise of God in Israel can be seen in declarative (or confessional) praise. It is the center inasmuch as in it (in retrospect of the peril) the danger which has just been overcome still is heard, and is connected to the earnest pleas then made in dire need. It is the center, however, in another entirely different connection. Declarative praise breaks through the boundary between set and free speech (poetry and prose), between the speech of everyday life and the cultic speech of the Psalms. The declarative Psalms of praise have in their simplest form the same structure as the *bārūk* sentences in the historical books. And it is out of the declarative praise of the people that the writing of history in Israel grew.[104]

This work built on Gunkel's demonstration that a Psalm is to be understood only as a branch on the tree of the category; that this tree, moreover, is rooted in a soil, that is, that the Psalm categories are not merely literary categories, but have a Sitz-im-Leben. Gunkel's thesis that the Sitz-im-Leben of the Psalms is the cult is here accepted only conditionally. I have pointed beyond that all too common and indefinite word *cult* to the basic occurrence which transpires in "cult" when men speak to God: the polarity of speaking to God as plea and as praise.

This is the real Sitz-im-Leben of the Psalms. As an occurrence from man to God each Psalm is a unit. Thus its structure can

---

103. Cf. Wendel, *op. cit.*
104. Cf. in this connection Martin Noth, *Überlieferungsgeschichte des Pentateuch,* Stuttgart, 1948, and my discussion of it in *Zeichen der Zeit,* 1951, p. 10.

be recognized, the structure of a live occurrence. It is a unit, whose members show that they belong to the whole. Never however does this whole become an external scheme, into which a living content is pressed.

Thus the beginnings and transitions to praise of God are seen even in the laments of the people and of the individual. Thus the confession of confidence, which is in Israel such a meaningful and richly developed part, is not to be sharply separated from praise of God. Thus the vow of praise directly points the way to the Psalm of praise.

On the other hand, in the declarative Psalms of praise of the individual and of the people there are echoes of the lament and the pleading of the Psalms of lamentation, and even in the descriptive praise of God, the activity of God, who saves out of the depths, is never forgotten.

Therefore the praise of God in Israel never became a cultic happening, separated from the rest of existence, in a separate realm, that had become independent of the history of the people and of the individual. Rather it occupied a central place in the total life of the individual and the people before God, as for instance the concept of faith does for us. (Cf. Grimme's reference, above, p. 42.) The praise of God occupied for Israel actually the place where "faith in God" stands for us. In Israel it was a fundamental of existence that God was and that therefore they believed in him, and as such it was not disturbed. On this still unshaken basis the clearest expression of the relationship to God was the act of praising God.

This may be shown finally by a peculiar expression of the Psalms concerning praise of God.

THE DEAD DO NOT PRAISE YAHWEH

hōdāh:

Ps. 6:5, "For in death there is no remembrance of thee; in Sheol who can give thee praise?"

Ps. 30:9, "What profit is there in my death, if I go down to the Pit? Will the dust praise thee? Will it tell of thy faithfulness?"

The Categories of the Psalms

Petition of the people	Declarative praise of the people	Petition of the individual (open)	Petition of the individual (heard)	Declarative praise of the individual	Descriptive Praise
Introductory petition	(Let Israel say so)	Introduction	———		
Lament	Looking back to the time of need ↑ ↓	Lament	Lament		
Confession of confidence	Report of the deliverance ↓ →	Confession of Confidence	Confession of Confidence		
Petition		Petition	Petition		
(Double wish)		Double wish	(Double wish)		
		(Confidence of being heard)	(Confidence of being heard)		
Vow of praise		Vow of praise	Vow of praise ←	→ Announcement	
				Introductory summary	

Praise (declarative) → Report of deliverance
1. Looking back to the time of need
2. I cried
3. He heard
4. He drew me out

Vow of praise ← → Call to praise

Praise (descriptive) ↑ → Praise
1. Yahweh is great
(a) the Creator
(b) the Lord of history
2. Yahweh is good
(a) he saves
(b) he gives bread

Conclusion

Ps. 88:10, "Dost thou work wonders for the dead? Do the shades rise up to praise thee?"

11, "Is thy steadfast love declared in the grave, or thy faithfulness in Abaddon?"

Isa. 38:18 f., "For Sheol cannot thank thee, death cannot praise thee; those who go down to the pit cannot hope for thy faithfulness. The living, the living, he thanks thee, as I do this day."

hillēl:

Ps. 115:17, "The dead do not praise the LORD, nor do any that go down into silence. But we will bless the LORD from this time forth, and for evermore."

Isa. 38:18 f., see above.

sippēr:

Ps. 88:11, see above.

Cf. Ps. 118:17, "I shall not die, but I shall live, and recount the deeds of the LORD."

Ps. 119:175, "Let me live, that I may praise thee."

Ecclus. 17:27 f., "Who will sing praises to the Most High in Hades, as do those who are alive and give thanks?" S has instead of this, "For what use to God are all those who have perished in the world, in comparison to those who live and praise him?"

Cf. Erman, *op. cit.,* p. 374; "Hymn to the Sun God":

"All who sleep praise together thy beauty, when thy light shines before their faces . . . When thou hast passed by, so darkness covers them and each one lies down [again] in his coffin."

The vocabulary of praise is found almost always in the vocative. Only in the later period are statements about praise numerous. In the earlier period, apparently the only way in which praise can be spoken of is by calling to give praise. The single, clear exception is this sentence, which is repeated in so many ways and given such emphasis that it must be of especial meaning. And just at this point a sentence from an Egyptian psalm says the exact opposite (see above, p. 50). Reference should be made here to the work of Chr. Barth.[105]

The sentence had its origin in the Psalm of petition of the individual as a motif in support of the petition, which should move God to intervene (Pss. 6; 30; 88). From there it passed over into the declarative praise of the individual, where it was spoken in retrospect, Isa. 38. In the liturgy of Ps. 115 the form can no longer be identified with certainty.

The positive expression of these negative sentences is found in Isa. 38:19, "The living, the living, he thanks thee." The expression "but we" (the *waw*-adversative which indicates the turning point in the petition, see above!) in Ps. 115:18 is to be understood in the same way. Ps. 118:17 and 119:175 express the same thing positively.

All these sentences have the meaning that *only* there, where death is, is there no praise. Where there is life, there is praise.[106]

The possibility that there could also be life in which there was no praise, life that did *not* praise God, does not enter the picture here. As death is characterized in that there is no longer any praise there, so praise belongs to life. The conclusion is not expressed in the O.T., but it must still have been drawn. There cannot be such a thing as true life without praise. Praising and no longer praising are related to each other as are living and no longer living. In the late period the existence of the godless (there is however not yet any name in the O.T. to correspond to it) has become a greater and greater temptation, but the belief is always firmly maintained that such an existence *must* be destroyed by God (Ps. 73). Nowhere is there the possibility of abiding, true life that does not praise God. Praise of God, like petition, is a mode of existence, not something which may or may not be present in life.

That is very hard for us to understand. For us the word has a much too greatly altered, feeble, weakened sound.[107]

---

105. *Die Errettung vom Tode,* esp. p. 151.
106. Cf. Chr. Barth, *op. cit.,* p. 151. "It should be noted, however, that the praise of Yahweh has at the same time the function of a sign of being alive."
107. In the O.T. the verb *hōdāh* has only Yahweh as its object. There is no clear

The essential element of the concept is that of exaltation (see above). The sentence in Isa. 38:9 is also to be heard in this way, "The living, the living, he thanks thee [exalts thee]." In this the whole meaning of the concept the O.T. becomes perhaps somewhat clearer. Exalting is a part of existence. It is so much a part of it, that when one has ceased to exalt God, something else must be exalted. Then God can be displaced by a man, an institution, an idea. Exalting remains a function of existence. World history demonstrates this. Man *must* exalt something, and without such exalting there can apparently be no existence.

But hereby the distance between our present concept "praise" and that of the O.T. is still not shown with sufficient clarity. This "praise" still includes our words "to honor" and "to admire" and "honor" and "admiration." Rilke, for example, felt this when he sought in his concept of "praise" to revive the original, fuller sense and sound of the concept.

Not everywhere where God is no longer truly praised will men of necessity fall into the extremity of the deification of man. But they must surely exalt, admire, honor something. There is no real, full existence that does not in some way honor, admire, look up to something. All this was originally meant in the vocabulary of praise. God is so real, so much alive and mighty for man in the Old Testament that all this is directed toward God. In all ages, however, when this full, living praise turns away from God or becomes withered, thin, and pale, it can be shown how exaltation, admiration, and honor turn away from God to other subjects.

If the praise of God, as the Psalms express it, belongs to existence, then the directing of this praise to a man, an idea,

---

passage in which a man might be the object of *hōdāh*. That the "praise of God" can be completely misunderstood in our modern language is shown by a verse of Hermann Hesse, ("Abends" in *Trost der Nacht*, p. 64):
". . . Summe dumme Gassenlieder
Lobe Gott und mich, . . .
Sage ja zu meinem Herzen
(Morgens geht es nicht),
Spinne aus vergangnen Schmerzen
Spielend ein Gedicht . . ."

or an institution must disturb and finally destroy life itself. The Psalms say that only where God is praised is there life.

The praise of the Old Testament remains in its center, in the declarative praise, a praise in expectation. This is true of the praise of the individual (Job 1:21) as well as of that of the people (the eschatological Psalm). Here and there God is really praised in the midst of trial, but this praise is at the same time a waiting.

We may surmise that the imperative call to praise in the late Psalms is given such great prominence because behind it there is hidden anxiety, whether God will really be praised enough, whether he will be praised aright.

This imperative call to praise, that has such significance for the history of religion,[108] served in its very preponderance as a sign that in this people all voices called for a praise that was yet to be given. This imperative too awaited the fulfilling of praise.

The expectation of the Old Testament is fulfilled in Jesus Christ. So must also the "praise in expectation" be fulfilled in him. The Gospel according to John says in its whole structure that Christ is come to "honor" the Father among men. This *doxazein* can also be translated as "praise."

Christ is come to honor the Father in his life and in his death. At the turning point of his life stands the word, John 17:1, "Father, . . . glorify thy Son that the Son may glorify [=praise] thee." Verse 26, "I made known to them thy name, and I will make it known." Cf. Ps. 22:22, "I will tell of thy name to my brethren." This is the intent of the vow of praise of the Psalms. In the Prologue the work of Jesus Christ is summed up in "The only Son, who is in the bosom of the Father, he has made him known." He has done that which it was the intention of the praise of the people of Israel to do.

108. The caesura between the second and third Babylonian motif of address. See above.

The totally new, the decisive, element lies in the fact that, in contrast to the unanimous declaration of the Psalms, Christ praises the Father through his death, in death. This is the "hour" for which the whole of the Gospel of John waits (John 2; 7; 12; 13; 17).

In that Christ has honored and praised God by his death, the concept of the praise of God has been altered in an essential point. Among the followers of Christ, who honored God by his existence and his death, there is the new possibility of praise by existence (Eph. 1:12), which includes the possibility of praising God through death in following Christ, John 21:19. This is the meaning of a passage which is decisive for the praise of God in the New Testament, John 4:23.[109]

This is also what is meant in Rom. 12:1-2. It has been shown above that the structure of the Letter to the Romans corresponds to that of the declarative Psalm of praise, and Rom. 12:1 ff. corresponds to the vow of praise. The congregation of Jesus Christ is called on to praise God by standing in the world as followers of Jesus Christ, who praised the Father in his life and death. It praises God by confessing in its whole existence "what God has done for us." In such praise of the congregation, in which and by which it confesses before the world God's deed in Jesus Christ, exactly the same thing happens which this investigation established as the basic, central praise of God in the Psalms: declarative praise. The proclamation of the church can then be only a way in which this praise is expressed by the congregation through its existence. It must fail if it sets out to be something else than the *hōdāh* of the one saved in the declarative Psalms of praise. One difference is that the individual no longer proclaims before the congregation, but in the voice of an individual the community proclaims before the world what God has done. The other is that the proper witness to the deeds of God occurs in the existence of the community in the world, and that the proclamation is only a way of bearing this testimony.

---

109. This proceeds from the exegesis of the concepts *pneuma* and *aletheia*.

BOOK TWO

LAMENT
IN THE
PSALMS

Translated by Richard N. Soulen

PART FOUR

The Structure and History
of the Lament
in the Old Testament

The purpose of this essay is to further at a single point the task undertaken in Gunkel's *Introduction to the Psalms*. Research since its publication has in my opinion turned too quickly from the then newly discovered path of understanding the categories of the Psalms as a whole and each in terms of its parts only to proceed in the direction recently taken by Mowinckel, that is, to inquire thoroughly into their "Sitz-im-Leben." Gunkel had already identified this setting in Israel's life to be the "cult,"[1] though, of course, with limitations. Mowinckel radicalized this thesis, contested the limitations and mistakenly placed the weight of the question totally upon the cultic events and practices underlying the Psalms.[2] At the same time scholarly inquiry of necessity moved toward the wider horizon of the basic phenomena surrounding the cult in the ancient Orient. Research in the following period concentrated upon these phenomena, based upon a tremendously enlarged body of material from new discoveries and newly interpreted texts.[3] The results of these investigations for the understanding of the Old Testament, and above all the Psalms, go far beyond the new perspective regarding the Psalms provided by Mowinckel's *Psalmenstudien*. A good example of this is the opinion which Ivan

---

1. Gunkel-Begrich, *Einleitung in die Psalmen*, Göttingen, 1933, p. 10.
2. S. Mowinckel, *Psalmenstudien* I-VI, Kristiania, 1921–1924.
3. Consult the bibliography in Ivan Engnell, *Studies in Divine Kingship in the Ancient Near East*, Uppsala, 1943, pp. 223–46.

Engnell shares at the conclusion of his *Studies in Divine Kingship*.[4]

It is characteristic of this chapter of research, centering on the concept of the cult, that at times a whole profusion of phenomena is reduced to a *single* explanation, that is, attributed primarily to a *single* cultic event. The classic example of this is still Mowinckel's *Psalmenstudie* II, in which he attributes a number of highly varied Psalms to the enthronement festival, thinking that he has thereby given them their essential interpretation.[5] This tendency was extensively expanded in the "cultic pattern" approach of the English school surrounding S. H. Hooke[6] and in the explanation of all or almost all of the Psalms as royal Psalms used in the ritual of the king. It is basically this same interpretive tendency which also permits Artur Weiser for example to attribute a number of different Psalms to *one* specific festival (the Covenant Festival), and to interpret the Psalms on the basis of the ideology of this festival, the heart of which is the "theophany of the God of the Covenant."[7] It is a tendency which continues to find a succession of varying formulations.

Under the dominance of this perspective, the work initiated by Gunkel (of analyzing the characteristics of *individual* Psalm categories and their *individual* motifs) was all but completely abandoned. Yet such a task, it seems to me, is indispensible for any further discussion of the relationship of the Israelite Psalms to the Babylonian and Canaanite psalms and to their over-all interpretation. This is shown to be the case at two points in particular.

1. The question of the relationship of the Psalms of the indi-

---

4. *Ibid.*, Conclusion, pp. 174–77: "Anticipatory Summary of the Subsequent Treatment of the O.T. Material." For a contrasting view, see John Gray, "Canaanite Kingship in Theory and Praxis," *VT* II, 1952, pp. 193–220.

5. Cf. S. Mowinckel, *Offersang og sangoffer*, Oslo, 1951, pp. 118ff.; English trans. *The Psalms in Israel's Worship*, 2 vols., tr. D. R. Ap-Thomas, New York, 1962, pp. 106ff. Cf. also S. Mowinckel, *Religion und Kultus*, Göttingen, 1953, pp. 71ff. A clear statement of the thesis of the Uppsala School is found on p. 74.

6. S. H. Hooke, *Myth and Ritual*, London/Oxford, 1933, and *The Labyrinth*, London, 1935.

7. A. Weiser, *Die Psalmen* (AT Deutsch, 3. Aufl., 1950), Einleitung, pp. 9–61. English trans. by Herbert Hartwell, *The Psalms*, Old Testament Library, Philadelphia: Westminster Press, 1962, Introduction, pp. 19–101.

vidual to the Psalms of the people (thus the question of the "I" of the Psalms) has been taken up anew,[8] and of course with the intention of playing down of what up to now had seemed to be generally recognized, viz., the formal distinction between laments of the individual (LI) and laments of the people (LP).[9] Whether this is justified can be determined, in my opinion, only on the basis of the precise definition of the motifs of the two types of Psalms. This is possible, however, in terms far more exact and comprehensive than, let us say, the position taken in the Introduction by Gunkel-Begrich. There it is demonstrated that the distinction between laments of the people and laments of the individual can be discerned within every motif and in the relationship of the motifs to each other, and for this reason at least such leveling down of the distinction is unjustified.

2. Whenever all (or nearly all) of the Psalms are treated as royal Psalms, the lament of the king takes on great significance. The same is true of the lament for the dead king, who in the cult is identical with the dead god. In this case, however, the fundamental distinction between a lament for the dead and a lament of distress is not to be overlooked. They are in their origin and in their nature different phenomena. The lament for the dead god or king,[10] of such decisive importance for the Babylonian and Canaanite cults, is, of course, mentioned in the Old Testament polemically,[11] but in the Psalms this type of lament is not to be found.[12]

8. E.g., Engnell, *op. cit.*, p. 48, note 5; cf. also note 22.
9. E.g., Engnell, *op. cit.*, p. 48. Here he quotes Jastrow, *Die Religion Babyloniens und Assyriens*, Giessen, 1905–12, vol. 2, p. 106, "The distinction between public and personal songs of lament . . . is not due to the nature of the subject."
10. Cf. the analytical study by M. Noth, "Gott, König, Volk im AT," *ZThK*, 1950, 2, and H. H. Schrey, "Die alttestamentliche Forschung der sog. Uppsala-Schule," *TZ* 7, 1951, pp. 321–41.
11. Thus, e.g., Hos. 10:5 and Jer. 5:7; see also J. Pedersen, *Israel, Its Life and Culture*, vol. 4, London, 1947, p. 470, note 3.
12. In the O.T., the lament of the dead is a phenomenon differing from the lament of distress which has its own structure and history, as H. Jahnow has shown in his work, *Das hebräische Leichenlied im Raum der Volkerdichtung*, BZAW 36, 1923; also Paul Kahle, "Die Totenklage im heutigen Ägypten," in *Eucharisterion (Festschrift for H. Gunkel)*, Göttingen, 1923, pp. 346ff. Additional literature is cited by E. Littmann, "Abessinisches zum AT" in *Bertholet-Festschrift*, Tübingen, 1950, p. 342.

But beyond this we must ask: What after all is a lament?
What happens in it? What are its components? Without this
kind of clarification it would seem to me impossible to answer
the question of what the lament of the king within the cult
could mean, or what happens in such a lament, or whether and
how the subject of this particular lament could be changed
around (either in transference to the king or in the so-called
"democratization" of the subject). We shall have to pursue these
questions further. The same would have to occur for the most
important of the other motifs.[13] Only then would there be a
sufficiently firm basis for a comparison. Of course such a comprehensive comparison of motifs makes sense only from the
perspective of a single presupposition, viz., that the lament is a
phenomenon of human existence which received its special,
one may even say its peculiar character in the cult, but which
nevertheless extends beyond it and which therefore must be
investigated in terms of its wider occurrence as well.

The investigation which follows proceeds from the assumption that *the lament has a history.* The lament in the Psalms has a
historical antecedent and a sequel. We find evidence of it as a
phenomenon of life both in the historical narratives and in the
prophetic writings. We encounter it as early as the Exodus traditions (and even here, as a lament of the mediator, in an especially strong and vivid form), and encounter it still in the
Apocryha which bear witness to a highly curious reawakening
of the lament. The laments of Moses, Samson, Elijah, Jeremiah,
Job, and the Apocalypse of Ezra all belong within this larger

---

The essential characteristics of the lament of the dead in contrast to the lament of distress are:
1. The lament of the dead is not addressed to God; the name of Yahweh never occurs in
it.
2. Characterizing the lament of the dead is the address to the dead, the call for lamentation, the announcement of death, and the description of suffering.
3. The lament of distress is combined with supplication, i.e., it looks to the future for the
time of deliverance; the lament of the dead confronts the fact of death and looks to
the past.
13. For example, J. Begrich, "Die Vertrauensäusserung im israelitischen Klagelied des
Einzelnen und in seinem babylonischen Gegenstück," *ZAW*, 46, 1928; now in *Gesammelte
Studien zum Alten Testament (Theologische Bücherei* 21), 1964, pp. 168–216.

context. They all, like the laments contained in a Psalm, are either laments of an individual or of the people.

What do all these texts have in common while so distinct from each other in time, content, and literary character? What is the connection between the non-cultic lament and that of the cult? The texts in the O.T. show that throughout its history (that is, both in the Psalms and in its earlier and later develop- ment) lamentation is a phenomenon characterized by three de- terminant elements: the one who laments, God, and the others, i.e., that circle of people among whom or against whom the one who laments stands with a complaint. In the case of the lament we are not dealing simply with the utterance of an individual reacting to a situation of distress, but rather with an event which from the beginning has these *three* components.

The lament in the Psalms is threefold. It is divisible according to its three subjects: God, the one who laments, and the enemy. For example, as found in a lament of the people:

Ps. 79:1–3, the enemy; vs. 4, we; vs. 5, Thou, Yahweh.

Or, in a lament of the individual:

Ps. 13:1: "How long, O LORD? Wilt thou forget me for ever?
How long wilt thou hide thy face from me?
    2: How long must I bear pain in my soul,
and have sorrow in my heart 'day after day'?[14]
How long shall my enemy be exalted over me?"

These three parts or dimensions alone constitute the lament as complete. What a lament is, the relationship of these three components to each other alone will reveal. Of course, they are not always as obvious as in the two examples cited. Nor are we saying that every one of the laments must contain every one of these elements. Nevertheless, as an event the lament is by na- ture threefold. In every lament there are "the others" and— expressed or implied—they always have something to do with

14. *BH,* Kittle; see apparatus *ad loc.*

the lament. For the one who utters the lament is never an isolated individual standing alone; the lamenter is always a member of a group. This fundamental structure is the common feature of all the laments in the O.T.; it unites all their varied expressions.[15]

Because the lament has this structure, it has a history, for the relationship of these three dimensions of the lament (God, the one(s) who lament, and the others) is not always the same. And, though the relationship of the three elements varies in several respects, the structure as such—that is, that which constitutes the lament as a lament—remains. It connects the lament contained within a Psalm, or the cultic lament, with its historical antecedent and its subsequent development.

Let us first of all sketch this history in very broad terms. At its center stands the lament included within a Psalm. Here it is but one part of a more comprehensive whole. This larger unit, the lament Psalm, is structured (here greatly stylized) as follows:

Address (and introductory petition)
Lament
Turning toward God (confession of trust)
Petition
Vow of praise

The unit as a whole is a call to God. It can also be termed a

15. The German word *Klage* ["lament"/"complaint"] corresponds to this phenomenon only approximately. On the one hand it is too broad, since it includes both lament for the dead and lament arising from distress. On the other hand it is too narrow insofar as for us it is an individual "act of self-expression" and not an event containing the three above-named components. In a way this is reflected in the fact that these three components of the lament brought about special linguistic formulations. The lament [*Klage*] directed at a court of law became an indictment [*Anklage*]. When the lament refers back to the one who is lamenting, it is called a lament over personal suffering [*Sich-Beklagen*]. When it is directed at the opponent, it is called an accusation [*Ver-klagen*]. Thus, these three concepts are included within the word "lament" when we apply it to the phenomenon investigated here in the O.T. In this case we must be aware, however, that the German usage has become somewhat blurred. We no longer make a sharp distinction between *anklagen* ["to indict, to accuse"] and *verklagen* ["to accuse," "to bring action against"]. [Translator's note: Corresponding to German parlance and in deference to common practice, no absolute distinction is made in the translation between *anklagen* and *verklagen*. Generally speaking the former is here rendered "to complain against" and the latter "to complain about," but both denote an accusatory complaint.

prayer. The lament is a part of those prayer Psalms in which the petition must follow the lament, the lament precedes the petition. By contrast, the lament in the early period (for example, Samson's lament in Judg. 15:18) is in itself a self-contained supplication to God. It requires no explicit petition since a petition is already included in the lament itself.[16] In the later period the lament again becomes detached from the lament Psalm as a unit and exists independently. The Psalm from which it separates then becomes a prayer of petition. But the lament of this later period, emancipated from the Psalm of lament, is something essentially different from the lament of the early period which *remained* independent. This early form is the call to God, prayer in the strictest sense of the word, whereas the later lament emerged *along side of* and outside of prayer. On the other hand, prayer (the call to God) was fundamentally altered when the lament was cut off from it.

Corresponding to this change in the external history of the lament is a change within the lament itself, specifically a change in the relationship of its three parts. In the early period, the dominant one of the three components constituting the lament is the lament directed at God, the complaint against God. In the middle period, that is, in the Psalms, the three components of the lament are on the whole held in balance. In the later period, the complaint against God falls almost totally silent. How and why it becomes silent can easily be observed. The theology of the Deuteronomic school—which declared the history of the wilderness sojourn (esp. Deut. 9:7ff.), and even more the history of established Israel, to be a history of disobedience, and which sought to prove that political annihilation was the righteous judgment of God—began to formulate a way of thinking in which complaint against God was absolutely disallowed. The guilt of the Patriarchs was so earnestly and consciously taken over that, in place of the complaint against God formerly found in laments concerned with the fate of the na-

16. On Judg. 15:18, see below, p. 195.

tion, now the exact opposite appeared, viz., the justification of God's righteousness or simply praise of the righteous God. Nevertheless, over and beyond this theological conviction, perplexity at the incomprehensible judgments of God remained. The accusatory questions "Why?" and "How long?" could not be silenced altogether. They erupted with force again outside the prayer.

Major Foci in the Transmission of the Lament

The middle of the tradition lies in the Psalter in two category types: the Psalm of the lament of the people and the Psalm of the lament of the individual. Outside the Psalter the most numerous and extensive examples of the lament of the people are to be found in Second Isaiah. The prophet's message of salvation reflects so thoroughly the lament of the people[17] voiced during the Exile that the motifs which can be recognized there presuppose a far greater number of such Psalms than have been handed down to us in the Psalter.

In the early period we know of laments only within the historical traditions. One focal point to be recognized here lies in the lament of the leader and mediator, particularly the laments of Moses (and Joshua) and the laments from the period of the Judges. Later it occurs only in allusions (as with Elijah, Amos, Hosea) and reaches its full development in the laments of Jeremiah.

In the later period, the focus lies in the laments over the fall of Jerusalem beginning with Lamentations up to 4 Ezra. In Lamentations a totally new type of song of lament appears which is characterized by an admixture of motifs from the lament of the dead.[18]

In two instances the lament motif has led to large compositions of its own. Underlying the book of Job as its leitmotif is the lament of the individual, and underlying 4 Ezra is the la-

---

17. J. Begrich, *Deuterojesaja-Studien*, *BWANT* 25, Stuttgart, 1938, esp. p. 11; republished in *Theologische Bücherei* 20, 1963.
18. H. Jahnow, *op. cit.*, pp. 168f.

ment of the people. The latter is transmitted in the Psalter only rarely, whereas by contrast its motifs and references to the phenomenon itself are found quite frequently.[19] It must have played an important role in Israel during the pre-exilian period, for the laments collected in Lamentations, which with certainty began to appear after 586 B.C.,[20] already represent a mixed form[21] which presupposes the pure form of the lament of the people and is possible only after it. The prayers of lament or repentance in the Chronicles and in the Apocrypha prove by their radically altered form that the ancient lament of the people had experienced in the Exile a profound transformation which we can properly describe as its collapse. For the lament of the individual there are no historical points of reference of this sort. Only the laments of Jeremiah possess fixed dates. It will be shown, however, that for them as well changes can be noted which justify speaking of a history of the lament.

THE LAMENT OF THE PEOPLE

The arrangement of the lament of the people according to its three subjects is discernible in the few Psalms of this type preserved in the tradition.

One will note that the three subjects of the lament are present in a somewhat similar fashion in Pss. 79, 44, 80, 89; Isa. 63; and Hab. 1. They have no fixed sequence and one of the subjects can appear more than once in a single Psalm. Thus we are not dealing here with a set pattern.[22] The summary below shows primarily only that in the laments of the people, the lament directed at God (subject 1) is clearly dominant.

19. Cf. Gunkel-Begrich, *Einleitung*, pp. 117–139 (par. 4). On p. 117, Gunkel cites as pure laments of the people only Pss. 44, 74, 79, 80, 83, and Lam. 5.
20. M. Haller, *Die fünf Megilloth*, HAT, 1940, p. 92.
21. *Op. cit.*, p. 92.
22. In the bracketed verses the subject involved appears in connection with another subject or with another motif. In Ps. 89, the entire lament found in vss. 38–46 is a complaint against God; the two other subjects are incorporated into it. In Ps. 44 the structure has probably been disturbed. Verses 16–17 are a fragment of a LI. Ps. 60 contains only parts of a lament of the people, and only subject 1 at that. Hab. 1:2ff. is formally a lament of the individual. Within the context of the whole book, however, only a lament of the people can be in mind; vs. 4a is possible only within a LP.

Lament[22]	Subject 1 Thou, God	Subject 2 we	Subject 3 the enemy
Ps. 79	5	4, 8b	1–3, 7, (10)
Ps. 74	1, 11	9, (19–21)	4–8, (10, 18, 22, 23)
Ps. 44	9–12, 14, (19), 24	13, (14), (17–22), 25	10b, 13–14
Ps. 80	4–6, 12	(5–6, 12–13)	12b–13
Ps. 89	38–46	(40–41, 44–45)	(41–42)
Ps. 83	(1)	—	2–8
Ps. 60	1–2a, 3, 10	—	—
Lam. 5	20, 22	1b–18	(8, 11–13)
Jer. 14	8–9 19	(2–6) 17–18	Confession of Sin
Isa. 63:7—64:12	15b–17 64:12	(17), 19 64:10–11	18b —
Hab. 1	2–3, 13b	(3), 4a	4b

Important variations are found in three passages.

(1) In the two laments of the people occasioned by drought in Jer. 14, the third referent (the enemy) is naturally absent. In both cases a confession of sins appears in its place. One also notes that in the first of the two laments, the second subject is simply described and thus falls outside the prayer.

(2) The lament in Ps. 83 is completely dominated by references to the enemy. Even the petition in the Psalm is a petition *against* the enemy. Moreover the situation is quite different. The enemy have only made threats (3–9); the battle has not yet begun. Elsewhere these two features are found only in a group of LI (see below). Ps. 83 probably belongs close to this group and is for this reason a mixed form. Certainly it is to be considered a postexilian Psalm.[23]

(3) By contrast, Lam. 5 is totally dominated by subject 2. Here the balance has been so radically disrupted that we really have to speak of a transformation of the form. As Lam. 1, 2, and 4 indicate, the context of this transformation was the inter-

---

23. A conclusion supported by other evidence as well. See Gunkel, *Kommentar, ad hoc,* p. 365.

mixing of the lament of the people with the lament of the dead.[24]

In Second Isaiah's prophecy of salvation (which Begrich has convincingly shown to belong to the category of the "oracle of salvation of hearkening,") we can also clearly discern the three parts of the lament of the people.[25] They stand behind the three sides of the proclamation of salvation to Israel:

Subject 1: God's wrath has been withdrawn; God has forgiven the people.

Subject 2: The specific need, the imprisonment of the people, is thereby removed.

Subject 3: The enemy is no longer able to detain and oppress Israel.

The clearest example is Isa. 54. Its structure is determined by the three subjects of the lament:[26]

54:1–3: Eschatological song of praise
4–5: Subject 2: The Lamenter (Israel)
6–10: Subject 1: God
(11–14): Subject 2 repeated; but these verses are uncertain in themselves and in terms of the chapter as a whole.

24. F. Willessen, "The Cultic Situation of Psalm LXXIV," *VT* 11, 1952, pp. 289–306. The author finds parallels in Pss. 79 and 74 to the Babylonian-Canaanitic temple lament which functioned within the context of a purely ritual destruction and re-establishment of the temple. Here the profanation (i.e., the destruction) of the temple and the death of the god are directly inter-related (p. 295) and thus the lament for the dead god and the lament over the destruction of the temple as well. Proof for the parallels is conclusive. Nevertheless, the conclusion that Pss. 79 and 74 can in no wise be understood as Psalms of the lament of the people (p. 289) is not. That would mean that these laments were also uttered in Israel as laments for a dead god. In this regard Pedersen (*Israel*, IV, p. 472) refers to ". . . the lamentations over the dying God, which the Israelites always regarded as militating against the nature of their God." For the same conclusion see also Mowinckel, *Religion und Kultus*, p. 77. Moreover, in making this identification there is a blending of the lament of the dead and the lament of distress which in any case cannot be the original one for Israel.
25. Begrich, *op. cit.*, pp. 6f.
26. Here, certainly, both text and context pose great difficulties. Begrich (*op. cit.*, p. 6) deals with very small units: Isa. 54:1–3, 4–6, 7–10, 11–12 + 13b, 14a + 13a + 14b–17. Apart from vss. 1–3 he attributes them all to the literary category "oracle of salvation" or "oracle of hearing." If our thesis of the threefold division of the lament should prove to be valid, then we would naturally assume that in Ch. 54 (and in other passages of Second Isaiah as well) we are dealing with larger units of tradition.

15–17: Subject 3: The enemy.

An impressive example of the lament being reflected in the message of salvation is found in Isa. 45:(14) 15–17.[27]

45:15: "Truly, thou art a God who hidest thyself,
O God of Israel, the Savior.
16: All [his adversaries] are put to shame and confounded, ...
17: But Israel is saved by Yahweh
with everlasting salvation;
you shall not be put to shame or confounded to all eternity."[28]

Second Isaiah's proclamation of salvation is thus brought into very close relationship with the lament of the people, enabling us to clarify the structure of the proclamation considerably at several points.

The component parts of the lament of the people

The complaint against God is dominant in the lament of the people (cf. the above table). Its most frequent form is the question directed at God, usually introduced with "Why?" less frequently with "How long?"

The question "Why?" asks why God has rejected (Ps. 74:1; Jer. 14:19), abandoned (Lam. 5:20), or forgotten (Ps. 44:24; Lam. 5:20) his people.[29] In the blow he has suffered, the la-

---

27. Begrich assigns vss. 14–17 to the oracles of hearing; he is not certain of its authenticity.
28. Other passages as well contain all three subjects of the lament:

	Subject 1	Subject 3	Subject 2
Isa. 49:14–23:	14–16	17, 19c	19–23
51:17–23:	17b (20b, 21)	18–21	22–23
51:9–16:	9, 10, 12	12, 14	12, 13

Elsewhere the three subjects of the lament are found in Second Isaiah reflected in the promise of salvation:
Subject 1: (40:7); 40:27; 41:17; 42:14; 43:25; 45:9–13 (?); 45:15; (48:9); 49:14; 50:1, 2b; 51:17, 20b; 52:9; 54:6–8, 9b.
Subject 2: (40:6–7); 41:14; 41:17; 42:22; 45:17; 49:9; 49:19–21; 51:3; 51:18–21; 52:1–2; 54:1, 4–5, 6, 11, 14b.
Subject 3: 41:11, 12; 45:16; 49:17, 19c, 24, 26; 51:7; 51:22b, 23; 52:5; 54:15, 17.
29. "Why ... are [thou] silent?" Hab. 1:13b.

menter has experienced God's denial. The experience is utterly
unnerving and incomprehensible. The question "Why?" is like
the feeble groping of one who has lost the way in the dark. It
has the sense of finding one's own way;[30] it assumes that what
has been suffered has its origin in God's alienation.

The question "How long?"[31] implies distress of some dura-
tion. It is not complaining about a sudden blow just suffered
but about constant duress. In the Israelite Psalms it appears less
frequently than the why-question, in the Babylonian psalms
more frequently. In the early history of the lament in Israel it is
not found at all (see below). The question "How long?" just as
the question "Why?" asks about the absence of God. In them
verbs of anger predominate.

Beside these accusatory questions are complaints in the form
of statements. They appear frequently in the LI and often with
startling bitterness.[32] They tread that thin line between reproach and judgment. But never do they condemn God, for
the utterances are never objective statements. They always remain personal address.

The heart of the lament of the people in ancient Israel lies in
these accusatory questions and statements directed at God.

"Why sleepest thou?" Ps. 44:23.
"Why dost thou hide thy face?" Ps. 44:24.
"Why dost thou look on faithless men?" Hab. 1:13b.
"Why shouldst thou be like a stranger?" Jer. 14:8.
"Why hast thou smitten us?" Jer. 14:19.
"Why . . . thou seest it not? . . . thou takest no knowledge of it?" Isa. 58:3.
"Why does thy anger smoke?" Ps. 74:1 (Exod. 32:11).
"Why shouldst thou be like a man confused?" Jer. 14:9.

30. In Gen. 25:22, after virtually the same question ("Why?"), comes the sentence, "So
she went to inquire of the LORD."

31. How long wilt thou be angry? Ps. 79:5; 80:4; 85:5; 89:46; Jer. 3:5. "How long shall I
cry for help, and thou wilt not hear?" Hab. 1:2. "How long . . . wilt thou hide thyself?" Ps.
89:46. The question, "How long wilt thou be angry?" corresponds to the question, "Wilt
thou be angry with us for ever?" Ps. 85:5; Jer. 3:5.

32. Thou hast cast us off, rejected us. Ps. 44:9; 108:11; 60:10; 89:38.
Thou hast chastened me. Jer. 31:18; Ps. 90:15 (afflicted).
"Thou hast utterly deceived us." Jer. 4:10.
"Thou hast given us wine to drink that made us reel." Ps. 60:3.
"Thou hast made thy people suffer hard times." Ps. 60:3.
Thou hast restrained thyself, kept silent. Isa. 64:12.
"Thou hast not forgiven. Thou hast wrapped thyself with anger and pursued us,
slaying without pity; thou hast wrapped thyself with a cloud so that no prayer can
pass through. Thou hast made us offscouring and refuse among the peoples." Lam.
3:42b–45.

There are no laments of the people in which they are totally absent. Indeed, the phenomenon of lamentation is concentrated in this one motif.[33]

The lament of the people which lies behind Second Isaiah's proclamation corresponds in an astonishing degree to the situation found in the Psalms.[34] Here, too, the dominant complaint is that God has turned away from his people. Almost all the verbs present are found in the Psalms as well. Just what form these accusations took we are no longer able to tell from their reminiscence in Second Isaiah's message of salvation. On the basis of the summary in note 34, the assumption is that the first group were why-questions.[35] In the second group, which is comprised of verbs of anger, we can infer the question "How long?" The third group contains strikingly bitter accusations. They are closest to laments expressed in the form of statements.

The lament over personal suffering obviously assumes less significance than subject 1 of the lament. It is not so pronounced and its structure is not so fixed. It is still wholly dependent upon the complaint against God and is closely tied to it (e.g., Jer. 31:18;

33. In many Psalms this part of the lament is joined with other parts. The clearest example of this is Ps. 89:38–46. The whole Psalm is a complaint against God, but it contains the we-lament (vss. 40, 41, 44, 46) and the lament against the enemy (vss. 42, 43). Cf. the table on p. 182. This combination is often found, e.g.:

	with Subject 2	with Subject 3
In the question, "Why?"	Hab. 1:3	Hab. 1:13b
In the question, "How long?"	Hab 1:2	Ps. 94:3; 74:10
In the accusatory statement	Ps. 80:5	Ps. 89:42

The complaint against God can also include other motifs, as for example reference to God's earlier acts of salvation as in Ps. 89:49, Isa. 63:15.

34. 1. God has abandoned, forgotten Israel. Isa. 49:14; 41:17; 54:7.
    God has turned away from Israel. Isa. 40:27.
    God has held his peace, restrained himself. Isa. 42:14.
    God has not listened. Isa. 41:17.
    God has hidden his face. Isa. 45:15–17; 54:8.
  2. God has poured out his anger upon the people. Isa. 40:7; 42:25; 48:9; 51:17, 20b; 54:7–9.
  3. God has cast off, sold Israel. Isa. 50:1–2; 52:3; 54:6.
    God has given up Israel as booty to robbers. Isa. 42:24.
    God has delivered Israel to utter destruction. Isa. 43:28.

35. Isa. 40:27 provides the means for confirming this. Here the question, "Why?" is taken from the lips of the people and turned against them by the prophet. The people had lamented, "My way is hid from the Lord, and my right is disregarded by my God." To which the prophet replied, "Why do *you* say . . ."

Ps. 44:17–22). It is possible that a lament of the people did not even contain the subject "we" explicitly at all, even though in meaning it is present throughout, as in Ps. 80. Here the we-lament is contained in the indictment of God, as e.g., vs. 5.*

The we-lament always has two sides: It laments the suffering and the disgrace of suffering.

> Lam. 5:1: "Remember, O LORD, what has befallen us;
> behold, and see our disgrace!"

Moreover, the lament over disgrace is at least as frequent and as emotionally charged as the lament over suffering, e.g., Ps. 79:4.[36]

But whereas in the earlier laments, statements in the first person are infrequent and often limited to the disgrace of suffering, in the later laments the "we" section is greatly enlarged by a description of the *situation* created by the blow suffered (explicitly bewailed in the earlier laments). It is in fact merely a "description of affliction."[37] Lam. 5 is illustrative.[38] The extensive, even excessive description of affliction in the book of Lamentations diverges so radically from the lament of the people that we can no longer speak of it as a lament in the real sense. Here the lament simply flows over into a description of what is lamented. The basic contours of the form are consequently lost. The three parts of the lament can, of course, still be discerned, but they are quite fluid and able to merge with motifs from the lament of the dead, as Lam. 1, 2, and 4 show.[39]

In the case of Second Isaiah the message of salvation points to a very distinct and fully developed lament with the subject "we." It seems to fall halfway between the laments of the Psalms and those of Lamentations. In terms of the extensive develop-

---

*[Translator's note: Here Westermann follows the Septuagint.]
36. Other passages are Ps. 89:41b, 50; 123:3b, 4; 44:15f., 79:10; 115 2; Jer. 3:25; Joel 2:17; Mic. 7:10; Exod. 32:11; also Ps. 74:10.
37. F. Stummer, *Sumerisch-akkadische Parallelen zum Aufbau alttestamentlicher Psalmen*, Paderborn, 1922.
38. Cf. Jahnow, *op. cit.* and the commentary by Haller, *ad loc.*
39. So Jahnow, *op. cit.*, p. 98.

ment of the "we-lament," it approximates Lamentations, yet it is less a detailed description of a particular situation than reference to a fact. Cited are the ruins and barren places,[40] the imprisonment,[41] plundering and robbery.[42] Of course here, too, the lament, so profusely bemoaning the blow Israel has suffered, flows over into a complaint about the situation—particularly as expressed in the image, so common to Lamentations as well, of Israel as the lonely, childless widow.[43] The image is simultaneously one of suffering and the shame of suffering: "the reproach of your widowhood" (Isa. 54:4).

What we see in the movement of this motif from the Psalms through its reflection in Second Isaiah's message of salvation to Lamentations is the increasingly dominant emergence of subject 2, the we-lament.[44]

The complaint about the enemy constitutes a basic component of the lament of the people in time of war. This is shown by the wholly uniform structure of this part of the lament in Pss. 79, 74, 83, and 80. It is also closely related to the complaint against God, as revealed in a number of Psalms in the uniting of both elements (see note 33) and in the frequent use of the second person suffix in the following constructs: "your inheritance," "your servants," "your holy temple," "your (!) enemy," "your possession," etc. The accusation against the enemy has two sides: a) what they have done to the people of God, and b) their slander and abuse.[45] The latter stands in the closest possible

---

40. Isa. 49:19; 51:3; 44:26, 28; 52:9.
41. Isa. 49:9, 24–26; 52:2; 42:7, 22; 45:13; 51:14; 40:2; 52:5.
42. Isa. 42:22, 25; 49:24–26; 51:19b.
43. Isa. 54:1, 4, 6; 49:20, 21; 51:18, 20.
44. Still one other group of laments in Second Isaiah also describe a situation, but in terminology they really belong to the LI, using words such as "afflicted," "poor" (Isa. 48:10; 51:21; 54:11), "weary," "without strength" (40:29, 31; 50:4), "deaf" and "blind" (42:18–20; 43:8).
    A third group can be added which are actually laments related to a drought (Isa. 41:17; 44:3a; 49:10; 51:1, 14, 19); in this case, however, it is only one part of a lament over the political catastrophe and its consequences.
45. a) Conquest of the land (Ps. 79:1, 7), destruction of Jerusalem (80:16), desecration of the temple (74:4–7), killing and terrorizing (94:6; Lam. 5:11–15), crushing and afflicting (Ps. 94:5), Joel 1 speaks of the enemy as locust (vs. 4) and fire (vss. 19–20).
    b) Ps. 79:10; 74:10; 44:13–16; 89:41, 50–51; 94:3; 123:4; Joel 2:19c.

connection with the two other subjects. Psalm 123 is the most impressive example of this type of lament.

In Second Isaiah the complaint about the enemy recedes into the background. It is found mostly in such terms as the destroyers and desolatorers (Isa. 49:17).[46] But it is easy to see that they are accused before God. The second part of the accusation, the reproach and abuse of the opponent, is explicitly mentioned only in Isa. 51:7 and 51:23; elsewhere it appears only in declarative sentences which have the people as the subject, i.e., in the lament over personal suffering. The situation is quite similar in Lamentations, especially chap. 5, where the enemy appears only in the description of Israel's suffering.

In the configuration, Yahweh-Israel-the enemy, the vehemence of the complaint about the responsibility for Israel's ignominy diminishes. It appears more and more as a part of the burden placed upon Israel itself.

THE LAMENT OF THE INDIVIDUAL

In the LI the three components of the lament can be discerned in the table below:

We could scarcely base our thesis concerning the threefold division of the lament on these relatively few laments. Nevertheless, the picture immediately changes when we recognize that the "negative petition" in the LI ("Be not silent, O God of my praise!" "Do not cast me away!" etc.; see below) is a modified complaint against God. The result, then, is a large group of Psalms in which this negative petition stands in the place of the lament with the first subject. An example for this group is Ps. 109 (see table below). Also in this group are Pss. 6, 27, 28, 35, 38, 55, 69, 71, 102, 143.

46. Other passages are Isa. 49:24, 26; 51:23; 41:11–12; 45:16; 54:15–17; cf. 52:5.

Lament	Subject 1 (Thou, God)	Subject 2 (I)	Subject 3 (the enemy)
Ps. 6	(1), 3	6–7	7b
Ps. 13	1	2a	2b, 4
Ps. 22	1–2	6–8, 14–15, 17a	6–8, 12–13, 16, 17b–18
Ps. 35	17	12b, (15a)	7, 11–16, 19–21
Ps. 38	1–2	3–10, 17–18	11–12, 19–20
Ps. 42	9a	3a, 9b–10	3b (9b–10)
Ps. 43	2b	2c	2d
Ps. 88	6–7	3–5, 8b–9a	8a
Ps. 88	14–18a	15, 18	(17–18)
Ps. 102	10	3–7, 9, 11	8
Ps. 109	(1a)	(16b) 22–25	2–5, 20, 25
Jer. 20:7–11	7a	7b–9	7f, 10

That the lament of the individual is also by nature trichotomous is above all demonstrated by the laments in the book of Job. Unfortunately, we still do not possess a comprehensive comparison of the laments of Job with the laments in the Psalms. To my knowledge Gunkel in his Introduction was the first to parallel all the laments of both in rather broad terms. Yet, even here the comparison was carried out only from one side, that of the Psalms.

In the book of Job, the three-dimensional character of the lament is not perfectly obvious either. Yet it is readily apparent in the long summary lament at the end, chaps. 29–31. The recollection of former happiness (chap. 29) and the oath of purity (chap. 31—which corresponds to the protestation of innocence in the Psalms) frame the actual lament in chap. 30. It begins with Subject 3, vss. 1–15.[47] The next clearly discernible section is found in vss. 21–23 with the subject, "Thou, O God." However, it probably begins in vs. 16. Vss. 21–31 are characterized by the subject "I." Here again we are reminded of many similar

---

47. Vss. 1–10: the mocking of the neighbors; 11–15: the attack of the enemy. It should not be supposed that we are dealing here with different groups. Vss. 12–15 (vs. 11 is uncertain) speak of the attack of the enemy with very vivid images but this must be ascribed to the set terminology of the Psalms of lament.

expressions in the corresponding section of the lament in the Psalms. This three-part division of the lament in chap. 30 is confirmed by the fact that it recurs in chap. 29 in the recollection of former happiness: vss. 2–6: God's treatment of Job; vss. 7–11 and 21–25: the relationship of others to Job; and vss. 12–20: Job's own actions.

This division according to the three subjects occurs elsewhere as well.[48] It can even be found in the overall structure of the speeches. The three dramatis personae of Job (treating the friends as one person) represent the three subjects of the lament. The structure seems to point to them as well. The lament in chap. 3 stands *before* the controversies with the friends, and it is dominated by the subject "I." The controversies with the friends are dominated by subject 3, and of course in such a way that the friends become enemies. In the great lament at the end Job stands alone before God. In the course of the drama the lament essentially becomes a pure complaint against God. Such remarks can only be suggestions which would require substantiation through precise form-critical analysis of the speeches. Nevertheless, we have already demonstrated that the three subjects of the lament shape the underlying form of the speeches of Job.[49]

The component parts of the lament of the individual

The complaint against God does not have the dominant role in the LI as it does in the lament of the people. We do, of course, find all of its characteristics here, too, including the uniting of the complaint with the two other components, but much less

---

48. They can be clearly discerned in chap. 3:
   1–10: The desire to be cursed (the day of birth replacing the enemy).
   11–19: Why me . . . ? (also 24–26).
   20–23: Why God . . . ?
   In addition, the three subjects are found in chaps. 6—7; 13—14; 16:7—17:8; 19. In these passages the three subjects of the lament cannot always be neatly separated from each other, nor do we really have here an original lament. One point in particular distinguishes the laments of Job from the LI: in the former God himself can be the enemy. Job confronts God precisely with what the enemy is accused of in the LI, e.g., Job 10:13–17; 19:6.
   49. Cf. C. Westermann, *Der Aufbau des Buches Hiob*, Tübingen, 1956.

frequently and obviously with less force and vigor. Only in Ps. 22 do we meet the question directed at God, "why ... Thou?"[50] accompanied by the same verbs as the corresponding section in the LP.

Ps. 13 is dominated by the question, "How long?" (see above, p. 169). The two verbs in vs. 1 are the same as in the question, "Why?" The question is expanded in vs. 2a in connection with subject 2 and then in vs. 2b with subject 3. This in itself demonstrates how the question, which originally belonged only to the complaint against God, affected the two other subjects. Thus it is all the more surprising that the question which so completely dominates Ps. 13 only rarely reappears in all the other laments of the individual. The full interrogatory sentence is found elsewhere only in Ps. 35:17; in abbreviated form it appears in Ps. 6:3 and 90:13.[51] The accusatory question directed at God recedes into the background. It is a risk no longer taken. This is also indicated by the abbreviated form in Ps. 6:3, "But, thou, O LORD—how long?" which now sounds like a formula. This is shown above all by the peculiar joining together of the why-question with the avowal of trust in two Pss. 42 and 43:

Ps. 42:9: "I say to God, my rock:
"Why hast thou forgotten me?"
Ps. 43:2: "For thou art the God in whom I take refuge;
why hast thou cast me off?"

One feels here that the petitioner is afraid of simply confronting God with his question, "Why?" and therefore covers it with an avowal of trust.

50. Ps. 10:1; 22:1; 42:9; 43:2; 88:14. Examples of combinations involving subject 2: Ps. 42:9a (= 43:2a); involving subject 3: Ps. 10:13.
51. Ps. 90:13 states, "Return, O LORD! How long?" Stummer has shown on the basis of Babylonian parallels that when used with the imperative, this "How long?" can assume the more precise meaning of "finally" (*op. cit.*, p. 93; there he refers to Ps. 94:3 and 90:13). This interpretation of "How long?" is certainly correct in Ps. 90:13, although it is rarely noted by exegetes. It is also confirmed by studies of the lament. It is a part of the tendency so frequently seen of watering down the lament to the level of a simple petition (see below). The weakening and subsequent alteration of the meaning of "How long?" is highly characteristic of this process. Ps. 90:13 shows that a lament, having once been uttered, could by such a change in meaning become a petition.

Complaints in the form of declarative statements are also few in number.[52] They appear in two Psalms which also contain accusatory questions (Pss. 22:2; 88:6–8, 15–16), elsewhere openly only in Ps. 102:10, 23. In Pss. 31 and 51 the verses in question contain simply a report of the complaint and are no longer direct accusations. The wording of Ps. 31:22 is illustrative: "I had said in my alarm, 'I am driven far from thy sight'" (instead of "You have driven me ..."). A similar shifting of the direct accusation over to subject 2 can be observed in a number of places.

This retreat from the complaint against God, or the fear of uttering it, is evidenced most clearly in a mixed form which formally belongs to the petition but belongs here in terms of content. It is the "negative petition" mentioned at the beginning of this chapter. It is found in the LI with striking frequency, much more so than in the LP. In every instance the negative petition contains within it, concealed or paraphrased, a complaint against God. It is formed throughout with verbs that are elsewhere found in the complaint: to hide, drive out, cast off, forsake, be silent, be far off, etc. To a certain extent the complaint lies hidden in the petition:

Ps. 27:9: "Hide not thy face from me.
            Turn not thy servant away in anger, ...
            Cast me not off, forsake me not."[53]

The appearance of the negative petition constitutes one of the most important places for observing the gradual curtailment of the lament to the level of a petition. The significance of this phenomenon becomes apparent only within the context of the whole history of the lament. Of course no fixed dates can

52. Ps. 22:2; 31:22; 51:9; 88:6, 7, 8, 15, 16; 102:10, 23.
53. Do not hide: Ps. 27:9; 55:1; 69:17; 102:2; 143:7.
   "Be not silent": Ps. 109:1; 28:1 39:12.
   "Be not far from me.": Ps. 22:11; 35:22; 38:21; 71:12.
   "Forsake me not": Ps. 71:9; 38:21; 27:9, 12.
   Chasten, strike me not: Ps. 6:1; 38:1; 39:10–11.
   "Rebuke me not": Ps. 6:1; 38:1; 39:11.
   "Cast me not off": Ps. 27:9; 51:11.

be established for it. It is obvious that throughout most of the period of Psalm composition the complaint and the negative petition stood side by side (as, e.g., in Ps. 22). Only in the late postexilic period did the complaint disappear completely from the prayer of the congregation, leaving only the negative petition.

The lament over personal suffering. In the LP the relationship of the second subject of the lament to the third is clear: It is the enemy who has caused the suffering of the one who laments. Conversely, in the LI it is not the enemy, at least not primarily, who is the cause of the problem. In a few Psalms this becomes immediately evident in the opening petition:

> Ps. 69:1: "Save me, O God!
>   For the waters have come up to my neck."
> Ps. 86:1: "Incline thy ear, O LORD, and answer me,
>   for I am poor and needy."

This corresponds to the "looking back on the time of need" in the declarative Psalms of praise of the individual,[54] e.g., Ps. 40: 1–2. Here the relationship of the second and third components of the lament to each other is therefore different and more complicated.

It is not necessary to examine in more detail all the possible types of lament over personal suffering. They extend from graphic representations of physical suffering (Ps. 22:14, 15, 17a; 102:4) or spiritual suffering (Ps. 119:143), to various depictions of the immanence of death (Ps. 102:11; 109:23), to very general laments such as "I am poor and needy" (Ps. 86:1; 109:21, etc.), to predictions of personal despondency such as "I am a worm and no man" (Ps. 22:6).

An appropriate term for this part of the lament is "description of need," a term with which Stummer[55] chose to designate the lament in the Babylonian psalms. The selection of this term

---

54. Concerning the term "declarative Psalm of praise" (instead of Psalm of thanksgiving), see above pp. 81–90.
55. Cf. Stummer, *op. cit.*, p. 55, note 1.

itself indicates that in the Babylonian psalms of lament this description of need played a dominant role. Widengren[56] calls them "laments concerning various evils," and Castellino "esposizione del caso." From each of these characterizations it is clear that the heart of the lament is seen to lie in the personal complaint itself. This is certainly justified with regard to the Babylonian psalms. For the laments of the Psalms, however, it is not appropriate in the same way. Castellino emphasizes this in his comparison of the Babylonian psalms with those of Israel.[57] The Babylonian psalms in this regard are much more detailed and concrete;[58] they often approach being a kind of diagnosis. At no time do the Israelite Psalms come close to diagnosis. No one could say that any of these laments implies a description of a specific situation. There is a fine distinction to be made between an "esposizione del caso" and the "pouring out of the heart" (Ps. 62:8; I Sam. 1:15). The "pouring out of the heart" happens "before God" and is a word directed to God. But the more prolix the lament becomes, and the more it enters into details, the more the addressee recedes into the background leaving alone the one who is laying out his case alone by himself.

When we review this part of the lament as a whole, it becomes clear that it is an essential and necessary component of the LI. In each of these Psalms it is either present or implied. It contains two parts, the lament of suffering and the shame of suffering.[59] As a consequence the lament of suffering can be expanded still further by a description of the complaint or affliction.[60] But this then constitutes a further development of the lament which presupposes a certain amount of reflection. It

---

56. Geo Widengren, *The Accadian and Hebrew Psalms of Lamentation as Religious Documents*, Uppsala, 1936.
57. R. G. Castellino, *Le lamentazioni individuali e gli inni in Babilonia e in Israele*, Turin, 1940, p. 151.
58. Cf. the summary in Widengren, *op. cit.*, pp. 93ff.
59. E.g., Ps. 22:6b, 7, 17b. In this case there is no sharp distinction between the mockery of the enemy and that of the on-lookers. It is simply accepted as an actual part of suffering and is poured out to God as such.
60. Ps. 31:9b, 10; 6:6–7; 55:17; 102:5, 7, 9, *passim*.

is exhibited far more widely in the Babylonian laments than in those of the Old Testament.

In the Psalms this part of the lament always remains on the fringes. Never does the lament sink into a broad, wide-ranging description of suffering; never does the mere phenomenon of suffering as such thrust itself into the foreground so as to dominate the Psalm; never does the we-lament develop into an independent Psalm of its own.

The complaint about the enemy. The problem of the enemy in the LI has recently been taken up again in quite a series of studies. Mowinckel's *Psalmenstudie I* initiated the discussion, and in his comprehensive work, *The Psalms in Israel's Worship,* he once again turned to the subject.[61] The problem and its discussion cannot be dealt with here, but this analysis of the lament can perhaps be a methodological contribution to it.

The question of the enemy cannot take as its point of departure the isolated motif, "the enemy." Even less can it start with one of the many terms used for the enemy. Such attempts fail to see that the statements about the enemy as a whole can be understood only as one part of the *lament.* Prior to the question, "Who are the enemy?" is the question, "What happens in the complaint about the enemy?" And this question cannot be answered apart from looking at the other parts of the lament. So understood, then, the question concerning the enemy stands from the start between two others: Who is the enemy in terms of the suffering of the one who laments? Who is the enemy in terms of the relationship of the one who laments to God?

In the extant Psalms of lament the dominant subject is "the enemy," and it is also the most elaborately developed part of the lament. Taken together, statements about the enemy can be divided into two large groups: Statements concerning an *act* on

---

61. Oslo, 1951, pp. 249ff. For an important observation in this regard, see also Mowinckel, *Religion und Kultus,* Göttingen, 1953, p. 140, note 28. Cf. esp. H. Birkeland, *Die Feinde des Individuums in der israelitischen Psalmenliteratur,* Oslo, 1933; G. Marschall, *Die Gottlosen des ersten Psalmbuches,* 1929; A. R. Johnson, "The Psalms" in *The Old Testament and Modern Study,* pp. 197–203; also A. F. Puukko, *Der Feind in den altestamentlichen Psalmen (Oudtestamentische Studiën,* Teil VIII), Leiden, 1950.

the part of the enemy directed against the one who laments, and statements concerning the true nature of the enemy.

Concerning the relationship of the two groups, we can say with certainty that statements dealing with the activity of the enemy are primary. This is a necessary outgrowth of the nature of the lament itself. Interpretation must therefore begin with these two groups.

Of the statements concerned with the *actions* of the enemy, the most frequent and important deal with an attempt against the life of the lamenter. Approximately thirty-six Psalms speak of these attempts. Such laments can be summarized under a very few headings:

1. The enemy sets nets or traps, e.g., Ps. 140:4b–5.
2. Wild beasts fall upon the lamenter, e.g., Ps. 17:11–12.
3. The enemy are attacking soldiers, e.g., Ps. 7:13 (or accusers before the judge).

In all three groups there are, in addition, preparatory acts:

1. They conspire together, take counsel, utter threats, e.g., Ps. 56:6;
2. They surround, encircle, e.g., Ps. 22:12, 13, 16.
3. They approach, draw near, arm themselves, e.g., Ps. 27:2–3.

Each passage refers to an act of the enemy. The act is not, as is the case in the LP, an accomplished fact; it is a threat. Hence, in these Psalms, the threat itself—that is, annihilation or something similar—is almost always mentioned only in the final phrases, e.g., Ps. 140:4: "to trip up my feet."[62] These final phrases are related to the image of the trap or the stalking lion.

One of the acts of the enemy is what they say. But whereas statements about the actions of the enemy refer to acts which are only intended, what the enemy has said is an already ex-

---

62. So also Ps. 7:2; 27:2; 64:4; 140:4; 17:11; 31:13; 37:14, 32; 62:4.

isting fact. The enemy mocks the lamenter,[63] rejoices at his stumbling and falling,[64] revels in his or her misfortune.[65] All of this obviously relates to the present suffering of the lamenter (mockery must have an occasion!), of which nothing is said to suggest that it is caused by the enemy.[66]

One group of statements about what the enemy has said represents the transition from statements concerning an act to statements about the true nature of the enemy. In this group what the enemy is saying is described in very general terms, e.g., Ps. 10:7: "His mouth is filled with cursing and deceit and oppression."[67]

Almost all these statements are characterized by two interrelated concerns: (1) The speech of the enemy seeks the destruction of the lamenter. (2) The enemy's actual intention is hidden behind lies and false friendliness.[68]

This group of generalizing statements about what the enemy is saying is of special importance. As the complaint about the enemy for a specific act passes over into a description of their speech in general, the speech form of the lament is technically abandoned. As it becomes more expansive, this descriptive speech ceases being a call to God in the real sense. It is a meditation upon one's predicament which has the enemy as its subject.

This is even more true of *statements concerning the nature of the enemy*. Such statements are characteristically overstated. They are expansive and verbose. The extraordinary number of assertions which belong here can be gathered into two groups:

     a) The enemy is perverse.[69]
     b) The enemy is sacrilegious and godless.[70]

---

63. Ps. 42:10; 69:9; 119:42; 89:51; 102:8; 22:7; 35:16; 119:51; 39:8.
64. Ps. 35:15; 13:4; 22:17; 35:19, 24–26; 38:16.
65. Ps. 22:17b; 35:21.
66. In several places the enemy claims that the lamenter's life is finished, thus possibly Ps. 41:8; 22:18; 35:21. In Ps. 71:11 the enemy risks seizing the lamenter only after first establishing that God has forsaken him.
67. Similarly Ps. 5:9; 55:21; 59:13; 31:18; 35:16, 20; 36:3; 41:5; 52:3–4; 59:7, 12; 64:2–6; 73:8–9; 109:2, 20; 119:69; 120:2; 140:3, 9; 144:11.
68. Cf. Ps. 28:3; 41:6; 52:2–4; 55:21; 62:4; 119:69; 144:11.
69. Ps. 14:1, 3–4 (=53:1, 3–4); 28:4; 26:10; 36:4; 52:1; 55:10, 11, 15; 73:6; 109:17, etc.
70. Ps. 5:10; 10:3; 14:1, 4; 28:5; 36:1; 52:7; 54:3; 55:19; 73:27; 86:14; 119:85, 139.

In group a) the concepts remain general and indefinite. Least of all could one infer from them an answer to the question of who the enemy might be.[71]

In the passages of group b) concerning the wickedness or "godlessness" of the enemy, we are in no way dealing with objective statements. They remain just as vague as those in the preceding group. But they do say something essential to us about the relationship between those who lament and their opponents, i.e., the "enemy." What we find here is one of the roots of atheism, of existence without God. The possibility of existence without God is met here—in any case in the world out of which the Psalms come—not primarily in the confession of an atheist, but rather in the accusation of those who are powerless to avoid suffering at another's hands and who are now able to see their enemy only as some one separated from them at the deepest level of existence, that is, as one who no longer acknowledges God as God: "the fool says in his heart, 'There is no God' " (Ps. 14:1).

What is to be noted here is how the lament, transformed into a descriptive meditation on suffering, continues to move away from its original form. The description of the true nature of the enemy is expanded by reflection on his fortune. In contrast to the dire situation of the lamenter, the enemy is powerful and rich, always successful, never knowing want, beyond the reach of God's judgments.[72] This abandonment of the speech form of the lament as a call to God is clearly indicated where the enemy is addressed, e.g., Ps. 52:1: "Why do you boast, O mighty man, of mischief done against the godly?"[73] The enemy is now so much the subject of the lament that its content is centered totally on him. The future collapse of the evildoer's good fortune is predicted (Ps. 52:5-7).

---

71. Among the names offered is *pōc alē 'āwän*, which Mowinckel translates "magician" and in which he believes to have found the key for explaining the LI. Gunkel had already noticed that the decisive link in the chain of proof was missing. In not a single passage can it be proved that the sickness from which the lamenter suffers has been caused by the enemy (cf. note 66).

72. Ps. 10:5-11; 17:14; 37:7, 35; 49:6; 52:7; 73:3-5, 12; 92:7. Cf. Mal. 3:15!

73. Ps. 4:2; 6:8; 52:1-4; 58:1-5; 119:115.

Thus, a new polarity appears: The good fortune of the evil doer versus the fall of the evildoer. This polarity can so dominate the lament Psalm that it destroys the normal framework and creates a Psalm type of its own, one which, however, approximates the language of wisdom. The best illustration of the separate development of this motif into an independent Psalm is Ps. 52. Also belonging to this type are Ps. 14, Ps. 36, Ps. 53, and Ps. 58, plus the major portion of Ps. 37. Although the structure of these Psalms is quite varied, in each is found the three motifs characterizing this type of Psalm: a) a description of the evildoer, b) the fate of the evildoer and, in contrast, c) the fate of the pious. Ps. 1 is in line with this Psalm type, which is found in the Psalms of Solomon as well.[74] In the book of Job, the motif is amply developed in the speeches of Job's friends. In all of this, then, we have sketched the path of a single motif which begins with its separation from the LI and passes over into the language of wisdom.

For our history of the lament, we have learned from this brief overview of its third component that no part of the lament, either of the LP or the LI, branched out in as many directions or as broadly as this one. In Israel, the lament of the individual developed very strongly in the direction of the complaint about the enemy. The expansion of this part destroyed the framework of the lament.

The transition from the complaint about the enemy to a generalizing description of the nature of the enemy constituted a departure from the strict form of the lament. The expansion of the description by meditation on the fate of the evildoer, com-

---

74. In the Psalms of Solomon, Pss. 4 and 12 show their derivation from the LI. Pss. 6 and 14 evidence the independent development of single motifs of the LI. Ps. 12 is close to the group of LI just discussed, in which the single subject of the lament is the enemy. Similarly, Ps. Sol. 4 belongs to this group. (The reproach of the evildoer is found here as well, Ps. Sol. 4:1.) Psalm 1 is so similar to the Psalms of this group that it must belong at least close to the time of the Psalms of Solomon (first century B.C., the end of the Hasmonian period), in any case in the late postexilian period (*contra* Engnell, who considers all the Psalms of the Psalter up to Ps. 137 to be pre-exilian, *op. cit.*, p. 176). The description of the righteous and the godless (Ps. Sol. 14) or of the righteous alone (Ps. Sol. 6) can become a separate Psalm of its own. Ps. Sol. 14 is so much like Psalm 1 of the Psalter that here again the temporal proximity of the two seems probable.

paring his present good fortune with his future fall, led to a breaking away of the motif and the formation of a Psalm type of its own. The one-sided development of this third subject in the lament (as the Psalms of Solomon in particular reveal) probably stands at the end of the history of the lament of the individual in a way similar to the one-sided development of the second subject which stands at the end of the pre-exilic lament of the people (cf. note 74).

Thus, to the question, "Who is the enemy in the LI?" we can say:

1. The enemy in the LI is totally different from the enemy in the LP. In the LP the enemy is clearly recognizable as political enemies who *have* dealt a severe blow to the lamenter (i.e., Israel). In the LI the enemy *threatens* the lamenter.[75]

2. The hostility of the enemy is totally directed only at the one who is lamenting (the first person singular suffix appears seventy-two times). The lamenter alone is under duress. Never is it even implied that the lamenter belongs to a circle of friends who are being assailed; never are companions in misery mentioned. Moreover, the enemy so absolutely overwhelms the lamenter, so completely undoes him, that the idea of opposing the enemy never comes to mind. In spite of the many belligerent images, battle between two opponents is never seriously considered.

3. The relationship of the lamenter to those whom he accuses is one which remains within the community to which both belong. The outer fabric of the community remains. The enemy in fact speaks with the lamenter in a friendly way (Ps. 55:21); they greet one another (Ps. 144:8), visit one another (Ps. 41:5–6). But such words, which appear to hold the community together, are not genuine, and it is precisely in them that the lamenter sees its collapse (Ps. 55:21). Thus, the façade of com-

---

75. Widengren, *op. cit.*, pp. 197ff., notes the same phenomenon in the Babylonian Psalms.

munity still stands, but the foundations on which it is built are shattered.

4. The foundation of the community is its relationship to God. Herein lies the greatest temptation for the lamenter, as Ps. 73 in particular shows. The evildoers (in the opinion of the lamenter) no longer take God seriously, and yet God does not condemn them. The lamenter takes God seriously, yet the enemy is able to mock with impunity.

Of course these observations do not provide a definitive answer to the question of who the enemy is, but they do enable us to see the relationship of the enemy to the one who laments. It is not in any case the relationship of two nations. The complaint is totally devoid of any political point of view.[76] But it is also not the kind of opposition which would exist between two groups or parties within a nation. The second point above makes this quite clear. It is also all too obvious that the lamenter stands alone in suffering. That the enemy is thought of as a group is possible in a number of Psalms, but what is certain is merely that several persons are involved. The description of the enemy contains nothing that would indicate a group representing a specific matter or one bound together by any particular thing. Therefore, what is said concerning the enemy in the LI in no way permits the conclusion that there were two groups, either of a religious or political nature, international or domestic. What can be seen reflected in them, however, is the phenomenon of the gradual disintegration and decline of a community in which antagonisms (which we are no longer able to discern in detail) become simply overpowering. The only thing certain is that they were rooted in the nation's relationship to God.[77]

---

76. The Babylonian Psalms are different. Cf. the summary statements in Widengren, *op. cit.*, pp. 197ff., 216ff. One simply cannot apply to Israel conclusions drawn from her environment, as Engnell wants to do, *op. cit.*, p. 49.

77. The division of the lament in terms of its three subjects is also to be found in the *laments of Jeremiah*, and most clearly in Jer. 20:7–11 (cf. the table, p. 174). The relationship of the laments of Jeremiah to the LI of the Psalter is complex. I concur with Baumgartner's opinion that the LI as a literary category preserved in the Psalter stands behind the laments of Jeremiah, but he thinks that in their present form they are more recent than

THE EARLY HISTORY OF THE LAMENT:
THE LAMENT IN EARLY NARRATIVE TEXTS

In his book *Das freie Laiengebet im vorexilischen Israel* (Leipzig, 1931), A. Wendel views the prayer of lament[78] as a form of the early prayers of the laity alongside the prayer of petition, the prayer of praise, and others. As far as the lament is concerned, I can essentially concur with the results of this investigation. The texts with which Wendel deals are all said to be from the period of the Judges (apart from the questionable text in Hos. 8:2).[79] All pertain to the affliction of the people, even when they are laments of an individual, as in Judg. 15:18 (a lament of Samson).

In addition to the group discovered by Wendel, it is my opinion that an early form of the lament of the individual can be identified in the early narrative texts. There are, to be sure, only two texts, but laments corresponding exactly to them are found frequently in later texts. What we have here must, therefore, be a fixed form:

> Gen. 25:22 (J): "And she [Rebekah] said, 'If it is thus, why do I live?'[80] So she went to inquire of the LORD."
> Gen. 27:46 (J): "Then Rebekah said ..., 'If Jacob marries ... what good will my life be to me?'" (or, "why should I live?").

A very similar type of lament is found in Jeremiah:

> Jer. 20:18: "Why did I come forth from the womb to see toil and sorrow, and spend my days in shame?"

This same lament is then found repeatedly in the Apocrypha.[81] What we have in this primitive form of the lament is precisely

---

the laments of Jeremiah (W. Baumgartner, "Die Klagegedichte des Jeremia," BZAW 32, Giessen, 1917, p. 91). Nevertheless, the laments of Jeremiah belong in that special line of the lament of the mediator (see above, p.   ), which warrants special investigation.
78. *Op. cit.*, pp. 123–138.
79. Jos. 7:7–9; Judg. 6:22; 15:18; 21:3; Hos. 8:2 (?).
80. *BH*, Kittle; see apparatus, *ad loc*.
81. Tob. 3:15; 1 Macc. 1:7; 4 Ezra 5:35. For the same form of the accusatory question between people, see 1 Sam. 17:28.

what in our western way of thinking we call the question of the meaning of existence. The difference is that here we do not have the theoretical question of an objective observer, but the question of one whose existence has been shattered. This is the primordial lament. It is the simple question which comes from the pain of affliction: "Why?"[82] It can arise as easily from the needs of an individual as from the needs of a people, but the primitive form of the lament ("If this be so, why do I live?") is most likely the lament of an individual.

As a third group, we must mention the lament of the mediator. It is a special form inasmuch as it deals with the affliction of the people, but the one who laments is an individual whose position among the people is ordained by God. The lament of the mediator in the Old Testament is expressed most vigorously in the laments of Moses. In the period of the judges, next to the lament of the leader appears the lament of the deliverer. In this group as well, however, belongs the lament of the prophets, from Elijah through Amos and Hosea, to Jeremiah and the Servant of God in Second Isaiah.

In the transmission of the Old Testament, however, the lament of the king as mediator, in contrast to the environment of the O.T.,[83] receded surprisingly but emphatically into the background. Wherever such a lament is repeated (e.g., Isa. 37:15–20), its content corresponds completely with these other laments of the mediator in the Old Testament. The thesis regarding the lament Psalms of the Old Testament—that the one who laments is the king—needs to be tested against the background of the lament of the mediator in the O.T. This would require a special investigation of its own.

---

82. A similar lament is found in Gen. 42:28 (E ?). To be sharply distinguished from this is the cry of woe, an interjection bound together .08with a simple exclamation of what has happened (Judg. 6:22—which Wendel mistakenly considers a lament—and Isa. 24:16), and the cry of pain, as in 2 Kings 4:19 ("Oh, my head, my head!") or Jer. 4:19.

83. For this reason alone it is very questionable whether there is any basis for the hypothesis that in the Psalms of the O.T., the one who originally uttered the lament was in every case the king. Cf. Engnell, *Divine Kingship*, p. 46 and esp. p. 50. In any case, the O.T. tradition as a whole does not speak for it.

The structure of the early laments

The essential characteristic of the early laments is that they are a self-contained call to God. They require no subsequent petition because they already imply a supplication to God. Since in the first group we are always dealing with some desperate need on the part of the people, it follows that we also find here the three elements found in the laments of the Psalms. This is obviously the case in the lament of Joshua.

> Josh. 7:7–9: Alas, O Lord GOD, why hast *thou* brought this people ... to give us into the hands ... to destroy us? Would that *we* had been content to dwell beyond the Jordan! O Lord, what can I say, when Israel has turned their backs before their enemies! For the *Canaanites* ... will hear of it, and will surround us, ... ; and what wilt thou do for thy great name? [italics added]

However, it is not certain whether this lament has been preserved in its original form. The other laments of the early period are shorter and more concise. An unquestionably old and probably unaltered lament is

> Judg. 21:3: "O LORD, the God of Israel, why has this come to pass in Israel, that there should be today one tribe lacking in Israel?"

Here mention of the enemy (subject 3) is totally lacking. It is excluded by the event out of which the lament itself has arisen. The lament consists of three parts: the address, the question, and the explanatory clause opening with a demonstrative pronoun. The lament in its simplest form consists only of the why-question and corresponds exactly with the original form of the lament of the individual.

One of Samson's laments is quite different in form but very similar in content:

> Judg. 15:18, "And he was very thirsty, and he called on the LORD and said, 'Thou hast granted this great deliverance

by the hand of thy servant; and shall I now die of thirst,
and fall into the hands of the uncircumcised?' "

This lament consists simply in Samson reproaching Yahweh
with a contrast. He confronts God with the "howling" contradiction between what God had done earlier to him and what he
was presently doing. The contrast itself implies the question
"Why?" without explicitly stating it. In the Psalms as well, we
found among complaints against God simple declarative
sentences alongside the interrogative form (see above, pp.
176f.). The first sentence corresponds to the reference to God's
earlier acts of deliverance, just as it also appears in the LP (e.g.,
Ps. 80) in contrast to the lament. A petition does not follow
even here where it seems so obvious. The contrast, which here
in its simplest form constitutes the entire lament, is an essential
element of the complaint against God and is present throughout the whole history of the lament. What this motif of chal-
lenging God with contradiction may have meant in Israel for
the "call to God in time of need" can be illustrated by a text
which is perhaps a thousand years younger:

> 4 Ezra 8:14: "If, then, with a light word thou shalt destroy
> him who with such infinite labour has been fashioned by
> thy command, to what purpose was he made?"

All the texts in question and those mentioned here are without exception complaints against God. If one adds the laments
of Moses, then the basis for making such a statement is in sub-
stance even broader. *The lament of the early period is essentially a
complaint against God.* The early lament is almost always in the
form of a question, most often introduced with "Why?"[84] When
we compare this why-question with those of the Psalms, we are
immediately struck by a difference in the verbs. In the Psalms
the questions center on God's absence or remoteness. By con-

84. Josh. 7:7–9; Judg. 6:13, 22; 21:3; Exod. 5:22; 17:3; Num. 11:11.

trast, the early laments ask directly why God has brought the lamenter into this specific situation of affliction:

Judg. 21:3, "O LORD, the God of Israel, why has this come to pass in Israel, that. . . ."

Num. 11:11, "Why hast thou dealt ill with thy servant?" (cf. also 2 Kings 3:10)

The difference lies in the fact that the early prose laments always pertain only to a given situation, whereas the prayers in Psalm form endeavor to encompass any number of situations.

The question "How long?" does not appear in the early prose laments because they are always simply reactions to something which has just been experienced.

In the early prose laments *the two other parts of the lament* either recede completely into the background behind the complaint against God, or they are present but remain undeveloped. Samson's lament quoted above (Judg. 15:18) is indicative. The lament itself speaks only in the second person but it contains the other two elements. The development of the complaint lies in the description of the situation of need, hence subject 2. But the situation is that of the people being confronted by the enemy, subject 3. The enemy itself is not yet accused; the objection pertains only to God. The third dimension of the lament still lies completely within the complaint against God. Another example of this is the lament of the mediator:

Exod. 5:22–23 (J), "O LORD, why hast thou done evil to this people? Why didst thou ever send me? For since I came to Pharaoh to speak in thy name, he has done evil to this people, and thou hast not delivered thy people at all."

Sometimes a late tradition can reproduce a lament in a very early form:

Deut. 1:27–28, "and you murmured in your tents, and said, 'Because the LORD hated us he has brought us forth out

of the land of Egypt, to give us into the hand of the
Amorites, to destroy us. Whither are we going up?' "

This is a complaint in the form of a declarative statement.[85]
The expanded form includes the two other parts of the lament.
The subject "we" is explicit, the subject "the enemy" is merely
implied.

These same characteristics are also to be found in several laments of the people preserved in the prophetic books. They
are, of course, stylized, in some instances only implied. Nevertheless, their proximity to the early laments is still clearly
recognizable.

> Jer. 4:10: "Oh Lord GOD, surely thou hast utterly deceived[86]
> 'us', saying, 'It shall be well with you'; for now the sword
> rests on our necks" (Westermann).

The close relationship which this lament has with the early laments is here seen in the bitterness of the complaint, in the
contrast form itself, and, above all, in the fact that the whole
lament is *pure* accusation against God in the development of
which the other two elements of the lament are merely implied.

One of these early laments seems to indicate the way in which
the lament evolved from the one subject form into a form containing all three subjects. It is the lament of Gideon in Judg.
6:13, which is strikingly close to the lament Psalms: "Pray, sir, if
the LORD is with us, why then has all this befallen us? And
where are all his wonderful deeds . . . ? But now the LORD has
cast us off, and given us into the hand of Midian."

In summary we can say that the structure of the early prose
laments contains but one subject and that it is throughout a
complaint against God. The other two parts of the lament are
implied in the complaint but in different ways. Subject 2 (the
we-lament) has to be seen as an essential element of the early

---

85. *Einleitung des deuteronomistischen Geschichtswerkes;* cf. M. Noth, *Überlieferungsgeschichtliche Studien,* I, 1943.
86. Read *lānū, BH,* Kittel, see apparatus, *ad loc.*

laments. It then began to be separated from the complaint against God and to exist independently, although it always remained in close connection with it. Subject 3 (the enemy) has not yet taken on an independent existence of its own. There is still no actual complaint about the enemy. Reference to the enemy resides in the motif that God ought to become involved.

THE LATE HISTORY OF THE LAMENT:
LAMENTS IN THE APOCRYPHA AND PSEUDEPIGRAPHA

In the later traditions we are able to distinguish four different types of prayers of lament:[87]

A. Those in which the structure of the lament Psalm is essentially retained (with variations);

B. Petitionary prayer without a lament (or merely with traces or fragments of the lament);

C. Prayers of repentance; and

D. Independent laments which emerge from the prayer.

Of these four groups, B is unquestionably the most prevalent. Only in a small group has the essential character of the lament Psalm been preserved (A). In most cases the lament has been reduced to a petition (B). No firm line can be drawn between A and B; there are many transitional forms. The same applies to the relationship between B and C. The motif of repentance is present in many of the prayers of petition, and when it dominates the whole Psalm, it is called a prayer of repentance. What is new and essential in the lament of the late period is the existence of B and D side by side. These two groups deserve special attention.

---

87. The following texts provide the basis for this section: 1 Esdras (3 Ezra) 8:73–90; 1 Macc. 2:7–13; 3:45, 50–54; 4:30–33; 3 Macc. 2:1–10; 6:1–15; Tob. 3:1–6, 11–15; Judith 9:1–14; Bar. 1–3; 4–5; Sir. 33 (= 36); Wisdom 2; Prayer of Manasses; Add. to Dan. 1 (The Prayer of Azariah); Add. to Esther C:1–10, 12–30 (13:8–17; 14:1–19 in RSV); Pss. Sol. 2, 4, 5, 7, 8, 9, 12, 14, 18; 4 Ezra (2 Esdras) 3, 4, 5, 6, 8, 9, 10; 2 Bar. or Syr. Apoc. Bar. 10–12; 48. [Translator's note: The German translation quoted by Westermann is that of Kautsch, *Die Apokryphen und Pseudepigraphen des AT*, 1900; the English translation follows R. H. Charles, *The Apocrypha and Pseudepigrapha of the Old Testament*, 2 vols., Oxford, 1913.]

A. Laments like those in the Psalter

The lament as a special section of a Psalm, divided according to its three subjects, is still discernible in Additions to Daniel 1, and in Additions to Esther C:12–30.[88] These texts contain all three parts of the lament. More numerous are laments preserved in relative clauses attached to petitions, as e.g., 3 Macc. 6:1–15.

The complaint against God in its pure form never appears here. One can no longer address God in this manner, but the motif itself does not simply disappear. It is added (in six of eighteen prayers) to a confession of sins or to a defense of God's righteousness:

> Add. Esther C:17: "And now we have sinned before Thee, and Thou hast delivered us into the hands of our enemies, because we have given glory to their gods. Righteous art Thou, O Lord."[89]

In each instance these statements, which outwardly still resemble the complaint against God, are carefully guarded to ward against being misunderstood as such. The complaint against God is silenced by the constantly repeated acknowledgement that "everything that has happened to us is justified. God had to treat us this way." Such statements are frequently accompanied with praise for the righteous God.

This development is evidenced most clearly by the Prayer of Azariah, Add. Dan. 1, one of the most impressive of the post-canonical prayers. In it one immediately senses the tremendous struggles which stand behind this development. The three parts of the lament are clearly discernible in it.[90] The basic atti-

---

88. The structure of Add. to Esther C:12–30 (14:1–19 in RSV) is as follows: Introduction: 12–14a; address and introductory cry for help: 14b; lament, subject 2: 15; looking back at God's earlier acts of salvation: 16; lament, subject 1: 17–18; lament, subject 3: 19–21; petition: 22–30. In between is the motivation and protestation of innocence.

89. So also Add. Dan. 1:9; Tob. 3:4; Prayer of Manasses 9–10; Pss. Sol. 2:15–18; 8:25, 26, 29, *passim*.

90. Address and praise of God: 3–4; instead of a lament with subject 1, a confession of sin and justification of God: 5–8; lament, subject 3 (bound together with subject 1): 9; petition: 11–13; lament, subject 2: 14–15; petitions, etc.: 16–22.

tude which brought about the cessation of any direct complaint against God is very movingly expressed in the words: "And now we cannot open our mouths . . ." (vs. 10a).

In Ps. Sol. 8:7, this acknowledgement of God's righteousness is consciously introduced with pious expressions:

> "I thought upon the judgements of God . . ."
> "I held God righteous in His judgements which have been from of old . . ."

By way of this kind of self-conscious piety which is forced to justify God's actions, what heretofore had been an occasion for lament now becomes an occasion for praising the righteous God. Thus, the polarity between lament and praise is abolished. Where complaint against God is disallowed, there can be no lament in the strict sense of the word. The lament is excluded from prayer. Instead of complaint against God there perforce arises the doctrine of the righteousness of God. This is the ground out of which the doctrine actually arose.

Concern for the righteousness of God, as found in late Judaism, grew from the soil of the lament precisely at that point where the complaint against God fell silent. In its place appeared the praise of the righteous God.

The lament over personal suffering appears as a clearly discernible part of the lament only in Add. Dan. 1:10, 14, 15. It consists of the two elements of the we-lament, viz., suffering and the shame of suffering. In most cases, however, the we-lament no longer appears independently in declarative sentences, but only in subordinate clauses attached to petitions or other motifs; e.g., 3 Macc. 2:2 in which a relative clause is added to a petition (as in 6:3 and 9), and vs. 14 in combination with a confession of sins. Whenever the lament is limited completely to relative clauses, it does not appear as a part of the structure of the prayer itself, thus causing the prayer to lose the clear outline which it has in the Psalms. The dissolution of this part of the lament goes a step further in Pss. of Sol. 5 and 8. Here it is no

204 LAMENT IN THE PSALMS

longer found even in subordinate clauses, but only in parts of sentences (e.g., 5:5; 8:28).[91]

The complaint about the enemy is usually associated with the desecration of the sanctuary.[92] It also occurs because the enemy has oppressed Israel, mistreated her, etc.[93] But even here we find the complaint as an independent clause only rarely; it occurs mainly in subordinate clauses or explanatory phrases. Here too, then, we can see the tendency toward reducing the complaint to the level of a petition.

B. Petitionary prayer without lament

Pure petitionary prayer, i.e., prayers which consist purely of a series of petitions, are few in number—in fact, only in Sir. 36 (= 33). There are some, however, in which the petition plays such a dominant role that they approximate the pure prayer of petition.[94] Nevertheless, the pure petitionary prayer is the rare exception. Another prayer form is the predominant one, and it is *the petition introduced with praise of God*. With this structure we have one of the few really certain indicators for a temporal classification of the Psalms. In the case of the early laments it is unthinkable that they would begin with the praise of God. Only after the structure of the lament Psalm had been dissolved did it become possible for praise of God to precede a lament. This took place in Israel rather late. It occurs only very rarely in the Psalms of the Psalter,[95] although it is indeed found in the prayers of Chronicles. The long prayer in Neh. 9 is explicitly introduced as praise to God (9:5ff.), the major part of which consists of descriptive (vs. 6) and declarative (vss. 7–31) praise of God. In terms of its intention, however, it is a lament of the

---

91. In several of these prayers the lament is clearer since it arises out of the specific situation of an individual: Add. Esther C:15; Tob. 3:6b, 15b; Pr. of Man. 10.
92. Judith 9:8b; 3 Macc. 2:14–16; Pss. Sol. 2:19, 21; 7:2; Add. Esther C:19.
93. 3 Macc. 2:2; 6:9; Sir. 36:9–10 (= 33:11–12); Pss. Sol. 7:1; 8:30; Add. Dan. 1:9.
94. 3 Macc. 6:1–15; 4 Ezra 8:20–36; Ps. Sol. 12; Tob. 3:1–6; here, too, should be added the *Šemonē 'esrē* and the Eighteen Petitions of the synagogue. It is, of course, introduced by the praise of God and interspersed with statements of praise, but they have the character of the framework in which they have been placed. The actual prayer itself consists of a series of petitions.
95. Pss. 89, 106, 120 (?); 144 (?).

people, as vss. 32–36 clearly show. These verses are petition mixed with lament. 2 Chron. 20:6–12 is also a lament of the people introduced with praise (vs. 6). In the late period, the introduction of the prayer of lament or petition with praise of God now becomes the norm; it is a rule which scarcely knows an exception.[96]

With this addition of the praise of God before laments and petitionary prayers, the late form of the lament Psalms in Israel corresponds in a most remarkable way to a large number of Babylonian psalms.[97] This correspondence applies as well to specific characteristics. In these late prayers of Israel, the introductory praise is sometimes placed in apposition, as in 4 Ezra 8:20–23, where fifteen appositives stand at the beginning of the text. Such a piling up of predicates of praise never occurs in the Psalter; it is very common among Babylonian psalms.[98] There is only one explanation for this. The Babylonian psalms in the main and in spite of their unquestionably great antiquity represent a late form whose prehistory we know very little about. Israel itself arrived at this late form only in the postexilian period. This may in part have to do with a borrowing of the Babylonian form (e.g., the piling up of predicates of praise). On the whole, however, this development within the prayers of Israel is to be explained on the basis of the history of the Psalms of lament in Israel itself. A peculiar combination of praise and lament also occurs in the psalms of Qumran. In the fourth of the earliest published psalms, the main section of the psalm is a (greatly altered) lament which has, however, been set within declarative praise.

96. It consists either of a declarative sentence (Ezra 3:11) or of a relative clause added to the address (3 Macc. 6:2); it is, however, usually more detailed, a series of declarative sentences, relative clauses, appositions (4 Ezra 8:20–23).

97. Cf. the examples presented in Widengren, *op. cit.*, where in contrast to the Psalms of the O.T. a whole list of words and sentences of praise strangely appear at the beginning of the Babylonian Psalms of lament.

98. Cf. here Begrich, "Vertrauensäusserungen im israelitischen Klage psalm des Einzelnen . . . " *ZAW*, 1928, pp. 221–260; esp. pp. 230ff.; now in *Gesammelte Studien zum Alten Testament (Theologische Bücherei* 21), 1964, pp. 168–216. From this Begrich draws the conclusion (p. 234) that "the formal address and the description of majesty are nothing but a *captatio benevolentiae.*"

C. The prayer of repentance

The prayer of repentance in its fully developed form is not to be found in the Psalter. Only in a few Psalms (such as Ps. 51) does the motif of the confession of sins begin to shape the whole Psalm. In spite of traditional usage, we still cannot speak of a Psalm of repentance as a *literary category* in the Psalter. Prayers of repentance in the real sense of the word first appear in the late prose prayers, as in Neh. 9 and Dan. 9. Here the whole prayer is a repeatedly rephrased confession of sins, which finally leads up to petition. It bears resemblance to the lament, but the lament is replaced by the confession of sins. Thus, the prayer of repentance is also a transformation of the Psalm of lament in which the lament recedes completely or almost completely into the background and in its place another motif comes to dominate the Psalm.

Among the post-canonical prayers, the genuine prayers of repentance are 1 Esdras (3 Ezra) 8:73–90, The Prayer of Manasses, Ps. of Sol. 9, and Bar. 1:15—3:8. Yet, in these prayers as a whole, the confession of sins is a more powerful and pervasive motif than any other. It is totally absent in only a few of these late prayers, and the transition between a prayer of petition (lament) and a prayer of repentance is quite fluid. However, we need not pursue the subject of the prayer of repentance any further here.[99]

D. The exclusion of the lament from the prayer

The most surprising phenomenon in the history of the lament generally is the appearance during the final epochs of the free-standing lament, or rather, its emergence *alongside* the prayer. The lament, which was gradually pushed more and

---

99. Considering the wealth of preliminary detailed investigations in Engnell's work *(Divine Kingship)*, we can say that the significance of the prayer of repentance for the royal cult has been amply proved. Cf. the summary in *Divine Kingship*, p. 35, then also pp. 46, 47, 66f., 73f., passim. However, the notion that the Psalm of repentance has its immediate origin in the ritual surrounding the king is, in my opinion, unproved. If the Psalm of repentance is merely a late form of the Psalm of lament (at least in Israel), then an explanation based on the royal ritual alone would not be sufficient.

more into the background and finally excluded altogether from the prayer, broke forth anew. It obviously could not be suppressed. And a confirmation of the history of the lament as it has here been brought to light lies in the fact that when the lament re-emerged, it did so essentially as a complaint against God.

The exclusion of the lament took place in a variety of ways:

1. The lament became independent by assuming the form of the lament of the dead.[100] This happened in Bar. 4—5, a lament of Zion upon the deportation of its children. The song reveals clear reminiscences of the funeral song. The lament is divided according to the three subjects: (1) 4: 9b–10, God (but not in direct address); (2) vss. 11–13, I (Zion); and (3) vss. 15–16, the enemy. In the words of consolation (4:30—5:9), this threefold division is unmistakably reflected: (1) 4:36—5:5, God; (2) 5:6–9, Israel; (3) 4:31–35, the enemy. The way in which the lament is reflected in the word of deliverance is here similar to that found in Second Isaiah.

2. The beginning verses of 1 Maccabees bear witness to the re-emergence of the lament simply as a result of the overwhelming burden of national calamity.

> 1 Macc. 2:6 (RSV): "He [Mattathias] saw the blasphemies being committed in Judah and Jerusalem, and said,
>> 'Alas, why was I born to see this,
>>> the ruin of my people, the ruin of the holy city,
>> and to dwell there when it was given over to the
>>> enemy . . . ?' "

There follows, in vss. 8–13, part of a poetic song of lament similar to the kind found in Lamentations; it concludes with the lament: "Why should we live any longer?" (RSV). Thus, the ancient lament of the individual (see above, pp. 181–195) is the starting point for the history of the Maccabean period. The

---

100. The joining together of the lament of the people and the lament of the dead occurs already in Lamentations (see above).

lament by no means signifies resignation, but rather a new departure. Beginning with this lament, Mattathias arrives at the public confession in 2:19–22.[101] We must note, however, that the lament has been set loose from the prayer. What follows is not a supplication to God for help, but an act on the part of Mattathias himself.

A bit later (1 Macc. 3:50–54) there is a prayer which consists purely of lament. With fallen Jerusalem in sight, the faithful few gather, open the book of the Law, spread out the altar paraphernalia, perform the rites of mourning,[102] and pray:

> 3:50b: "What shall we do with these?
> Where shall we take them?
> 51: Thy sanctuary is trampled down and profaned,
> and thy priests mourn in humiliation.
> 52: And behold, the Gentiles are assembled against us to
> destroy us;
> thou knowest what they plot against us.
> 53: How will we be able to withstand them,
> if thou doest not help us?"

The three subjects of the lament are clearly present. The complaint against God is, of course, only implied, but the whole passage has the sound of such an accusation. Both texts are examples of the free-standing lament. At the point of extreme duress, the lament which had been excluded from the prayers of the congregation reappears in the power of a historically momentous event between humankind and God.

3. The Psalms of Solomon reveal the separation of the lament from the prayer in still another way. What holds Pss. Sol. 1 and 2 together is not the formal structure of a Psalm, but rather the sequence of historical events which are presented in close connection with the motifs of the Psalm. Ps. 2 can still be

---

101. It is the lament of an individual in the midst of national calamity; so also 4 Ezra 5:35.

102. Cf. T. Worden, "The Influence of the Ugaritic Fertility Myth," *VT*, III, 3 (1953), p. 288. Worden quotes Canaanitic texts describing acts of mourning which correspond exactly to those here.

recognized as a Psalm of lament with all three elements in it,[103] but it is one which has been transposed into an account.

Ps. Sol. 8 illustrates the separation of the lament from the prayer even more clearly. The chapter is composite. The actual prayer consists only of vss. 30–40. The situation to which the prayer addresses itself is the enemy's attack against Jerusalem described in vss. 1–6 and reflectively interpreted in vss. 7–29. The lament, which here has been transposed into a description of the event, stands outside the prayer. The prayer itself (vss. 30–40) contains no lament; in its place appears a confirmation of the event (vss. 31f.: "Our eyes have seen Thy judgements ... ") which is then followed by praise of the righteous God.

4. It is in the Apocalyptic writings that the full significance of this severance of lament from prayer in the late period becomes most evident.

In the Syriac Apocalypse of Baruch (2 Baruch), chaps. 10—12, Baruch laments over the city. The lament is similar to those of Lamentations. The three subjects of the lament are clearly discernible. Chap. 10:6–19 contains the we-lament (along with 11:4–6) governed by the question why life should continue, considering what has happened. Behind the question stands the original form of the lament of the individual though here it pertains to the people. Chap. 11:1–3 is a complaint about the enemy which has been transformed into an account of an observer. But in the middle of the account there suddenly appears a direct accusation against God: "O Lord, how hast Thou borne (it)?" (11:3c). This one sentence is the clearest sign that the heart of the lament beats within the complaint against God. The fundamental elements of the lament are still there, but the lament itself is no longer a part of prayer. It is an independent phenomenon; it is that dark backdrop against which the revelation of future things stands out so boldly. The lament simply would not let itself be completely silenced. But now it is risked

---

103. (1) God: 2:1b, 4, 7–9; (2) Israel: 5, 6, 20–22; (3) the enemy: 2:1–2, 11–13, 20a.

only as the dark background for a new answer, the answer of apocalyptic. The petition follows only after the elucidation of the future, at the very end, in the free-standing prayer of petition (chap. 48).

The most astonishing example of the exclusion of the lament in the late period is found at the beginning of 4 Ezra.[104] The point of departure is the incomprehensible fact of the destruction of Jerusalem (3:1). From there Ezra turns over in his mind the events of world history, beginning with creation (vs. 4) and the story of divine election (vss. 13ff.) and continuing up to the destruction of Jerusalem (vs. 27). The result of his reflection follows in vss. 28–36. It is already implied in 3:3 ("in my agitation I began . . ."), and at several points in the account it suddenly breaks forth:

> 3:8: "(every nation . . . behaved wickedly before thee, and were ungodly—but thou didst not hinder them."
>
> 3:27: "and so thou gavest thy city over into the hands of thine enemies."

This very obvious complaint against God is developed in vss. 28–36 in the form of reflective doubt. Thus, when the lament is no longer speech actually addressed to God, it gives birth to doubt. Ezra adduces an objective comparison (vs. 28) which reaches the conclusion that neither Babylon nor any other nation had acted any better than Israel. God is challenged to weigh the sins of the inhabitants of the world against the sins of Israel. God will, of course, find individuals who have kept his commandments, "but nations thou shalt not find" (vs. 36). On the other hand, God cannot deny that Israel has believed in him. Such faith has, however, apparently become meaningless (vs. 32).

The whole introductory chapter of 4 Ezra is a singularly radical complaint against God. Clearly there is a parallel here to the book of Job with the difference that 4 Ezra is concerned with

---

104. Concerning the relationship of the Syriac Apocalypse of Baruch to 4 Ezra, cf. H. H. Rowley, *The Relevance of Apocalyptic*, London, 1950 (1944), pp. 141–144.

the fate of the nation. The attack upon God's actions is certainly no less audacious. The criticism even starts with primordial history! The resolution of the matter, it is true, is here completely different. The lamenter, or doubter, receives a twofold answer through an angel:

> 4:11: "thou art incapable of understanding ... how, then, should it be possible for a mortal in a corruptible world to understand the ways of the Incorruptible?"
> 4:26: "If thou survive thou shalt see ... ; for the age is hastening fast to its end."

This is the answer of apocalyptic which is subsequently developed in detail.

The structure of the first part of the Apocalypse is clearly determined by the three parts of the lament. Whereas chap. 3 is completely dominated by the complaint against God, the we-lament (with the questions "Why?" and "How long?" in vss. 23 and 33) follows the counter-arguments and objections of Ezra.

The second vision begins as the first with a complaint against God, but here it is even more reflective, more question than accusation. God's present actions are contrasted with his earlier acts of deliverance (vss. 23–27).[105]

> 5:28: "And now, O Lord, why hast thou delivered up the one unto the many ...? And (why) have they who denied thy promises been allowed to tread under foot those that have believed thy covenants?"

Here the complaint against God is joined together with subject 3, the enemy.

The third vision is also introduced with an accusatory question directed at God, this time with reference to the whole world. Again, both questions are present: "Why?" "How long?" (6:55–57). There follows a long discussion between Ezra and the angel about the meaning of world history, the righteous and the godless, and the judgment of the world. The prayer

---

105. As in the earliest lament (!), e.g., Judg. 15:18; see above.

which brings the vision to a close (8:20–36) no longer contains a lament. The change that has occurred is clearly obvious: *The lament has been eliminated from the prayer.*

In the fourth vision a lament once again stands at the beginning, but it is a lament of a different type. In his vision Ezra sees a woman lamenting. In response to his question, she complains of her suffering. She has lost her only son, for whom she had long prayed and suffered. But Ezra points to a greater suffering, to the suffering of Zion. Then the woman is transformed and in her stead Ezra sees a city: it is Jerusalem restored (10:44). The transformation of the woman into the reconstructed city is indicative of the theological changes occurring in the lament. In the lament of the Psalms, the transformation of suffering is never at first expected by the one who makes the complaint; rather the matter rests with God, that is, with him at whom the lament is directed. The decisive event rests with God, who must turn away his wrath and once again turn to the one who laments. The same assumption is undoubtedly present in 4 Ezra, but the change is in fact awaited at the superficial level of what is happening. In the book of Job the numerous laments all lead up to God's response. The whole emphasis rests on that answer, and Job's restoration is simply the result of it. By contrast, the various laments in the first part of 4 Ezra lead up to the transformation of the weeping woman into the restored Zion. Herein lies the significance of the lament's being separated from the prayer. With this transformation of the weeping woman into the new Zion, the lament in 4 Ezra comes to an end. In the following visions, to the very end of the book, the lament never again appears.[106]

CONCLUSION

The practice of calling on God in time of need in order to secure his help existed in Israel from the earliest to the latest

106. For the wider significance of the lament, cf. A. Bentzen, "Daniel 6; ein Versuch zur Vorgeschichte der Märtyrerlegende" in *Festschrift für A. Bertholet,* Tübingen, 1950, pp. 58–64, esp. pp. 62f.. Bentzen derives the legends of the martyrs from the motifs of the Psalms of lament.

periods of her history. Nothing ever caused this to change. But the way in which one called upon God changed dramatically. In the early period the bare lament, without a following petition, constituted this call. In the Psalms the lament is consistently followed by a petition, i.e., a supplication for help. In the late period the petition is separated from the lament, and an associated phenomenon is the gradual disintegration of the Psalm of lament as a whole.

The lament is an event between the one who laments, God, and "the enemy." It arises from a situation of great need and, for the people of the Old Testament, this need took on a three-dimensional character. The experience itself, however, did not remain the same throughout Israel's history. In the laments of the early period the complaint against God is dominant. In the late period the lament is gradually excluded from the prayer, seemingly in order for it to come to life again *alongside* the prayer. Where it is but part of a larger composition, the lament in the Psalms stands halfway between the early and the late period, yet discernibly related to both. In the Psalms the three parts of the lament are given roughly equal treatment. But we have observed that in the LP the second element of the lament is especially developed, and in the LI it is the third.

Our investigation has led us to this question: What is the significance for the relationship of the nation and the individual to God in the Old Testament that the lament, whose central nerve in the early period had been the complaint against God, receded into the background until finally reduced to a simple petition while the complaint against God fell altogether silent?

Similarly, what is the significance for understanding prayer in the New Testament that the prevailing prayer in post-exilic Israel arose out of praise (thanksgiving) and petition, and that the lament remained silent?

PART FIVE

The "Re-presentation" of History in the Psalms

In recent years considerable attention has been given to the historical motifs[1] in the Psalms, and much has been said concerning the portrayal of the events of salvation history in the form of a cultic drama.[2] The latter has centered particularly in the supposition that there was within the cult a dramatic representation of God's acts of salvation, such as the Sinai theophany, the Exodus events related in the Passover legends,[3] or (now going far beyond these) the portrayal of myths or mythic events of a common semitic or Near Eastern nature, such as the victory of a god over the powers of chaos, his enthronement as king and the *hieros gamos*[4] subsequent thereto. However, little research has been done on the "re-presentation"* of the events of history as they are revealed in the Psalms themselves, that is, in the texts of the Psalms just as they come down to us, apart from any preconceived theory about them.[5] This is what we shall endeavor to do here.

The question is: What do the Psalms *themselves* say to us, just

---

*Translator's note: The German terms, *Vergegenwärtigung* and *vergegenwärtigen*, are used by the author as technical terms and are translated here as "re-presentation" and "to 're-present' " following common practice. The German words carry both the notion of "presenting to the mind" and of "actualizing or making relevant to the present," for which no single English word is a happy translation.

1. Aarre Lauha, *Die Geschichtsmotive in den alttestamentlichen Psalmen*, Helsinki, 1945.
2. Sigmund Mowinckel, *Religion und Kultus*, Göttingen, 1953, esp. 73ff., the "Kultdrama" and Section C, "Die Wiederholungen der Heilstatsachen und der Heilsgeschichte," pp. 78ff. Additional bibliography is listed.
3. Johannes Pedersen, "Passahfest und Passahlegende," *ZAW*, 52, NF 11, 1934.
4. Geo Widengren, *Sakrales Königtum im Alten Testament und im Judentum*, Stuttgart, 1955. Contains additional bibliography.
5. Martin Noth, "Die Vergegenwärtigung des AT in der Verküdigung," in *Probleme Alttestamentlicher Hermeneutik*, München, 1960 [English tr.: *Essays on Old Testament Hermeneutics*, edited by James Luther Mays, Richmond, Va.: John Knox Press, 1960, 1966].

as we read them today, concerning the "re-presentation" of history?

THE "RE-PRESENTATION" OF HISTORY IN THE CONTRAST:
THE LAMENT OF THE PEOPLE

The "re-presentation" of history receives its most direct and tangible expression in the Psalms of the lament of the people.[6] The past forces itself into the present precisely in its contrast to the present. What *has* happened is heard as the antithesis of what *is* happening. I am aware that such an impersonal description of the phenomenon is not really accurate. The contrast cannot be so described, for properly speaking it is a contrast between what God has done earlier and is now doing. We need to be aware of why the concept "history" neither appears nor could appear in the Bible. It is simply that the consciousness of the One who is active in what is happening is still too strong. *God* is confronted with former deeds in order to persuade him to do now, not what he is doing but what by contrast he had done earlier.

Since this contrast-motif is found in so many places in the laments of the people,[7] we need look at only one example, viz., Psalm 80. The structure of the Psalm readily enables us to discern the place and function of that part of the Psalm called "looking back at God's earlier acts of salvation":

80:1, Address: "Give ear, O Shepherd of Israel, thou who. . . ."
1–3, Introductory call for help: "Give ear. . . . shine forth. . . . Restore us!"
4–6, Lament: "How long wilt thou be angry? . . . Thou dost make us the scorn of our neighbors. . . . "
8–11, Looking back at God's earlier saving deeds (in the imagery of the vinedresser and the vine).

6. Gunkel-Begrich, *Einleitung in die Psalmen,* Göttingen, 1933, par. 4, "Die Klagelieder des Volkes," C. Westermann, "The Structure and History of the Lament in the Old Testament," see Part Four above.
7. Ps. 44:1–8, (74:12–17), (77:11–20), 80:8–14, 83:9–11, 85:1–3, 126:1–3, Isa. 63:11–14, and once in a lament of the individual, Ps. 22:4–5.

12–13, Continuation of the lament, set in the imagery of vss. 8–11.

14–15, Petition.

16–17, A twofold wish (i.e., a wish directed toward two sides).

18, A vow of praise.

19, Repetition of the petition in vss. 3 and 7 (rhyme verse).

The "looking back at God's earlier saving deeds" forms the middle of the Psalm. It is set in the midst of the lament which confronts the present with the past, or which reproaches God for the present by pointing to the past. This happens in the following words:

"Thou didst bring a vine out of Egypt;
    thou didst drive out the nations and plant it.
Thou didst clear the ground for it;
    it took deep root and filled the land.
The mountains were covered with its shade,
    the mighty cedars with its branches;
it sent out its branches to the sea,
    and its shoots to the River" (Ps. 80:8–11).

And the lament continues in vs. 12:

"*Why* then hast thou broken down its walls,
    so that all who pass along the way pluck its fruit?"

Later we shall look at the parable in which this passage is set. For the moment let us test the statements of the analogy with the question: What do they tell us about the history of Israel? When we do, we quickly discover that here passing in review are the events handed down in the "historical Credo."[8] But the statements in the parable can be traced back even more directly to a *single* text, viz., the promise out of which the whole history of Israel had come (Exod. 3:7–8):

1. The deliverance from Egypt.

8. G. von Rad, "Das formgeschichtliche Problem des Hexateuch," *Ges. Studien,* 1958.

2. The settlement in the land of promise, which binds together two separate arenas of God's activity:
   a) God drove out, scattered the nations before her,
   b) God prepared the way before her.
3. The Sequel: Israel in the Promised Land,
   a) established
   b) in a land good and broad ... flowing with milk and honey (expanded in vss. 11–12).

In Ps. 80 the event of being brought out of Egypt and led into the promised and is included in the address to God. God is reminded of God's own "great deeds." They are held up so that God might "remember" them. Reference to the settlement of Israel is expanded with an eye toward the contrast that gives shape to the whole: *In those days* "thou didst drive out the nations" before her (vs. 8); *in those days* "thou didst clear the ground" before her (vs. 9)! These additions indicate the importance of developing perspective on the whole. The meaning of individual events could not be understood; their significance could not be passed on. They have meaning individually only as parts of the larger movement of events.

Up to this point everything in the address is stated in the second person: "Thou didst bring ... Thou didst drive out. ... " The effects of these initial acts of God could now be presented in a different way (vss. 10–12). In these verses the vine itself (Israel) is the subject. The magnificent miracle *at* the beginning is so determinative that it is clearly set off from what follows. Subsequent events can be "objectively" related in the manner of historical facts without losing sight of God as the hidden subject behind these events as well. Two such events are described in the parable: growth in depth ("it *took* deep root") and growth in breadth ("and filled the land"). The second is hyperbole, going beyond the limits of the image itself, since it is not something that can be said of a vineyard. It expresses the overpowering astonishment of a small group of people which by its own standards had grown so tremendously and so improbably. It is the same exaggerated speech found in the imagery of the progeny promised to the Patriarchs. Again, the effect of the contrast lies in what is implied: Shall that which has grown so miraculously now be destroyed? And in this way this final overstated development of the "review of the past" is automatically thrown back into the lament which follows in vss. 13–14.

All of this is set within the imagery of a vinedresser struggling with a vineyard, an image which, from Isa. 5:1–7 to John 15 receives a plethora of applications. What is its function here? The imagery describes in an impressive but almost unnoticed way the *entire* history of God's relationship with his people. Its function is not merely—or even primarily—aesthetic. It presents a concept of history out of which the Psalm itself grew and for which this image is but one of many possible forms of expression. Here history sprang with such obvious power from the actions of a Person or of a Will guiding the whole that every single event in history was always seen to have come from this whole, this "plan" of God. Hence, a past or present fact had meaning and could be understood only within the context of the whole. Corresponding to the oneness of the Lord of history is the *one* history which has its origin and its goal in the Lord. In Israel there were any number of ways to express the unity and wholeness of history, from the personification of Israel in the lament of Amos (5:1–2) to the visions of the apocalyptic writers who took the risk of looking at world history as a totality (Dan. 7).

It is against the background of this view of Israel's history as a coherent unity that we must see the contrast that comes to expression in Ps. 80. (In fact our abstract concept "history" has an important precursor in a parable such as this.)* What is to be recognized is that it is *precisely this unity,* this wholeness of history as something happening between God and his people that threatened to be torn asunder in face of the experience of God's actions which "went against the grain," acts directed

*Translator's note: In German *Geschichte* means both "history" and "story."

against the Lord's own vineyard! The Psalm bears witness both to the fact and to the way in which Israel, in face of such experiences and through such a desperate indictment of God, held fast to the unity of her history. The "look back at God's earlier saving deeds" in the lament of the people enabled Israel to hold on to this unity *in spite of everything*, even when it no longer seemed to make any sense.

But we must go a step further. The "re-presentation" of an earlier and happy event right in the middle of a lament enabled one to experience history as a totality and at a depth impossible when history was seen as merely progression from one success to another. Only with such experiences did Israel begin to understand where it stood, in what it participated, and the purpose of its admission into a covenant with God. The "re-presentation" of earlier events in the lament of the people had the effect of disclosing a deeper dimension of historical reality which made history comprehensible for the first time. It was Israel's experience that by clinging to God in desperate times, when former events were in danger of losing their meaning, history itself became a powerful, sustaining reality. Obviously this could be expressed in the lament of a single individual within the nation, as in Ps. 22:4–5.

It is altogether significant that this section, called "looking back to God's earlier saving deeds," can be so varied in its reference to or enumeration of these acts (cf. the passages cited in note 7). Yet, all of these passages have one thing in common. As in Ps. 80, the event in which the community of God has experienced an earlier act of deliverance is an event set within the context of the "primordial history" of Israel, i.e., that series of events by which Israel first became a people. They are the events surrounding the Exodus and the settlement of the Promised Land: liberation from Egypt, deliverance from the Reed Sea, guidance and preservation in the wilderness, territorial expansion in the Promised Land, victory over enemies who endangered their new existence—in fact the exact same series of events included in the imagery of Ps. 80.

Thus, we are able to establish an essential identity between the events contained in the "historical Credo" and those "represented" in the section, "looking back at God's earlier saving deeds." Or, to put it differently, in addition to the confessional recitation of the historical Credo, there was another *Sitz-im-Leben* for the summary "re-presentation" of these same events. It is this looking back at former acts which confronts God in the lament. What now seems to me to be of constitutive significance for the "re-presentation" of history in Israel is this: The events of history, remembered by Israel within a confessional setting, were kept alive on those various occasions not only in such a way that an individual could remember and cause others to remember, but also in a way that enabled the congregation to remind God of his acts of deliverance in the past. From the shock of contemporary (national) experience, what once had happened suddenly emerged as that which was now to be held up before God, in the assumption that by forcing God to remember, he might heal the ruptures in the present. Recalling history had the immediate purpose of influencing history. Of course this is possible only where history still stands in unbroken continuity with the activity of God. We may well ask whether there has ever again been a "re-presentation" of history with such immediacy and power to open the future since the end of this unity of history and divine activity in ancient Israel.

THE VOW OF PRAISE
AS A BASIC ELEMENT OF HISTORICAL CONTINUITY

Under the rubric, "The 'Re-presentation' of History," one might be inclined to think immediately of the "re-presenting" of single events as may perhaps be brought to mind in a nation's celebration of a military victory. "Re-presentation" of history in Israel from the very beginning was by contrast the "re-presentation" of the whole course of history surrounding an event, giving the event continuity. Ps. 80, with which we dealt so extensively above, concludes with a vow of praise (prior to the repetition of the rhyme verse in vs. 19):

"Give us life, and we will call on thy name;
Then we will never turn back from thee!"

(v. 18, Westermann).

We could also call this verse a vow of faithfulness. Just as in the section "looking back at God's earlier saving deeds" there is a binding together of the present moment of national lament with a moment in the past when divine deliverance occurred, so in the vow of praise a moment in the future is tied into the present moment of national lament. The hour of need in which the people voice their lament comes to life again later when they praise God for his new act of deliverance in which the promises given in the former times are now fulfilled.

The vow of praise[9] can illumine for us this element of continuity inherent in the praise of God in Israel. "I know that with the promise that I add to my petition, I have entered into a relationship with God" (see above, p. 78). Of course it is a world involving both words and actions. Originally the vow of praise and the pledge of sacrifice were interrelated (Ps. 66:13–16; 27:6; 54:6; cf. 51:15–19; 69:30–31). In Ps. 80:18 the vow of praise has been transformed into a promise of faithfulness. The affirmation of God in word (praise) and deed (faithfulness) is bound up together with the hour in which the commitment is made. The confrontation with God resulting from his response to those who make supplication in time of need is not intended to come to an end with deliverance. Out of this confrontation is supposed to come a relationship, or, if you will, a history which from the human standpoint is defined by faithfulness to God and the perpetuation of praise. The promise or vow of praise is *not* fulfilled simply by uttering God's praises a *single* time. Once intoned, it cannot be stilled: "Thou hast loosed my sackcloth and girded me with gladness, that my soul may praise thee and not be silent" (Ps. 30:11b–12a); "I will bless

9. Concerning the vow of praise in the lament of the people, see above, pp. 59 ff.; in the individual lament, pp. 75 ff.

the LORD at all times; his praise shall continually be in my mouth" (Ps. 34:1).[10]

This initial thrust for continuity inherent in the vow of praise is of momentous significance for the understanding of history in the Old Testament. The idea of a continuous event, and therewith historical time, is perceived when, in the context of God's relationship to humanity, two points in time are united in the reciprocal relation of word and deed (that is, in the sense of word and response). This is the case when a word spoken by God (a solemn vow uttered as a promise) bridges the time between the moment when the word was spoken and the moment in which it is fulfilled. From the human point of view the vow of praise corresponds to the promise in that here, too, the moment of promise creates a tension which lasts until the promise is fulfilled. In neither instance, however, either in the promise or in the vow of praise (and faithfulness) is that which is released exhausted in the moment; rather it initiates an on-going event.[11]

The psychological motivation for continuity inherent in the vow of praise is explicitly stated in another vow of praise found in a lament of the people:

Ps. 79:13, "Then we thy people, the flock of thy pasture,
     will give thanks to thee forever;
         from generation to generation we will recount thy praise."

Here the vow of praise is closely related to the affirmation of trust. In the hour of supplication God is assured that helpful intervention will be of real and lasting significance for the na-

10. This explains one of the motives for the constant repetition of the praise of God in the continually repeated performance of the cultus. It is the character of the praise of God that, once begun, it cannot ease, demanding continuation in perpetuity.

11. This compulsion for continuity avoids any misunderstanding either of the human or of the divine promise, i.e., that misunderstanding of the promise as "prophecy" insofar as this has in mind only a single point of realization. The promises have as their goal the realization of what is promised as a continuation of the gracious acts of God toward God's people. The promise of praise or the vow of praise does not seek a reward in the sense of the *do ut des,* but rather the continuation of praise as a response to God.

tion and its future course. The response of those who are saved cannot be exhausted in a single act of praise; it will be repeated again and again, beyond the generation that experienced it, even "from generation to generation." What is being said here so unambiguously is that the story of God's deed is to enter history so that it might forever (le'olam) be "re-presented," enabling it to speak to every new situation in the life of the people.

But now we must pursue our line of inquiry a bit further: What actually is promised in the vow of praise? How are God's deeds to be continually "re-presented"? In Ps. 79:13 two verbs are placed in parallel: "will give thanks to thee" and "will recount thy praise." This means that thanks is given when the praise, or the glory, or the glorious deeds of God are recounted: ledōr wādōr nesappēr thehillathākha. This describes perfectly what I have called "declarative praise," that is, praising God by recounting (or telling) the saving acts of God.[12] This glorifying, or extolling, or praising the mighty acts of God is the most basic way of "re-presenting" history in ancient Israel.

It has often been assumed in recent years that there was in Israel a "cult drama" which "re-presented" the events of Israel's history. Leaving aside the question of whether a royal cult ever existed, let me limit myself to whether or not and to what extent we are able, on the basis of Old Testament statements, even to speak of a dramatic presentation of historical events within the cult. In the Introduction to his commentary on the Psalms, Weiser speaks of "the recapitulation of Heilsgeschichte in the form of a cultic drama."[13] But it is not at all clear how such

---

12. See above, p. 81ff.
13. Pp. 42f:
   The view that the psalms are rooted in the cultic tradition of the Covenant Festival is furthermore corroborated by the fact that a number of them also include or allude to the *manifestation of the nature of Yahweh* in the form of the representation of his *saving deeds*, that is, the recapitulation of the *Heilsgeschichte* in the form of a cultic drama, following the familiar pattern of the Hexateuch tradition. . . . Such cultic recitals of the tradition of the *Heilsgeschichte* are indicated by passages in the Psalms in which the congregation testifies: "We have heard with our ears, O God, our fathers have told us, what deeds thou didst perform in their days" (Pss. 44:1ff.; 48:8, 13f.; 62:11; 75:1; 78:3ff.); here the

a cultic drama is to be conceived. The two passages which Weiser cites explicitly (Ps. 44:1; 9:14) speak quite clearly of an event involving narration. In both, the verb employed means "to recount" or "to tell" (RSV). To recount something, however, is not the same as to present it in the form of a cultic drama. Moreover, in none of the other Psalms cited by Weiser (see note 13) am I able to find unambiguous evidence of a cult drama. If he means that along with the narration, i.e., along with a purely verbal "re-presentation" (as described in Ps. 44:1), there was also within Israel's worship a dramatic presentation of these events, then it must simply be said that that is a hypothesis which would have to be based on other texts. There is no evidence in the Psalms themselves for the presentation of historical events in the form of a drama as Weiser envisions it.

In my opinion, however, the presentation of the saving events in the form of a cultic drama would not only have to do with some kind of "performance" which could accompany their verbal "re-presentation," but would have involved a basically different kind of "re-presentation" altogether. If we take the Tammuz cult as a clear example of "re-presentation" by way of a cultic drama,[14] then it is clear that what we have here is the incorporation of the primordial mythic event into the cultic act itself. The dying and rising of the god occurs *now*, *in* the cultic enactment of his dying and rising. The temporal distance, or lapse of time, between the primordial event and the cultic event is irrelevant at the moment in which it is "performed" in the cult drama.

But it is precisely this which is fundamentally and essentially different in the purely verbal "re-presentation" of past events. The temporal distance between the event in the past and the present is *not* dissolved in the retelling, it is *not* made irrelevant

---

cult community's duty to pass on and keep alive this tradition is explicitly confirmed (cf. Pss. 81:10; 96:3; 102:21; 105:1f.; 111:4, 6). The duty of passing on the tradition even affects the cultic prayers of the individual (Pss. 71:16ff.; 77:11ff.; 143:5f.) and is reflected in such solemn promises as "that I may recount all thy praises" (Ps. 9:14; cf. 9:11; 22:22, 30ff.; 26:7; 40:5; 73:28; 118:17, etc.).

14. M. Witzel, "Tammuz-Liturgien und Verwandtes," *An Or* 10, Rome, 1935.

by its "re-presentation" in narrative form. What is retained are the two points in time between which the narrative, or account, forms a bridge. The narrative, or the account, as a mode of presentation, presupposes two points in time: when the event occurred and when it is retold. "Re-presentation" in the form of a cultic drama is an essentially different event than "re-presentation" in the form of narration.[15]

That the Psalms have in mind the "re-presentation" of saving events by means of the word alone and not by means of a cultic drama is proved in the texts themselves, not only by the abundance of the verbs of telling, recounting, announcing used in this context, but also by the context itself, viz., the vow of praise and declarative praise. It is here that the two points in time are clearly held apart: that of the promise and the fulfillment of

<hr/>

15. Noth (*op. cit.*, p. 81; Eng. tr.) sees the dramatic re-presentation and the narrative re-presentation as complementary to each other:

> Certain features of "representing by performing" are surely present in the Israelite cult. . . . But there is something else to be said in this matter which is of its essence in the Old Testament. In the instructions given for the celebration of the Passover . . . (Exod. 12:24ff.), it is commanded that the act of worship should be interpreted by simply retelling the story of the Exodus from Egypt, . . . Thus, the narration of the event of God's wonderful act is a necessary part of the "re-presentation."

Here we must ask, it seems to me, what was "re-presented" in the performance? In the Passover rites it was *what people did* in response to the activity of God that became ritual through constant repetition; it was not the acts of God as such that were celebrated in the festival. Thus at this point we cannot speak of a dramatic "re-presentation" of God's deeds.

It remains to be said, however, that in Noth's case the whole emphasis falls upon re-presentation in the word. He speaks of dramatic re-presentation only indirectly and with reservation. I refer particularly to the conclusion of the article (in which Karl Barth is quoted) which begins, "And in what way do we 're-present'? By proclaiming the saving acts of God, by 'telling' them."

Mowinckel (*Religion und Kultus*, pp. 77f.) sees the relationship of history and cult quite differently. Of course he very consciously and emphatically dissociates himself from any dissolution of history in the cyclical structure of the cult, but his position does not seem to me to be sufficiently clear when he speaks merely of the emergence of a historical element. Mowinckel sees

> an essential difference between the cult drama of Israel and that of other religions of the ancient Near East. . . . And whereas in the other Near Eastern religions it was the most elementary necessities of life which were secured, recreated and experienced in the cult, . . . in the religion of Israel an historical element appeared. For Israel the basic foundation of life was their election by God and his covenant with them. . . . It is this which was re-experienced, confirmed, and made a living reality again in the coming of Yahweh in the cultic celebration. . . .

A "nature and fertility cult" (p. 74) cannot be merely enlarged by the appearance of a historical element. The nature of the "re-presentation" of events of salvation in the two instances are quite different. What Mowinckel sees as characteristic of the "re-presentation" of history, where "past, present and future flow together as one in the 'today' of the festival experience" (p. 79), does not at all hold true for this phenomenon as we find it in the Psalms.

promise. The worshiper consciously looks back from the moment in which the story is heard to the time of distress in which deliverance occurred. Declarative praise spans temporal distance by verbal recollection, not by dissolving it. The presentation of past events by way of a cultic drama has a totally different understanding of history undergirding it than does narration.

When importance is placed on the dramatic actualization of the primordial event, the basic conception of history is unipolar, i.e., history is concentrated in a *single* event, and the preservation of this *one* underlying event occurs in an "actualization" of the event which eliminates historical distance. In this *one* event—more or less removed from any notion of before and after—has occurred that which constitutes this history, and in the reproduction of this one event (in the cultic drama) its continued existence is assured. The relationship of these two moments is not one of cause and effect but of identity. What happened in the primordial past is present in the cult.

When importance is placed in the narrative word, the basic conception of history is bipolar or multipolar. In other words, *history cannot be made to fit into a single moment or into a single event. History always involves a whole range or course of events; it is never simply an event.* The clearest examples of this are those mentioned above which, like two tensive arches, span the whole of the Old Testament. On the one hand, there is the announcement of a future event and then its appearance, and, on the other hand, the vow of praise and then declarative praise. Here, too, there is quite assuredly that special event to be emphasized for its particular significance. But this act of God, so decisively and definitively bearing the fate of the nation with it, is enclosed from both sides within the movement of time. It is the appearance of that which (at a specific moment in history) had been proclaimed. It is the place where declarative praise originates in answer to God's deed, extending itself through time "from generation to generation." In Israel, too, there is this *one* act of God determinative of all subsequent history; but for Israel history was never absorbed into this "primordial event." It was never absolutized; it remained a link in a chain of events. If one wanted to "re-present" this "primordial event," he had to tell a story, to recount history; it did not exist within the present apart from the sequence of events, a sequence which can only be told, recounted.

Hence, the " 're-presentation' of history" never dealt with single events, but always with an event (or events) in historical context. The word which remains binding despite temporal distances is of essential significance for the understanding of history in Israel. To this extent, then, there is a connection between promise and vow of praise on the one hand and the great Israelite outlines of history on the other.

Using this analysis as our starting point, let me raise a question concerning the understanding of history in contemporary New Testament studies, for it is the case that worship in the Christian church also has to do with the "re-presentation" of a historical event. For a long time it has been quite common practice to absolutize the "Christ-event" so as to reduce it completely to Christ's death and resurrection, to which alone is attributed saving significance in the strict sense. The event is then abbreviatedly called "the cross," and it can also be said that to "the cross" alone is attributed a saving significance.

This absolutizing of "the cross" as the event of salvation, cut loose from all that went before and all that came after, does not correspond to the Gospels. The message proclaimed in the Gospels has more the form of a continuous story. But the same holds true of those condensed, confession-like formulations of the gospel message such as Phil. 2, or the second article of the Apostles' Creed, which retain the form of a report even if extremely condensed. In these basic documents, faith in Jesus Christ is not belief in an absolutized event, but rather belief in a story which has actually happened.

The proclaimed Christ (or "the Christ of faith" or "the Christ of the kerygma" or the "kerygmatic Christ"—to cite some of the linguistic malformations often used today) would then have to be the story of Christ, not the "Christ-event." Here too, then, the authentic and essential form of "re-presentation" can only be the telling, the recounting of what has happened. An absolutized "Christ-event," that is, one which has been isolated from history, cut loose from before and after, cannot be "re-presented" in the simple narrative mode. If the "Christ of faith" or the "kerygmatic Christ" is absolutized into a "Christ-event" or a "Christ-fact," then the whole understanding of history in the Bible is abandoned, and basically any connection with the Old Testament is surrendered along with it.

Corresponding to this is the fact that in the Psalms the "re-presentation" of history presupposes throughout, without a single exception, something constantly going on between God and God's people. Individual events in history are not called to mind—even though at first glance that may sometimes seem to be the case—in order somehow to make the event "real" for the present. It is rather that by evoking the past, what is proclaimed is the on-going nature of the relationship which God has begun with God's people.

DELIVERANCE AT THE BEGINNING OF ISRAEL'S HISTORY
AND DECLARATIVE PRAISE

In his book *Die Geschichtsmotive in den alttestamentlichen Psalmen* mentioned above, A. Lauha notes that we do not find in the Psalms individual historical facts mentioned at random, but that we can discern in them a specific "bundle" of facts. He asks, "Why do the Psalms constantly return to the Mosaic period, and when doing so, why do they always lift up the same motifs while completely ignoring other events so heavily emphasized in the historical books?" (p. 133). He finds the answer in the position taken by Anton Jirkus (*Die älteste Geschichte Israels im Rahmen lehrhafter Darstellungen,* 1917) that "in Israel there existed a doctrinal statement incorporating historical events, i.e., a schema involving doctrine and preaching had been formulated in which the same historical material was continually repeated and which was used as a kind of catechism" (Lauha, p. 133). Lauha couples this assumption with the thesis of G. von Rad "when he attempts to find the basic schema for the whole Hexateuch in certain agenda-like formulas which contain an enumeration of the historical facts of salvation and which, in von Rad's opinion, constitute an established part of Israelite worship in the form of a direct Credo or a paraenetic address to the congregation."[16]

If this is correct, we would then have to expand our statement above concerning the section of the Psalm called "looking back at God's earlier saving deeds," for it is not just this one Psalm category which in its looking back limits itself to one definitively circumscribed series of events. The same holds true, even if not so exactly and with several notable exceptions (particularly the royal Psalms), for the "re-presentation" of history in the Psalms generally. What is "re-presented" is not a number of especially significant events in Israel's history, but a single, relatively closed circle of events: "The cornerposts of this outline of historical facts were the miracle of the Exodus, certain occurrences during the sojourn in the wilderness, and the settlement of the promised land" (Lauha, p. 133).

Why precisely this exceedingly limited series of events was repeatedly brought to mind is easy to understand. It represents the very beginning of the nation's history. But, we may ask, wherein lay its fundamental meaning? Lauha explains: "Understandably, all the later religious ideology of history was oriented around that historical heritage which, from this fundamental period of time, was actively preserved by the tradition in the consciousness of the people." This basic argument was carried further and rooted more deeply theologically by von Rad (*Old Testament Theology*, I, pp. 121ff.) and M. Noth (*Überlieferungsgeschichte des Pentateuch*, 1948, pp. 48ff., esp. p. 52). Von Rad can then even say that "this span of time—and this alone—was regarded as the time of the saving history proper" (*Ibid.*, p. 123),

---

16. G. von Rad, *Das formgeschichtliche Problem* . . . (see note 8).

which he then demonstrates with reference to the historical Psalms 136, 105, and 78.

Nevertheless, when it is said that we see in this series of events "the religious and national beginning of Israel," or "the time of the saving history proper," this still does not explain what distinguishes this particular time or what makes it the authentic *Heilsgeschichte*. The question can be answered quite simply. The structure of the "historical Credo," as expressed in Deut. 26, is virtually identical with the structure of the declarative Psalm of praise:[17]

Looking back at the time of need	"The Egyptians treated us harshly, and afflicted us, and laid upon us hard bondage" (Deut. 26:6).
Supplication in time of need	"Then we cried to the LORD the God of our fathers" (vs. 7),
Hearing	"and the LORD heard our voice, and saw our affliction, our toil, and our oppression" (vs. 7);
Deliverance	"and the LORD brought us out of Egypt with a mighty hand and an outstretched arm, with great terror, with signs and wonders; and he brought us in to this place and gave us this land, a land flowing with milk and honey" (vss. 8–9).
Vow of praise and praise	(The response of service and praise in vss. 10f.).

What is the significance of the extensive similarity in these structures? The recitation in Deut. 26 summarizes in the briefest possibile way the events reported from Exodus to Numbers (or Joshua), but it summarizes them precisely into those points which constitute the structure of the declarative Psalm of praise. For all practical purposes, then, we can say that in this passage the outline of a historical report is identical with the structure of a Psalm. This fact, which from a form-critical point of view is really quite extraordinary, finds its explanation in the declarative Psalm of praise in which praise of God and histori-

17. I have already drawn attention to the structural similarity between the Credo in Deut. 26 and that of the declarative Psalm of praise (see above, pp. 114f.).

cal report have been united. As von Rad writes, "The exalted mood which lies behind this recitation is merely that of a disciplined celebration of the divine acts" (*ibid.*, p. 122). Just as the declarative song of praise in Exod. 15:21 (the Song of Miriam) incorporates the account in Exod. 14 and corresponds to it, so the Credo corresponds to the whole Exodus account, couching it in the language of praise for God's act of deliverance which laid the initial basis of Israel's history. In this summary the long list of events assumes the form of a single self-contained event, just as the event of divine deliverance spoken of in the declarative praise of the individual is in response to a single human being. We are no longer dealing with the simple enumeration of facts, but with a relationship in which both sides participate as partners in a story. Deliverance is at the same time just a hearing (as in Exod. 3:7f.), and a hearing which presupposes a prior supplication in time of need. The relationship (or the history) does not end with deliverance; part of the history is the response of the saved, viz., the declarative praise. It finds its classic formulation in Deut. 26 in the occasion surrounding the text itself. Instead of saying something about the sacrifice of his first fruits, the farmer tells the history of his people set within the story of initial deliverance.

In the Psalms, the "re-presentation" of history is drastically limited to the events of the beginning. The reason for this is that they set forth very simply *the* story of deliverance, just as in Deut. 26 these same events are reduced to a *single* account of deliverance. The same phenomenon appears again in Second Isaiah, where the Exodus with all its component elements seems to be retold in a startlingly similar way. What is going on here is not actually mere repetition in our sense of the word, but it is rather the continuation of that history of the beginning in spite of its apparent discontinuance. The language of Second Isaiah at the time of the Exile was possible only because, from the inception of Israel's history up to the Exile, the story of its beginnings had been kept alive in the Psalms.

We cannot consider the songs of praise, which are the spontaneous responses of those liberated to God's act of deliverance, to be the "re-presentation" of history in the proper sense. They are still too close to the event itself for that. The event is not yet history, it is still present. They are in the main very brief shouts of joy, which fall somewhere in that middle ground between prose and song. As such they are often part of an account (that is, when they have been preserved at all), as for example David's song in 2 Sam. 5:20: "The LORD has broken through my enemies before me, like a bursting flood." Another example is the Song of Miriam which is part of a historical account in Exod. 15:21, whereas in Exod. 15:1 it has been handed down at the beginning of a historical psalm. Also belonging to these shouts of joy, as spontaneous responses to an act of divine deliverance, are the very brief songs of victory, such as Judg. 16:23, 24 (a historical account) and Ps. 118:15–16 (part of a festival Psalm, cf. vss. 21–24):

> "Hark, glad songs of victory
>   in the tents of the righteous:
> 'The right hand of the LORD does valiantly,
>   the right hand of the LORD is exalted,
>   the right hand of the LORD does valiantly!' "

This shout of joy also lies behind the Psalter's only two songs of praise by those who have been delivered, Pss. 124 and 129.[18] These Psalms still reveal quite clearly that they were created out of very brief shouts of joy.

Even if these shouts of joy and short songs of praise voiced by those saved cannot, as we have said, be quite properly characterized as "re-presentations" of history, they, nevertheless, have considerable significance for the continuing existence of the events remembered in them. In these spontaneous reactions of joy, deliverance and/or liberation is celebrated as the work of God (they all have the structure, even if it is quite variable, "God has done. . . ."). They are ascribed to God and there-

18. See above, pp. 85–90.

by enter history. Each of these events was handed down in the tradition and could later be "re-presented" because as they happened they were added to the praise of the liberated and placed within the context of the activity of God in behalf of God's people. Just as these events were initially conceived in these joyous shouts of praise as deeds of God, so they were handed down in the tradition and "re-presented" as deeds of God.

We are confronted here again with what we have already observed in that section of the lament of the people called "looking back at God's earlier saving deeds." In the early period of Israel's history, whatever happened occurred in unbroken continuity with the activity of God. History is not preserved in the tradition for its own sake, nor is it restored to the consciousness of the people (that is, "re-presented") for its own sake. It is always the case, of course, that out of all the diverse aspects of an event only that is passed down and "re-presented" which is in some respect "significant" or seems to be significant. Here an event takes on meaning by being extolled and declared significant because it evokes the praise of God and is extolled as God's act. One cannot say that it became significant because it was perceived to be significant, being given a religious interpretation only subsequently, i.e., attributed to the activity of God. Such a view would derive from our understanding of history. Significant historical events were from the outset experienced in personal terms and written down in personal language: God has heard, God has seen, God has uprooted, God has hidden his face, God is angry, God has turned away. In Israel statements of this kind are the original language in which history is expressed. Herein lies the reason for saying that events which were significant for Israel in the positive sense were conceived, passed down in the tradition, and again "re-presented" within the context of the praise of God. The Psalms of praise are the original context for the "re-presentation" of history in the Psalms; the "historical Psalms" are secondary formulations. We should, therefore, expect God's deeds in Israel's history to be mentioned in the declarative Psalms of praise of the people (songs of thanksgiving of the people) and for these deeds to be traditioned in the declarative praise of the people. But such a tradition has not been preserved for us in the Psalter. Gunkel noted this surprising fact in his Introduction (pp. 315ff.), as indicated above (p. 81), and he ventured a possible explanation. The explanation lies in the fact that only the events of the early period were identified unconditionally and without reservation with divine activity; this is the period which von Rad calls "the time of the saving history proper." For this reason they were immediately taken up into the praise of God.

In the songs of victory the situation is quite different. In their case the account of the events is not exhausted in the jubilant recounting of Yahweh's act of deliverance. Of course here too it is the decisive fact, but there are essential and important political and military facts added as well—that is, human actions which clearly fall outside the unadulterated praise of God, as e.g., in the Song of Deborah, Judg. 5. Thus, with the appearance of names and dates the tradition begins to branch out. The song of victory branches off from the pure praise of God (the song of praise of those who have been saved) and develops its own tradition outside the Psalms. It can be no accident that this occurred precisely at the time when the series of events within "saving history proper" (viz., the events included within the historical Credo) came to an end. It is at this point that "history" in our sense of the word begins to be severed from the event which is still identical with the activity of God. It is here for the first time that one's own historical tradition is introduced into the songs of victory, which we know were collected and passed down ("The Book of the Wars of Yahweh," "The Book of the Upright," or "The Book of Songs"). In addition to and probably in close connection with the songs of victory, historical traditions in the form of prose accounts came into being, distinct from the historical traditions in the Psalms but which had a secondary effect upon them (hence, the historical Psalms).

This provides sufficient reason for believing, it seems to me, that a literary category identifiable as the declarative praise of Israel did not exist in the Psalms (with the exception of Ps. 124 and 129; see above), and that the Psalms essentially limited themselves to the transmission and "re-presentation" of those facts which fell within the history of Israel's beginnings. This did occur, however, in the descriptive Psalm of praise (hymn) and in an expansion of this category, the historical Psalm.

THE "RE-PRESENTATION" OF HISTORY
IN THE DESCRIPTIVE PRAISE OF GOD

The descriptive praise of God in Israel revolved around two poles: God's majesty and God's grace. The juxtaposition of the two motifs is not accidental. It is grounded in God's confrontation with Israel from beginning to end. Israel is confronted by God solely as the one of whom these two things must be said, as one who cannot be praised apart from making these two assertions: "Who is seated on high, who looks far down" (Ps. 113:5–6). In the polarity of these two principal expressions of the praise of God, the effect of God's presence in history is already laid out: "For though the LORD is high, he regards the lowly" (Ps. 138:6). From the tension created by these two aspects of God's being, there emerges an action, a spontaneous intervention. He reaches far down and lifts up the needy (Ps. 113:7–9; 118:22). But corresponding to exaltation there is humiliation: "he has put down the mighty from their thrones" (Lk. 1:52). And so his activity can be summarized: "Thou dost deliver . . . thou dost bring down" (Ps. 18:27)—as amply described in Ps. 107:33–42.

These two basic concepts of God's majesty and grace are developed in various ways. God's majesty is revealed in his work as Creator and as Lord of history; his grace in aiding his people (or, in more general terms, the oppressed and the needy). Psalm 33 clearly illustrates this development in the praise of God (see above, p. 122ff.). After the call to praise (Ps. 33:1–3), the two theses summarizing God's dominion (4–5) are developed: the Creator (6–9), the Lord of history (10–12): Yahweh "frustrates the plans of the peoples. . . ." This section is transitional, leading to the development of the grace of God (13–19): "The LORD looks down from heaven . . . on those who fear him."

These two dimensions of the activity of God in history (as Creator and as Lord) are frequently referred to in the descriptive Psalms of praise: Ps. 33:10–19; 65:5, 7; 66:5–7, 8–12; (68); 89:10–14, 15–18; 100; 111; 135:8–12; 136:10–24; 145; (146;) 147:10–14; 149:4–9. The important thing in each of these Psalms is to praise the One who works in history; this is their real intention. Consequently, broad generalizations predominate, permitting us to discern quite clearly a developmental path from the few summarizing sentences to the increasingly detailed descriptions of history, as when we compare the few generalized sentences in Ps. 33 with Ps. 66:5–7, then with Ps. 135:8–12, and finally with Ps. 136:10–24. From simple statements concerning God's activity in history gradually emerged a historical account. Standing at the end of this development are the historical Psalms (Pss. 78; 105; 106; Exod. 15; Deut. 32; Isa. 63:7–14), in which the detailed account has become the main section of the Psalm or in which this motif has become an independent Psalm of its own (corresponding to the Psalms of creation). But even in the case of these historical Psalms, their origin in the descriptive Psalm of praise is clearly discernible. Thus, in Ps. 105 for example, after a long imperatival introduction (vss. 1–6), the historical section (vss. 12–44) proceeds out of the praise of God as Lord and Judge (vs. 7) and as the gracious God who is mindful of God's covenant with Israel (vss. 8–11).

The meaning of the "re-presentation" of history in the descriptive Psalms of praise (and in the historical Psalms which come from them) is then not actually the remembrance of the facts of history, enumerated or implied; rather, meaning lies in extolling Yahweh who is *present* with the community in his actions in history. It lies in praising Yahweh *who is* as he has revealed himself to be in his dealings with the nations (majesty) and with Israel (grace).

This praise of the Lord of history (including both aspects of God's being) has to do less with the "re-presenting" of past historical facts for the sake of dwelling on them, than with "re-presenting" the One who is active as the Lord of history. Praising the Lord of history is not directed toward the past but toward the future. This corresponds exactly with the "re-presenting" of past events of history in the laments of the people. In the introduction to one of the historical Psalms this is expressed in a way which, though deeply reflective, nevertheless illumines the meaning of all such "re-presentations" of history:

> Ps. 78:2–8, "I will open my mouth in a parable;
> I will utter dark sayings from of old,
> things that we have heard and known,
> that our fathers have told us.
> We will not hide them from their children,
> but tell to the coming generation
> *the glorious deeds of the LORD, and his might,*
> *and the wonders which he has wrought.*
> He established a testimony in Jacob,
> and appointed a law in Israel,
> which he commanded our fathers
> to teach to their children;
> that the next generation might know them,
> the children yet unborn,
> and arise and tell them to their children,
> *so that they should set their hope in God,*
> and not forget the works of God,
> but keep his commandments;
> and that they should not be like their fathers,
> a stubborn and rebellious generation,
> a generation whose heart was not steadfast,
> whose spirit was not faithful to God"
>
> (italics the author's).

This is the most elaborate and beautiful description of what the Bible understands as tradition. In the middle of the passage, as the very real essence of what is to be handed down, are the words:

> "the glorious deeds of the LORD, and his might,
>   and the wonders which he has wrought."

This means nothing less than that the heart of the tradition is the praise of God, the handing down of the glorious deeds of the Lord and the wonders which God has wrought. This has to occur so that the coming generation will place its trust in God, so that its heart will be steadfast and its spirit faithful to God. What is here so precisely and clearly enunciated is that the "traditioning" of the events of past history within the contemporary scene has a meaning that is forward looking. By recounting the glorious deeds of God, the future is opened.

Thus Psalm 78, which is probably a late Psalm, confirms in a kind of reverse way that the "re-presentation" of history as it occurs in the body of the Psalm understands itself consciously and explicitly to be primarily praise of God. The introduction to the Psalm graphically illustrates as well how the major emphasis in the "re-presentation" shifted in the direction of historical *tradition*. The really important task now was to preserve from one generation to another what had been received. This process of "traditioning," however, still took place in the lively act of narration. Even these historical Psalms continued to live by virtue of their origin in declarative praise.

THE "RE-PRESENTATION" OF HISTORY IN THE HISTORICAL PSALMS

In the introductory verses of Ps. 78 there appears along with the miraculous deeds of God the tradition of the law. It too is listed among the deeds of God:

> "He established a testimony in Jacob,
>   and appointed a law in Israel" (vs. 5).

The two are closely interrelated; the gift of the law is one of

God's saving acts toward people—hence, the parallel injunction to teach the children to "not forget the works of God, but keep his commandments" (vs. 7). Here we have an expansion of the historical motif, for along with the praise of God's deeds in history appears the gift of the law and as a natural consequence obedience and disobedience. This is the primary difference between the historical Psalms and the historical sections in the Psalms of praise. Human response is now added, one which, as the introduction in Ps. 78 shows, was mostly negative:

> "and that they should not be like their fathers,
>   a stubborn and rebellious generation,
> a generation whose heart was not steadfast,
>   whose spirit was not faithful to God" (vs. 8).

In Exod. 15 this new element is still totally absent; praise for God's saving acts is merely expanded into historical description. In Deut. 32, however, the introduction (32:1–4) is followed by an indictment: "They have dealt corruptly with him, they are no longer his children . . ." (vs. 5), which is then developed further in vss. 15ff. Similarly, in Ps. 78 the two elements stand side by side with approximately equal emphasis. But in Pss. 105 and 106 they are thrust apart in an almost bizarre way. Ps. 105 describes the history of Israel, from God's covenant with Abraham down to the giving of the land of Canaan, as an unbroken chain of God's gracious deeds without the slightest hint of Israel's response. But Ps. 106 sees the same history from the perspective of a comprehensive confession of penance: "Both we and our fathers have sinned" (vs. 6).[19] The juxtaposition of these two Psalms (which were unquestionably placed next to each other deliberately) would seem to indicate that in the "re-presentation" of history in the Psalms these two elements did not originally belong together. It is more likely the case that the second element, the remembrance of Israel's repeated disobedience during her history, was added later and that, as Gunkel earlier assumed, this is probably due to the influence of pro-

19. This corresponds closely to the great prayers of repentance in Ezra 9 and Dan. 9.

phetic proclamation (as is especially clear in Deut. 32). Isa. 63:7–14 illustrates this as well. Isa. 63:7—64:12 is a lament of the people. It contains the section, "looking back at God's earlier saving deeds" (see above), which has been expanded into a self-contained historical Psalm (Isa. 63:7–14). Isa. 63:7 is the introduction to a historical Psalm and the general description of God's acts toward his people (vss. 8–9) is followed in vs. 10 by their disobedience and God's reaction to it. What we have here, then, is a very peculiar combination of motifs which demonstrate how the "re-presentation" of history contained in the "look back" of the lament of the people belongs together with the "re-presentation" of history in the historical Psalm (which, we have noted, grew out of the praise of God). This is evidenced in the fact that here, at a later stage in their development, they have been combined with each other.

In this connection, a few festival Psalms which recall events of the early period particularly demonstrate the disobedience of Israel:

> Ps. 95:8–9a, "Harden not your hearts, as at Meribah,
> as on the day at Massah in the wilderness,
> when your fathers tested me."

Ps. 81:7 recalls the same event. In both, recollection provides opportunity for admonishing and warning the nation:

> Ps. 81:8, "Hear, O my people, while I admonish you!
> O Israel, if you would but listen to me!"

The passage in Ps. 95 which speaks of Massah and Meribah is introduced similarly: "O that today you would hearken to his voice!" (vs. 7b). Ps. 106, a historical Psalm of repentance, recalls the same event in vss. 32f. The historical Psalms also point to the following events as evidence of the disobedience and apostasy of the people.

1. The miracle of manna in the wilderness falls under this perspective in Ps. 78:17–31: "They tested God . . . by demand-

ing the food they craved" (vs. 18). Ps. 106:13–15 refers to the same event from the same perspective but with different words. But Ps. 105:40 mentions the event without a single word about the disobedience of the people.

2. Ps. 106:19–23 speaks of worshiping the golden calf as one of the acts of disobedience: "They forgot the God who saved them" (vs. 21).*

3. The Psalm also includes the story of the spies (106:24–27), the revolt against Moses and Aaron (106:16–18; implied in Exod. 15:12), and the apostasy to Baal of Peor (106:28–31). Whereas in Ps. 106 the individual acts of disobedience are enumerated, Ps. 78 condenses them into generalized, all-encompassing statements: vss. 10–11, 17, 22, 32, 36–37, 40–42, 56–58: "Yet they sinned still more against him, rebelling against the Most High in the desert" (vs. 17). Similarly, Deut. 32:5–6, 15–18, 20b, 21a, 28, 32–33, which are furthest removed from the historical facts, show the same vagueness. *The* sin of Israel now lies in worshiping foreign gods (vss. 15–18), exactly as in Deuteronomic descriptions of the monarchical period.

We can say, therefore, that in the historical Psalms 78 and 106, as in the festival Psalms 81 and 95, Israel is confronted by her offences and disobedience which had begun to appear even in the early period, in the "time of saving history proper." This is in contrast to the pre-exilic prophets who have the story of Israel's transgression begin primarily with the settlement of the promised land or at least with the monarchy, speaking much more positively about Israel's early years. Yet, this dating of Israel's sins back to the time of her origin is strikingly similar to the prophet Ezekiel, as chaps. 16, 20, and 23 indicate: "But the house of Israel rebelled against me in the wilderness" (20:13).

The following observations can therefore be made. In the Psalms of praise those events are "re-presented" which are summarized in the Credo. They all have to do with God's mighty acts at the very foundation of Israel's history. In the

*Translator's note: Westermann here follows the Septuagint.

historical Psalms (and a few others), however, events pointing to Israel's disobedience in this same period of time are included to admonish and warn the contemporary generation and to call it to repentance. This whole development in the "re-presentation" of history in terms of indictment, admonition, warning, and call to repentance is a subsequent one and appears in the Psalms only in the later period under the influence of prophetic and historiographic traditions which were closely related to the Deuteronomic school.

The radical change that had taken place is particularly evident in the original contrast which we discovered in the lament of the people. Between God's earlier acts of salvation and his present absence, including the abandonment of his people to suffering and humiliation, there appeared in the historical Psalms a secondary contrast of an entirely different kind. It is the contrast between sinful behavior of the people and the preceding acts of divine salvation. The origin of this motif lies in prophecy.[20]

ADDENDUM: OTHER PSALM GROUPS

In the so-called *Enthronement Psalms,* the basic structure of the descriptive Psalm of praise is usually clearly discernible. Praise of God's majesty and grace is developed in terms of his activity in history toward the nations and toward Israel:

> Ps. 47:2–4, "For the LORD, the Most High, is terrible,
>   a great king over all the earth.
>   He subdued peoples under us,
>   and nations under our feet.
>   He chose our heritage for us,
>   the pride of Jacob whom he loves."

This correlation between God's majesty and work occurs in a similar way in Ps. 95:3 and 6b–7, in Ps. 97:1–7 and 8–11; in Ps. 98:4–9 and 1–3, and in Ps. 99:1–4a and 4b–8. In spite of all

20. In the judgment against Israel in Amos 2:6–11; or in Isa. 5:1–7.

the variations and differences between them, their derivation from descriptive praise can still be recognized, just as the many imperatival calls to praise also belong to the descriptive Psalm of praise. Nevertheless, the whole emphasis in these Psalms lies in celebrating God's rule as king, and for this reason they employ only very general and traditional statements concerning God's lordship over the nations and concerning the election of Israel. So far as these Psalms are concerned, it is better not to speak of the "re-presentation" of history. This is also true for Ps. 99, although in vs. 6 Moses, Aaron, and Samuel are named and vs. 4b alludes to the gift of the law. But these references are all very vague and not a single concrete event of history is "re-presented."

Descriptions of the "epiphany of God" are a part of the "re-presentation" of history in the Psalms. In these epiphanies,[21] the purpose of God's appearance (or more accurately, his drawing near) is in each instance an intervention on behalf of his people in need. A *single* form probably underlies their many variations:

1. God's coming from ... and (or) his going forth from. . . .
2. Cosmic disturbances which accompany his coming.
3. God's (wrathful) intervention for or against. . . .

The epiphany of God in Israel's early period must have been closely connected with specific events in history, as is indicated by the Song of Deborah in which it constitutes an important segment (Judg. 5:4–5). In the Psalms, where the epiphany appears in quite varied contexts, we undoubtedly have mere imitations of what was once a very powerful and meaningful motif. God's withdrawal is also coherent with the heavily mythological language in which the epiphany is depicted. The significance these motifs must have had at one time for the "re-presenta-

21. In this regard, see above, pp. 93–101.

tion" of history is indicated by a passage such as Ps. 80:1c–2: "Shine forth before Ephraim and Benjamin and Manasseh! Stir up thy might and come to save us!" Here the epiphany still resounds. Reminiscences of the epiphany are also indicated in oracles of salvation such as Hab. 3:3–15 and Isa. 59:15. Employed in this way, the epiphany approximates the "looking back at God's earlier saving deeds" found in the lament.

I suspect that at this point a profound transformation of how God's activity is talked about has occurred. The concept of divine intervention dominating the early period was of God coming forth from his dwelling place (which could be variously described) to his people in need in order to destroy their enemies. His dominion over the forces of nature and his power over history are one, as the epiphanies themselves show. Later, in place of this rather sudden and elementary intervention, there appears the King, who seizes power and is enthroned as the Lord of the earth before whom the nations tremble and who, as the heavenly King, elects and protects Israel as his people. This later concept—for which non-Israelite models certainly played a role—is present in the enthronement Psalms. This, it seems to me, enables us to explain the totally inappropriate conclusion found in Pss. 96 and 98: ". . . for he comes, for he comes to judge the earth." Here the basic motif of the ancient epiphany reappears, transformed by the new idea of the heavenly King who is also the heavenly Judge. But the idea of the heavenly Judge as the One who is to come goes back to the concept of divine epiphany.

The Songs of Zion, which speak of a victory over the enemies of Zion (Ps. 46:7–8, 9–11 [?]; 48:4–8; 76:1–6), do not properly belong to the "re-presentation" of history in the Psalms. The battles alluded to are not historical conflicts in which Israel was engaged, even if they were so construed. On the basis of Near Eastern parallels, we can now say with certainty that here we have the mythical notion of the city of God endangered by enemy powers, a notion which in its historical form was transferred to Jerusalem. (See Excursis 5 to Ps. 46 in H. J. Kraus, *Psalmenkommentar I*, pp. 343f.)

Of direct significance for our discussion, however, is the fact that this pre-Israelite tradition of the city of God and of God's victory over enemy powers has, particularly in Ps. 46, been fused with the motif "affirmation of trust," so that in its present form it is a "Psalm of confidence of the people." The Psalm falls within the "re-presentation of history" in that it gave to the historicized myth of the city of God in the North, the totally new function of making the victory in ancient times the basis for confidence, not in Zion itself but, in a very real and vital way, in Yahweh, the Lord of lords and the Protector of Zion. As the first verse of the Psalm says, "*God* is our refuge and fortress."* So understood, the affirmation of trust as a whole is related to the "re-presentation" of history, but it is an indirect one and does not need to be developed here.

The Royal Psalms (Pss. 2, 18, 20, 21, 45, 72, 89, 101, 110, 132) are, at least in a certain sense, concerned with the "re-presentation" of history. We have not dealt with them here because they constitute a self-contained body of tradition, the analysis of which would go beyond the limits of this discussion. I would instead draw attention to the work by K. H. Bernhardt, *Das Problem der altorientalischen Königsideologie im AT. Unter besonderer Berücksichtigung der Geschichte der Psalmenexegese dargestellt und kritisch gewürdigt*, Suppl. *VT* VIII, 1960.

CONCLUSION

The "re-presentation" of history in the Psalms is focused in the section, "looking back at God's earlier saving deeds" in the laments of the people and in the praise of the Lord of history in the praise of God. What is common to both is that the historical events "re-presented" in them are conceived as acts of God and are "re-presented" as such. What gives them contemporary

---

*Translator's note: Westermann translates here *"Burg"* (fortress) instead of the usual *"Stärke"* (strength).

significance is the same; that is, what enables them to enter into or be handed down as history is the activity of God experienced in them.

This is why the historical events "re-presented" in the Psalms (with the exception of the royal Psalms and the Psalms of Zion) are in essence limited to the beginning of Israel's history, for only in them could God alone be praised so unreservedly as the One who acts.

What is "re-presented" are not isolated incidents in history but rather something that had happened which was on-going and all-inclusive, viz., the deliverance at the beginning, as for example in the Credo of Deut. 26 where it is told as a unified story. It is a history which takes place between God and the people. It is to this on-going event that the "re-presentation" of historical events in the Psalms refers, even if only a single event is named. It is the same story of deliverance evident in the structure of the declarative Psalms of praise.

A new element appears in the historical Psalms and in several of the festival Psalms. In contrast to the acts of God, there now appear the responses (mostly negative) of the people in this early period. Their reactions are "re-presented" in order to admonish or to warn the people and to call them to repentance.

The "re-presentation" of history was intended neither to create interest in past events nor merely to preserve them in memory. The purpose of "re-presenting" the history of the beginning lay in continuing the story because the future of the nation was dependent upon its continuation. The phenomenon of looking back at God's earlier acts of deliverance occurred because the sense of continuity experienced by Israel threatened to collapse under duress. Praise for the acts of God in history occurred because the experience of God's acts evoked the kind of praise that had to continue and had to be passed on (Ps. 78). To cease praising God would be to forget his deeds, and forgetting would, of necessity, lead to the end of God's relationship with the people—a warning often expressed in the book of Deuteronomy.

By way of conclusion, let me cite a passage from the Old Testament in which the "re-presentation" of history has attained special beauty as well as poetic power. It is found in the introductory section of the Psalm of the lament of the people in Isa. 63:7—64:11, mentioned several times before. It is one of the later Psalms, probably composed soon after the destruction of Jerusalem in 587 B.C. (to cite Volz). It was subsequently expanded and in its expanded form incorporated into the collection known as "trito-Isaiah." The section, "looking back at God's earlier saving deeds," is actually contained in vss. 11–14, but it has been expanded into a historical Psalm complete in itself (vss. 7–14).

In sharp contrast to the present, in which the community experiences God in their daily lives as their enemy, as the One who fights against God's own people (vs. 10b), there is the past in which God had shown himself to be so completely different: "Then they [RSV: "he"] remembered the days of old ..." (vs. 11a). This "remembering" is a passionate evocation of the past: "Where is he who brought ... ?" (vs. 11). These verses constitute a totally independent version of the Exodus event. Here alone is Moses' name mentioned; here alone is the event traced to God's holy Spirit. (In an excursis on "Spirit" in his *Komm.*, pp. 270f., Volz calls it "the power active in the history of Israel.") Here alone is the deliverance from the Reed Sea bound up with the image of the shepherd. The image appears in the introduction to the lament of the people in Ps. 80 ("O Shepherd of Israel, thou who leadest Joseph like a flock!") and is here taken up and carried further. The shepherd leads the endangered flock on a path God creates ("who divided the waters before them ...," Isa. 63:12c) and takes them to a hidden place of rest. This is developed further in two fleeting images. The path through the divided waters is as secure and firm as the ground under the feet of a pack of horses on a hunt across the steppes; it is as peaceful as the return of cattle at sunset to the valley spring. The figure of the shepherd (which for Israel certainly meant originally the shepherd of the people as a whole and not simply the individual) is most powerfully and impressively depicted in this Psalm. Thus, Israel knew God and this experience lived on in the praise of goodness, in the remembrance of divine deeds. In this way the tradition of God's act of deliverance at the beginning was preserved throughout the centuries while its external form was allowed to change.

This passage in trito-Isaiah is an especially beautiful and impressive example of what ancient Israel's own history had meant to the nation. It was the arena of Israel's confrontation with God. And it was, of course, such that the movement of history, with its heights and depths, became, for Israel, vital evidence of God's activity, of his incomprehensible love and his terrible holiness. It was not that history itself reveals or had revealed God. Revelation was effected through his word alone. God had of course bestowed that word upon the people, he had spoken to them and his word accompanied his actions in history. But God's speaking was always bound up with his actions. God's speaking could never be separated from history as though one could possess the word apart from the wonders and tragedies of history. As the prophet says (Isa. 63:7–14):

"I will recount the steadfast love of the LORD,
    the praises of the LORD,
according to all that the LORD has granted us,
    and the great goodness to the house of Israel
which he has granted them according to his mercy,
    according to the abundance of his steadfast love.
For he said, Surely they are my people,
    sons who will not deal falsely;
and he became their Savior.
In all their affliction he was afflicted,
    and the angel of his presence saved them;
in his love and in his pity he redeemed them;
    he lifted them up and carried them all the days of old.
But they rebelled
    and grieved his holy spirit;

therefore he turned to be their enemy,
    and himself fought against them.
Then he remembered the days of old,
    of Moses his servant.
Where is he who brought up out of the sea
    the shepherds of his flock?
Where is he who put in the midst of them
    his holy Spirit,
who caused his glorious arm
    to go at the right hand of Moses,
who divided the waters before them
    to make for himself an everlasting name,
    who led them through the depths?
Like a horse in the desert,
    they did not stumble.
Like cattle that go down into the valley,
    The Spirit of the LORD gave them rest.
So thou didst lead thy people,
    to make for thyself a glorious name."

PART SIX

The Formation of the Psalter

According to the scholarship of the last few decades which has concerned itself with the formation of the Psalter, it seems certain that this process occurred in accordance with purely formal criteria, or—more cautiously stated—that in terms of the present Psalter, we are no longer able to move beyond formal criteria of classification to a classification arranged according to content.[1]

Although in recent research complete unanimity rules on this point, it still can be asked whether the final word concerning the formation of the Psalter has yet been said. Two significant arguments speak against it. First, in the book of Lamentations we are confronted with a small collection of Psalms which are uniform in content, i.e., it is a small collection of five laments of the people.[2] In addition to this material unity, perhaps even based on it, the collection's *Sitz-im-Leben* is also clearly discernible, viz., the service of mourning following the fall of Jerusalem and the destruction of the temple in the year 587 B.C.[3] The little book of Lamentations, therefore, proves that there once was in Israel a collection of Psalms uniform in subject matter.

Secondly, with the discoveries at Qumran, we now have in addition to Lamentations a collection of *Hōdajōth*.[4] Here the unity of the collection is not so clear because the Psalm form

1. Cf. the more recent Introductions to the O.T., the recent commentary by H. J. Kraus (*Biblischer Kommentar*, Neukirchen) and the articles, "Psalmen" and "Psalterbuch" by Kurt Galling in *RGG*, 3d ed., vol. 5, which also contains a bibliography of recent literature; and, for a detailed and accurate review of the status of research, see O. Eissfeldt, *The Old Testament: An Introduction*, pp. 445f.
2. One can say this, even if the style of the ancient lament of the people is no longer strictly preserved, and even if Lam. 3 constitutes the joining together of an LI and an LP.
3. H. J. Kraus, *Kommentar zu den Threni (BK)*, pp. 10f.
4. Article "Qumran" in *RGG*, 3d ed., vol. 5; see there additional bibliography.

250

involved is very late and in the process of disintegration. Nevertheless, there is preserved here as well a unified collection of *one* specific Psalm form, the clarity of which is surprising for the late period. They are even known collectively by the name given to the form: *hōdajōth*, the ancient *tōdah*, i.e., they correspond to the Psalm of thanksgiving (or, more accurately, to the confessional or declarative Psalm of praise).

If such collections of Psalms united around a single subject have been preserved, it follows that behind the Psalter as well, at least in part, there were collections uniform in content. Actually, form-critical research would have to come to this assumption as a matter of course. For certainly its intention is to locate the individual Psalm in its proper context within the group of which it is a part. By seeking the setting of a Psalm category within Israel's worship, the idea of the original homogeneity of a group of Psalms belonging to a particular festival or to a particular celebration seemed immediately compelling. That in the case of the laments of the people their original homogeneity should have played no role at all when they were collected is surely improbable. How are we to explain the fact that form-critical research has not changed in any way or even raised doubts about the thesis dominant up to this point concerning the categorization of the Psalms according to purely formal considerations?

The reason for this, it seems to me, lies simply in the fact that in laying the foundation for his interpretation of the Psalms, Gunkel above all had no interest in how the collection was handed down to us.[5] This is revealed all too clearly in the paragraph dealing with the collection of the Psalms in the Gunkel-Begrich *Einleitung* (par. 13, pp. 433ff.). The possibility of partial collections bearing a materially unified character was excluded from the beginning:

---

5. We can call attention here to a certain parallelism with Gunkel's treatment of Genesis where, due to his interest in the smallest literary units, the question concerning the larger compositions is completely overlooked.

That the arrangement of the Psalms is not the result of a classification system based on subject matter is easy to see. In any case they have not been grouped according to separate literary categories. Thus, for example, in Book One of the Psalms the hymns (Pss. 8, 19, 24:1–2, 29, 33) are not side by side; the royal Psalms (Pss. 2, 18, 20, 21) do not form a homogeneous group, and the songs of the lament of the individual, just to name one more, are scattered about (Pss. 3, 5, 6, 7, 13, 22, etc.). The remaining books produce the same results (p. 434).

One gets the feeling from this short paragraph, in which the question is dealt with once and for all, that a genuine interest in the problem simply did not exist. This alone would explain why there are so few really careful (and even fewer accurate) statements in this section. What is overlooked is that Book One of the Psalms contains almost exclusively Psalms of the individual; that, even at first glance, in the entire first book the LI (the lament of the individual) is absolutely predominant and that there is not a single lament of the people to be found in it. Certainly no effort is made to explain the peculiar placing of the Psalms of praise and the royal Psalms.

But if neither Gunkel's commentary nor the *Einleitung* by Gunkel-Begrich made any attempt to go beyond the traditional understanding of the formation of the Psalter, then it is understandable that those who followed by-passed the question as well. The two reasons cited above, however, at least make it worthwhile to ask whether groups of Psalms, united by subject matter, cannot still be discerned behind the partial collections which have been handed down to us, all of which contain Psalms of various types.

In the Psalter as we have it today, we are able to discern with certainty a small, formerly independent collection of Psalms, called the *ma'alot* Psalms ("Pilgrimage" Psalms?), Pss. 120—134.[6] Just before this collection in Ps. 119 which is unique in

6. And so all of the more recent Introductions, e.g., B. A. Bentzen, *Introduction to the Old*

the Psalter (only 19 B corresponds to it), being a Psalm in praise of the law. These two facts suggest that Ps. 119 once concluded a collection of Psalms.[7] Though not in terms of form, Ps. 119 does have a faint parallel in Ps. 1 in terms of content, the latter being an indirect praise of the law in that it deems the person happy who in his life affirms God's law and directs his life according to it. Both Psalms belong to religious wisdom or to the religion of the law; neither is a Psalm any longer in the proper sense of the word. We may assume, then, that Ps. 1 and Ps. 119 form a framework around the intervening Psalms, one which denotes a definite stage in the process which produced our Psalter. We can say, therefore, that there was once a Psalter which began with Ps. 1 and ended with Ps. 119.[8] Moreover, this framework bears witness to an important stage in the "traditioning" process in which the Psalter, as a *collection*, no longer had a cultic function primarily, but rather circulated in a tradition devoted to the law. The Psalms have now become the word of God which is read, studied, and meditated upon.[9] This same stage in the "traditioning" process is indicated for the prophetic books by the closing sentence of the book of Hosea:

> Hos. 14:9, "Whoever is wise, let him understand these things;
> whoever is discerning, let him know them;
> For the ways of the LORD are right,
> and the upright walk in them,
> but transgressors stumble in them."

When we ask about other collections in the Psalter of which

Testament, 2d ed., Copenhagen, 1952, p. 165: "The *ma-aloth*-Psalms certainly constitute an independent collection."

7. In his commentary to Ps. 119, H. J. Kraus in essence follows A. Deissler, *Psalm 119 (118) and seine Theologie. Ein Beitrag zur Erforschung der anthologischen Stilgattung im AT* (*Münchener Theolog. Studien*, I, 11, 1955). He writes, "In his extensive study of Ps. 119, A. Deissler has attempted to get a handle on the literary form of this large composition with the concept 'anthology.' He understands by this an authorial way of working which presupposes for itself a place among the sacred books." This corresponds completely with the function attributed here to the Psalm.

8. An explicit confirmation of this lies in the fact that neither Psalm has a title.

9. Precisely as Ps. 1 describes it.

we are quite certain, the first to be mentioned is the collection of Psalms of David (Pss. 3—41). As the doxology at the end of Ps. 41 shows, the latest division into five books corresponds with an earlier one (according to the superscription). In addition to these two marks of a collection, however, an objective criterion for the unity of this particular group of Psalms can be established with certainty. They are all—with the exception of Pss. 19, 24, and 33—songs of the individual. In the collection Pss. 3—41, the LI category is overwhelmingly predominant.

The Elohistic Psalter begins with Ps. 42 (Pss. 42—83). The identifying mark of the collection in this case is, to be sure, merely of a redactional nature, but it can be helpful in identifying older collections. Ps. 42 also begins a collection noted in the superscription, viz., the Psalms of Korah (Pss. 42—49). This clearly indicates that the superscriptions go back to earlier collections. In Pss. 42—49, Pss. 44—48 are songs of the community and were obviously at one time an independent, objectively defined collection now framed by the two Psalms, Pss. 42—43, and 49. The same is true of the Psalms of Asaph (Pss. 73—83). Like the Psalms of Korah (Pss. 42—49), they are framed by two Psalms of a different type (Pss. 73 and 83). Psalms 74—82 are all songs of the community (Ps. 77 only in the second part). It is a fact that almost all the laments of the people contained within the Psalter are found in these two collections.[10]   The Elohistic Psalms of David (Pss. 51—72) stand between these two collections.[11] Like Pss. 3—41, they are almost exclusively Psalms of the individual. The end of the collection coincides with the conclusion of Book Two of the Psalter.[12] Thus, the Elohistic Psalter included a collection of community Psalms at the beginning and at the end with the second collection of Davidic Psalms placed between. Appended[13] to these Psalms is a small group of the Psalms of Korah (Pss. 84—88, excluding Ps. 86) and Ps. 89,

10. The LP shows most clearly that closed character of the original collection.
11. Except Pss. 60, 65—67, 68.
12. Also excluding here the redactional conclusion at Ps. 72:20, "The prayers of David, the son of Jesse, are ended."
13. The majority of Introductions characterize it this way.

a royal Psalm, with which Book Three of the Psalter comes to a close. The observation made previously applies to these appended Psalms as well: Pss. 84—88 are, in the main, Psalms of the community.[14]

Thus, an additional framework now becomes evident. The two larger collections (Pss. 3—41 and 42—83 [+84—88]) are enclosed by two royal Psalms, Pss. 2 and 89.[15]

The next recognizable grouping is Pss. 93—99, the Psalms of the kingdom of Yahweh (excluding Ps. 94). Psalm 100 has been added as a concluding doxology. The Psalms in between (Pss. 90—92) evidence no connection to the others.

Pss. 93—99 (with 100) is the first of the larger groups of Psalms of praise to be found in the Psalter. The two additional groups follow: Pss. 103—107 and Pss. 111—118. (To the latter group also belong perhaps Pss. 135 and 136 which are now separated from it by Ps. 119 and Pss. 120—134). Again, individual Psalms stand between the groups. Ps. 108 is not an independent Psalm but rather is made up of verses from Pss. 57 and 60. Ps. 109 is a curse Psalm. Ps. 110 is a royal Psalm. The very short Ps. 117 is probably the concluding doxology to Pss. 111—118, to which Ps. 118 was subsequently added.

Psalms 120—134 constitute a self-contained book of Psalms which was later added to the collection framed by Pss. 1 and 119. These Psalms reveal a certain material unity; almost all the Psalms in 120—134 are Psalms of the community, and, of course, here explicitly, the worshiping community. The collection contains only one real pilgrimage song (Ps. 122), the only one in the Psalter, although songs of Zion (Pss. 125, 126, 132) are similar to it. These Psalms constitute the heart of the little book. The tendency toward some kind of material unity is particularly discernible in the fact that the two Psalms, Ps. 130 and Ps. 131, are explicitly Psalms of an individual which were subse-

14. Pss. 85 and 89 are LP; Pss. 84 and 87 are songs of Zion.
15. Ps. 89 represents a combination of a royal Psalm with a Psalm of the lament of the people and, with this in mind, has consciously been added to the collection, Pss. 73—88.

quently transformed into community songs.[16] Ps. 134 is the concluding doxology to the collection.

From here on the Psalter seems to be made up essentially of smaller groups and individual Psalms.[17] The next discernible collection is Pss. 140—143, that is, four Psalms which have the same superscription and form (LI), but which also evidence other characteristics in common. This small group is certain proof that the Psalter knew of groups of Psalms joined together according to content. It may be that Pss. 138 and 139, as Psalms of an individual, were added before the collection and Ps. 145 after. Pss. 135 and 136 belong to the Hallelujah Psalms (i.e., to Pss. 111—118 or they existed as a small independent group). Again, we are particularly able to see that Pss. 137 and 144 stand completely apart. Ps. 137 is not in fact a Psalm but is something rather like a folksong. Ps. 144 seems to be a secondary composition of different parts of Psalms. Its connection remains difficult to ascertain.

The Psalter closes with a series of Psalms of praise (Pss. 146—150), dominated by the imperative call to praise. Ps. 150 stands as the concluding doxology for the final book of Psalms, Pss. 107—150.

In the foregoing summary, we have described the Psalter only in terms of its most important features without delving into specific details. Our intention has been simply to reintroduce the question, which up to this point has been so unjustifiably ignored, concerning the original relationship of the Psalms when they were gathered together into collections.[18]

16. Through the addition of Ps. 130:7f. and 131:3. It is my supposition that we are dealing here with a refrain and that Pss. 130 and 131 are actually *one* Psalm.

17. Just as, on the whole, the first half of the Psalter contains more fixed, self-contained groups, so the second contains more individual Psalms.

18. In what direction our investigation probably should proceed may be suggested by two conjectures. In Ps. 85, verse 9 clearly points to an oracle of salvation; so say most recent interpreters. The question is, to what extent the kernel of Ps. 85, the oracle of salvation, could be derived from a lament of the people and therein have the reason for its inclusion in the collection, Pss. 73—89. More obviously, Ps. 81 could then be understood as having grown from the kernel of an oracle of salvation (vss. 6ff.) which was then deliberately added to Ps. 80, a lament of the people.

A second conjecture proceeds from the observation that in Pss. 18 and 19, 33 and 34, and 66 A and B (that is, where Psalms of praise have the function of a conclusion—see

WHAT ARE THE RESULTS OF THIS ANALYSIS?

1. At first glance we can see that the lament of the individual, the most abundant category in the Psalter, is almost totally concentrated in the first half, and that means, of course, in the two large collections, Pss. 3—41 and 51—72. To this we must add the small collection, Pss. 140—143. Apart from these three closely knit groups, the LI appears only in individual Psalms which have been inserted or added to various collections, such as Pss. 77, 94, 102, and 109.

2. Larger groups of Psalms of praise appear *only* in the second half of the Psalter. Except for Pss. 120—134 and 140—143, *all* the collections after Ps. 90 contain Psalms of praise. The resultant picture is quite clear: The first half of the Psalter is comprised predominantly of Psalms of lament, the second predominantly of Psalms of praise.

3. The superscriptions to the Psalms identify several specific groupings. *Each* of the collections of the Psalms of David contains an overwhelming majority of Psalms of the individual (mainly LI). Psalms of the people or the community appear almost exclusively in the fixed group of Korah and Asaph Psalms as well as in the *ma'alot* Psalms. This indicates that at a particular stage in the tradition the original division of the Psalms according to subject was still known to the traditionists.

4. In the smaller collections, the Psalms of praise usually have the function of closing the collection, hence the doxologies at the end of the various books (Ps. 41:13; 72:19; 89:52; 106:48; 150), and thus Ps. 134 (collection 120—134), Ps. 117 (111—118), Ps. 100 (93—99), Ps. 145 (?) (140—143). It seems probable that all the Psalms of praise prior to Ps. 90 have this function: Pss. 18 and 19; 33 and 34; 40; 65 and 66.[19]

5. The royal Psalms seem to suggest a collection of their

---

under point 4 above) a declarative Psalm of praise and a descriptive Psalm of praise (or hymn and Psalm of thanksgiving) sometimes stood side by side. That this is not accidental is in any case shown by the conscious joining together of the two literary forms.

19. Cf. note 18; Psalms pronouncing a blessing (such as Ps. 67) also seem to have this function of closing a collection.

258 LAMENT IN THE PSALMS

own;[20] they are found throughout the whole Psalter only as addenda. Pss. 2 and 89 frame the two larger collections, Pss. 3—41 and 42—83 (89). Pss. 20 and 21, 72, 101, and 110 are either added or inserted. This is an important fact for any understanding of the royal Psalms, which at a particular stage in the selection process were individually added or inserted into the various collections. This was obviously done when they no longer retained their original cultic significance for the reigning king,[21] having taken on a secondary messianic interpretation.

6. The Psalter does not contain a clearly discernible collection of liturgies. Where they are found (e.g., Pss. 24, 118), they have been added or inserted into existing collections. This seems to me very much worth considering when determining the significance of the liturgies in the Psalter.

7. The criteria discernible in the rise of the collections indicate that two basic distinctions were made: First, Psalms of the individual were distinguished from Psalms of the community; and, secondly, Psalms of lament were distinguished from Psalms of praise. Since we are able to discern these two differentiations with certainty, it follows that they must have been important to the collectors and traditionists in designating a Psalm. These two criteria correspond exactly to the two fundamental criteria used in determining the categories of the Psalms.

20. Cf. the quotation from Gunkel-Begrich cited above.
21. For this stage in the process there once were, of course, closed *corpora* of royal Psalms.

PART SEVEN

The Role of the Lament
in the Theology
of the Old Testament

The Old Testament cannot pin God down to a single soteri-ology; it can only speak of God's saving acts within a whole series of events, and that necessarily involves some kind of verbal exchange between God and man. This latter includes both the cry of man in distress and the response of praise which the saved make to God.

I

1) The deliverance from Egypt is of fundamental significance to the theology of the Old Testament. This is attested both by the so-called "historical Credo" (G. von Rad), which in a few sentences proclaims and traditions this event as the founding of the people of Israel (e.g., Deut. 26:5–11), and by the structure of the Pentateuch (or Torah), at whose center the account of the deliverance from Egypt stands (Exod. 1:1ff.). The first commandment recalls the event: "I am the LORD your God, who brought you out of the land of Egypt, out of the house of bondage" (Exod. 20:2).

When we inquire more closely and ask what happened in this event, the tradition in which it was preserved and handed down invariably gives us the same answer. The events making up the deliverance form a sequence which is always encountered (though it is not always the same) wherever a deliverance is

259

related: distress, a cry of distress, a hearkening (promise of deliverance), deliverance, response of those saved (the praise of God). This sequence appears both in the detailed account of the deliverance from Egypt in the book of Exodus and in the brief text of the Credo:

	Deut. 26:5–11		Exod. 1—15
Prehistory	26:5	1:1	"Who came to Egypt"
Distress	6	1:6–22	Oppression in Egypt
Call for help	7a	3:7–9	Cries of distress
Hearkening	7b	3:7–8	Hearkening and promise
A leading out	8	7:14	
A leading into	9		Exod. 16–Numbers
Response	10f.	15:1–21	The rescued praise god

What we have established here is *the place of the lament in the theology of the Old Testament*. It is set within the context of the account of the deliverance which became the basis of Israel's relationship with God; it is thus related to the saving acts of God. Whenever we want to explain precisely what happened when Yahweh delivered Israel from Egypt, we have to speak of the cry of distress uttered by those oppressed in the "house of bondage." In the Credo (Deut. 26:7a) as well as in the book of Exodus (3:7–9), the cry of distress (and hence the lament) belongs to the narrative of the deliverance from Egypt.[1]

Now, whenever a theology of the Old Testament attributes fundamental significance to the deliverance from Egypt (as e.g., the theologies of Gerhard von Rad, Walter Zimmerli and Th. C. Vriezen), it does so because Israel experienced God's presence throughout its entire history as one who saves (and Deutero-Isaiah for example speaks of God's saving action in much the same way as the book of Exodus). We can say, therefore, that a position of significance is thereby conferred implicitly upon the cry of distress, for it too belongs to the events of

1. The structure of Deut. 26:5–11 corresponds in turn to that of the declarative Psalm of praise; cf. C. Westermann, *Das Loben Gottes in den Psalmen* (Göttingen, Vandenhoeck und Ruprecht, 1961, 4th ed. 1968), 85; Eng.: *The Praise of God in the Psalms*, trans. Keith R. Crim (Richmond, Va.: John Knox Press, 1965), pp. 114f.

the deliverance. This has certainly not been widely seen or noted in Old Testament theology; the lament has held almost no special significance in the presentation of the theology of the Old Testament. The reason for this is readily apparent. We cannot discuss it here extensively but merely in outline. In the West, God-talk is characterized by objective thinking about God. In theology God becomes an object. But in the Old Testament, talk of God is characterized by dialogical thinking (Martin Buber). Accordingly, the object of theology is an event between God and man. When Western theology speaks of God's salvation or of a God who saves, God thereby becomes objectively tied to an event, and thus emerges a "soteriology." The Old Testament cannot pin God down to a single soteriology. It can only speak of God's saving acts within a whole series of events, and that necessarily involves some kind of verbal exchange between God and man. This latter includes both the cry of man in distress and the response of praise which the saved make to God.

2) In the Old Testament, from beginning to end, the "call of distress," the "cry out of the depths," that is, the lament, is an inevitable part of what happens between God and man.[2] We can catch sight of the theological significance of the lament in the Old Testament, however, only if we distinguish *the lament of affliction* from *the lament of the dead*.[3] The lament of the dead looks backward, the lament of affliction looks forward. A lament of the dead on the lips of one who mourns bewails the death of another, someone who belongs to him; in the lament of affliction the one who suffers laments what has happened to himself, he relates to his own life by way of his lamentation. In the lament of affliction the sufferer reaches out for life; he

---

2. To what follows, cf. Westermann, "Struktur und Geschichte der Klage im Alten Testament," ZAW, 1954, 66:44–80 and *Theologische Bücherei*, 24, 1964, pp. 266–305.
3. Hedwig Jahnow, *Das hebräische Leichenlied*, BZAW 36, 1923, and above (ftn. 2), p. 268; see also "Mourning," IDB, New York: Abingdon Press, 1962, III, 452–454; the latter contains additional bibliography.

begs that his suffering be taken away; it is the only possibility in life left for him as long as he has breath.

The fact that in the languages of the West the lament of the dead and the lament of affliction are designated by the same word is the result of a long development conditioned by the fact that the outward signs of lamentation, such as weeping, are the same for both. In Hebrew, as in all primitive languages, the lament of affliction and the lament of the dead are designated by different words and cannot be mistaken for each other. Another and more important distinction is that in the Old Testament only the lament of affliction is directed toward God. The lament of the dead on the other hand is a secular form, as David's lament over Saul and Jonathan for example indicates (II Sam. I:17–27).

3) *The significance of the lament in the Old Testament* is apparent in the way the pentateuchal narrative opens the book of Exodus with a cry of distress over the oppression in Egypt: "Then we cried to the LORD" (Deut. 26:7). The cry to God out of deep anguish accompanies Israel through every stage of her history. In his redaction of the book of Judges, the Deuteronomist says: "... they were in sore straits" (Judg. 2:15), but "the LORD was moved to pity by their groaning" (Judg. 15:18). And thus it happened over and over again in times of distress, up to the great catastrophe of the exile, times in which the laments of the book of Lamentations and many others (as, e.g., Ps. 89 or Isa. 63—64), up to and including 4 Ezra, brought before God the distress and suffering of the nation.

But in a like manner the distress and suffering of the individual is expressed in the personal laments that pervade the whole of the Old Testament. Psalm 130 begins: "Out of the depths I cry to thee, O LORD!" And Psalm 113 speaks of the God addressed in such laments: "... who is seated on high, who looks far down [into the depths]" (vss. 5–6). All the Psalms of lament in the Psalter revolve around this cry out of the depths, and the Psalms of praise declare that God has heard it. The book of Job is a mighty fugue based on the cry of lamentation; it alone indicates the underlying significance that the lament had in Israel for talk of God, that is, for theology.[4]

In order for us to see just how many of the texts of the Old Testament were lament texts, we must start with the fact that all the Psalms of lament in the Psalter (and in Lamentations) constitute only a portion of the laments contained in the Old Testament. We are able to discern three stages in the history of the lament: the short laments of the early period (e.g., Gen. 25:22; 27:46; Judg. 15:18; 21:2), the rhythmically structured laments of the Psalms, and the laments of the prose prayers of the later period (Ezra 9; Neh. 9). These three stages of the lament can be found throughout all the writings of the Old Testament. The short laments of the early period are preserved only in narrative accounts. The laments of the second stage are not limited to the Psalter (and Lamentations); they appear in the prophetic books (e.g., the laments of the nation in Jer. 14—15; Isa. 63—64; and, the laments of the individual in Jer. 11—20). We might draw attention here to the detailed discussion in Gunkel-Begrich, *Einleitung in die Psalmen* (1934). But, beyond that, the lament is an important structural element in the prophecy of Deutero-Isaiah, as is the lament of the individual in the book of Job. Any survey will show that laments pervade the entire Old Testament and that they are an essential part of what the Old Testament says happened between God and man.

The significance of the lament is rooted in the fact that the man of whom the Old Testament speaks is finite. He is not idealized or spiritualized. The Old Testament knows of man only within the limitations related in the stories of his creation in Genesis 2—3, the limitations of transitoriness and failure. The peril created by these limitations are part and parcel to his existence. This peril, and the plight to which it can lead, should and can be expressed in the lament. And just as it is a part of human nature that man can pour out his heart in lamentation, so it is a part of divine nature that God is concerned about this

4. Westermann, *Der Aufbau der Buches Hiob*, BhTh, 23, 1956.

LAMENT IN THE PSALMS

cry of distress. Praise of the God who hears this cry also pervades the whole Old Testament: ". . . because he has heard my voice and my supplications" (Ps. 116:1).

It is of great significance for what the Old Testament says of God that the account of the deliverance from Egypt in the book of Exodus gives *no* explanation either for the plight of the oppressed or for God's compassion regarding that plight ("I have seen the affliction of my people," Exod. 3:7). The former is given no historico-theological basis, unless perhaps it is the context of guilt and punishment. "It stands there as a primitive datum, totally unexplained" (Zimmerli). Following this primitive and yet unexplained fact, at the very beginning of the account, comes the lament, the language of suffering. In their cry the oppressed give voice to their plight. There is a striking similarity between the distressful cry of the oppressed and the wailing of Hagar's child in the wilderness (Gen. 21:16–17): "And as she sat over against him, the child lifted up his voice and wept. And God heard the voice of the lad. . . ." The lament implores God to be compassionate to those who suffer. This is its function: to appeal to God's compassion. All the multifarious forms of human affliction, oppression, anxiety, pain, and peril are given voice in the lament, and thus it becomes an appeal to the only court that can alter their plight.

4) At this point we must draw attention to *the difference between this usage and that of Christian tradition in the West.* In both the Old and New Testament the lament is a very natural part of human life; in the Psalter it is an important and inescapable component of worship and of the language of worship. In the Old Testament there is not a single line which would forbid lamentation or which would express the idea that lamentation had no place in a healthy and good relationship with God. But I also know of no text in the New Testament which would prevent the Christian from lamenting or which would express the idea that faith in Christ excluded lamentation from a person's relationship with God. Certainly in the Gospels the actions of Jesus of Nazareth are characterized by the compassion he evi-

denced for those who implored him to help them in their need. The cry of distress with which the afflicted besought him ("Oh, Thou Son of David, have mercy on me") is never rebuffed by Jesus. In the passion story the lament of the ancient people of God (Ps. 22) is placed on the lips of Jesus. Only in the paraenetic sections of the New Testament letters does the admonition to bear suffering with patience and humble self-resignation start to gain the upper hand. It would be a worthwhile task to ascertain how it happened that in Western Christendom the lament has been totally excluded from human relationship with God, with the result that it has completely disappeared above all from prayer and worship. We must ask whether this exclusion is actually based on the message of the New Testament or whether it is in part attributable to the influence of Greek thought, since it is so thoroughly consistent with the ethic of Stoicism.

II

1) The Psalms of lament in the Psalter stand at the center of the history of the lament of the nation and the lament of the individual. They can be distinguished from the earlier, very short laments (as encountered in the partriarchal narratives and in the historical accounts) and from the later prose prayers by their characteristic form—a form which evolved out of the worship tradition of Psalms of lament. They are poems and songs alike and have a fixed structure, one that obviously permitted an unlimited number of variations. Nevertheless, in each one of these Psalms we can discern a fixed sequence of elements which marks it as a Psalm of lament. The *structure* of the Psalm of lament is address (and introductory petition), lamentation, a turning to God (confession of trust), petition, vow of praise.[5]

The structure itself does not account for the difference between the lament of the nation and that of the individual; it

5. See ftn. 2 above, p. 270 *(Theologische Bücherei)*.

merely indicates what is essential to the Psalm of lament. What is of theological importance in the structure is that it exhibits an internal transition. There is not a single Psalm of lament that stops with lamentation. Lamentation has no meaning in and of itself. That it functions as an appeal is evident in its structure. What the lament is concerned with is not a description of one's own sufferings or with self-pity, but with the removal of the suffering itself.[6] The lament appeals to the one who can remove suffering. The transition is evident in the fact that the lamentation flows into petition (to secure God's attention and intervention)—or, that petition follows lamentation. In the early laments it is possible for the petition to be implied in the lamentation, as for example in Samson's lament (Judg. 15:18). This can be explained by drawing upon an observation from psychology. In the case of very young children the petition is contained in the lamentation; they can express what they want in no other way than by plaintive sounds or by crying. Only very slowly, as it matures, does the child begin to differentiate between lamentation and petition. For this reason we cannot agree with the view, recently proposed once again, that the petition is the very heart of the Psalms of lament.[7] The petition comes out of lamentation; the two cannot be separated nor can they be differentiated in meaning.

The transition in the structure of the Psalm of lament is also manifested by the fact that in spite of the vast richness and diversity of the Psalms, each one, without exception, can be recognized as being one step beyond simple lamentation. The transition is quite often indicated by a "but" (wāw adversative) which introduces a confession of trust or some similar statement.[8] Finally, the transition is shown at the conclusion of the Psalm, which either already anticipates the saving intervention of God with a vow of praise, or in a totally different way points

6. In modern times the lament has fallen into disrepute, in part because as an isolated I-lament it has degenerated into a self-pitying description of one's own afflictions.
7. Erhard Gerstenberger, *Der bittende Mensch* (Habilitation, Heidelberg, 1970; typewritten).
8. Westermann, *Das Loben Gottes in den Psalmen*, 4th ed., 1968, p. 52; Eng.: pp. 71f.

to a change which has taken place during the course of the Psalm itself.

This transition in the structure of the Psalm of lament is rooted in the lament's function as an appeal. Because the lament is directed toward the one who can change suffering, the change occurs in the Psalm or at least it is implied that it is. Understood in this way, the structure of the Psalm of lament, which enables us to see the path leading to an alleviation of suffering, is one of the most powerful witnesses to the experience of God's activity in the Old Testament.

The goal of the transition which we have observed in the structure of the Psalm of lament is the praise of God. This is indicated primarily by the fact that the Psalm of lament concludes with a vow of praise. Lamentation is turned into praise as the response to being saved (as in Psalm 22 especially). In the Old Testament lamentation and praise are juxtaposed to each other. Just as lamentation is the language of suffering, so the praise of God is the language of joy. One is as much a part of man's being as the other. But it is an illusion to suppose or to postulate that there could be a relationship with God in which there was only praise and never lamentation. Just as joy and sorrow in alternation are a part of the finitude of human existence (Gen. 2—3), so praise and lamentation are a part of man's relationship to God. Hence, something must be amiss if praise of God has a place in Christian worship but lamentation does not. Praise can retain its authenticity and naturalness only in polarity with lamentation.

2) A characteristic of the lamentation, which forms but one part of the structure of the Psalm of lament, is that it usually has *three dimensions*.[9] It is directed toward God (an accusation or complaint against God), toward others (a complaint against an enemy), and toward the lamenter himself (I-lament or We-lament). Since lamentation always has to do with life, whatever

---

9. See ftn. 2, pp. 269f. For an example of the lament of the nation, see p. 273; for the personal lament, see p. 280 *(Theologische Bücherei)*.

268   LAMENT IN THE PSALMS

the suffering lamented, the whole of one's being comes to expression in these three dimensions. For the lamenter it is not merely the isolated "I" that is threatened by the power of death which one experiences in suffering; threatened as well is one's standing in the community; that is, what one means to others and what they mean to him. But also threatened is one's relationship with God and with it the meaning of life. This is what the "Why?" of the complaint against God is all about. The answer to the question of meaning, to the question "Why" cannot be provided by the sufferer oneself; the question must be directed to God and only he can answer it.

The threefold character of the lamentation reveals an understanding of man in which the existence of an individual without participation in a community (a social dimension) and without a relationship with God (a theological dimension) is totally inconceivable. Using modern categories, we would say that the three elements of the lamentation presuppose an understanding in which theology, psychology, and sociology have not yet been separated from each other. We must note however that this understanding, which the elements of the lamentation express in a special way, is present throughout the rest of the Old Testament. It appears already in the J account of creation in which man is created, at one and the same time, as an individual for fellowship with others and in relationship to the Creator.[10] The same formulation appears again in the book of Job, where the drama of suffering is played out between God, Job, and his friends. We could also refer to other Old Testament passages in which it is equally apparent that these three dimensions are an essential part of human being.

The understanding of man manifest in the three elements of the lamentation could be important for the future. No anthropology that is purely theological or purely socio-political or philosophical or psychological can encompass man as a whole.

10. Westermann, *Genesis. Biblischer Kommentar I* (Neukirchen-Vluyn, Neukirchener Verlag des Erziehungsvereins, 1968—), pp. 245ff.

All three dimensions are a part of our total being. Comparing and contrasting the various "images of man" that absolutize one or another of these dimensions can no longer help a humanity whose very existence is at stake. The task for the future is to bring the three dimensions of man's self-understanding together again. Theology should forego creating its own separate anthropology in the sense of a doctrine of man; rather, it ought to try to bring to bear what the Bible says about man in its conversations with the social sciences. For the question of meaning cannot be answered by the social sciences; the voice of the theologian will always be indispensable. Yet it is the question of meaning that reveals the necessity for everyone to work together on the pressing intellectual questions that concern man.

3) In the Psalter, both *the lament of the individual and the lament of the nation* have their own particular forms; each is clearly distinguishable from the other.[11] But also in the other books of the Bible, the historical works and the prophets, both individual and national laments accompany the path of Israel, from her inception up to the post-canonical literature and the New Testament.

This, too, says something important for the theology of the future. We can no longer overlook the fact that the theology of the Reformation was one-sidedly individualistic. The justification of the sinner has to do with the individual, and the church consists of justified individuals. The "salvation of souls" is quite simply the salvation of the individual. The great social revolutions are responsible for restoring to society a position of primary importance in the history of humankind. In contemporary culture the society has become the dominant concept above everything else. Even theology can no longer ignore the fact that the lamentation of the oppressed was a factor in the great social revolutions. The task that lies before us involves a

11. Note the long discussion of "The I of the Psalms" by Emil Balla (*Das Ich der Psalmen*, Göttingen: Vandenhoeck und Ruprecht, 1912) and also that last, wise word from Sigmund Mowinckel, *The Psalms in Israel's Worship*, Oxford: Oxford University Press, 1962.

radical shift in our thinking, one that strives for a new and yet unrealized balance between the individual and society. It is the same task revealed to us when we juxtapose and conjoin the lament of the nation and the lament of the individual—which also tells us something about our relationship to God.

4) *The lament of the nation* opens the account of the exodus. It continues in the murmuring of the people throughout their sojourn in the wilderness. During the conquest and the first period of the occupation, the lament is of a people oppressed by superior enemies. During the period of the empire, the special laments that pertain to political catastrophe (enemy oppression) can be distinguished from those that deal with natural catastrophe (drought, locust). As a consequence of the fall of 587 b.c., the national lament took on special meaning, for after the destruction of the temple in Jerusalem lamentation became the only possible way left for worshiping God. The proclamation of Deutero-Isaiah refers to the recitation of the national lament at several points (e.g., 40:27). In postexilian times the recitation of the lament was changed into a service of repentance (Ezra 9; Neh. 9). The observance of the national lament is indicated by 4 Ezra, in which the lament, now separated from the service of worship, once again and with great pathos expressed the suffering of those who had survived catastrophe.

The theological significance of the national lament lies in its immediate relationship to the activity of God as Savior. Salvation is experienced as the hearing of the call of distress ("I . . . have heard their cry," Exod. 3:7). Even in its lowest moments the nation experienced its own history as a context that had meaning—or at least ought to have meaning. It took on meaning in that God was at work in it. Yet the nation experienced the plight it was in as an absurdity that confronted God with the question, "Why?" How can God bring such profound suffering upon people—if indeed they are his people—when he has previously done such great things for them? Insofar as the absurd is laid before God, the lament of the nation contains a dimension of protest, the protest of a people who cannot understand what has happened or has been done to them. It is a protest directed at God to be sure, but it is nevertheless a protest; it does not endure absurdity submissively and patiently: it protests! The protest itself arises out of the perception of fate as absurd, as for example the enslavement in Egypt; it lays the matter out before God so that he will do something about it. That the lament is heard implies that God has accepted their protest. Hence, we can see a connection between the lament (*Klage*) of the oppressed which God hears, and the prophetic accusation (*Anklage*) against society. For in their accusations against society, the prophets in a sense became the articulators of the lament of the oppressed and the defenseless.[12]

Among the many noteworthy instances of Israel lamenting her plight is the murmuring in the wilderness.[13] What characterizes the laments of these wandering people is that they are dominated by complaints against God (or Moses). They deal with elementary needs: hunger, thirst, exhaustion, and despair in a hopeless situation. The stories of the murmuring have one thing in common: God does not punish those who remonstrate or rise up against him; rather, he gives sustenance to those who hunger and water to those who thirst. In these narratives of the wilderness period, Israel preserved for all time the experience that when in elementary and mortal need, the lament of those who suffer is heard by God—even though in desperation their lament is turned against God, even though it is an accusation against God. Even those who despair of God are within range of God's ear!

In the lament of the nation, the contrast between God's former activity and his present activity is pointedly expressed in its "reference to God's former acts of salvation." The growing

---

12. This connection between the prophetic accusation and the lament of the Psalms should be investigated further. In any case it goes beyond social indictment. Its relation to the accusatory complaint against the rule of foreign powers is indicated by Hab. 2:11: "For the stone will cry out from the wall, and the beam from the woodwork respond."
13. Cf. G. W. Coats, *Rebellion in the Wilderness: The Murmuring Motif in the Wilderness Tradition of the Old Testament*, Nashville: Abingdon Press, 1968; Coats however understands the murmuring motif differently.

awareness of this contrast signified an awakening of historical consciousness which had begun to see history in its larger contexts. Since the "lament out of the depths" confronted God "on the heights" with what he was doing, since it faced him with his present actions while recalling what he had done earlier, we can say that it saw history in context. This is clearly expressed when the contrast is structured linguistically in parabolic form as, for example, the parable of the vinedresser in his vineyard: The parable presents history as a totality. In this contrast-motif, which we find in the national lament, lies one of the roots of Israel's historical consciousness.[14]

5) The *lament of the individual* appears as early as the stories of the patriarchs: the lament of Abraham (Gen. 15:2), the lament of Rebecca (25:22; 27:46), the lament of Hagar's child (21:16), and prior to these even Cain's lament in Gen. 4:13-14. In the period of the Judges we find it in the lament of Samson (Judg. 15:18), and in the time of the kings in the lament of the childless Hannah (I Sam. 1) or in that of the sick king (Isa. 38). In the Psalms the personal lament is the single most extensive form, and in Job it is the basic motif. Job's laments in chapters 3 and 29—31 provide the framework for the dialogues, and Job's speeches bear the stamp of the lament motif throughout.[15]

The theological significance of the personal lament lies first of all in the fact that it gives voice to suffering. The lament is the language of suffering; in it suffering is given the dignity of language. It will not stay silent! The introduction to Psalm 102 ("A prayer of one afflicted, when he is faint and pours out his complaint before the LORD") clearly states the meaning and function of the lament: to lay out one's own inner sufferings before the one who alleviates suffering, heals wounds, and dries tears. Human suffering, no matter what it is, is not something which only affects the sufferer alone and which he himself must overcome; suffering is something to be brought

14. Westermann, *Vergegenwärtigung der Geschichte in den Psalmen, Theologische Bücherei,* 24, 1964, pp. 306-35.
15. See ftn. 4 above.

before God. The true function of the lament is supplication; it is the means by which suffering comes before the One who can take it away. Seen from this perspective, we can say that the lament as such is a movement toward God.[16]

The lament reaches its climax in the book of Job in that instead of receiving consolation from his friends, Job is told to repent, to be prepared to answer for the sin which had caused God to punish him so severely. Job admits that he has sinned as others have, but he cannot admit that he has committed a crime as gross as his friends assume because of the terrible blows that have befallen him. Behind their assumption stands the doctrine that a bitter and cruel fate must unquestionably be the result of great sin, for God is just. For Job such a doctrine has disintegrated. He knows that his suffering is not punishment and that he can now no longer understand God. Forced into extreme isolation by friends who profess to speak in God's name, Job can do nothing but continue to hold on to a God he no longer understands. His lament is the language of one who clings to an incomprehensible God. In the case of Job the lament reaches the outermost limits of its function as supplication. It is the bitter complaint of one who despairs, who has no one else to whom he can turn. He clings to God against God. For this reason Job's lament is important for a world that has turned away from God. Doubt about God, even the kind of despair that can no longer understand God, receives in the lament a language that binds it to God, even as it accuses him.[17]

6) *The confession of guilt* can be a constituent part of the lament Psalms, whether in the lament of the nation or of the individual, but that is not generally the case. So far as the Old Testament is concerned, it is not true that every lamenter *eo ipso* (since he or she appears before God with a lament) would have

16. Because the lament as such can be a movement toward God, it became a component part of worship. This assumes that the experience of profound suffering can bring one to God, provided the experience is verbally articulated in the lament.
17. In his lonely adherence to a God he could not understand, against the theology of his omniscient friends, Job approximates the Old Testament figure of the mediator. His perseverance through suffering was not for himself alone.

to confess sins. There are even a number of laments which contain a protestation of innocence. From this we can conclude with certainty that wherever we meet a confession of sin, consciousness of a specific offense is presupposed. This differs with the Pauline doctrine which says that sinfulness is a part of the human condition and that the confession of sin is therefore a part of every approach to God. From the standpoint of the Pauline doctrine there can be no lament without a confession of sin; a lamenter appears before God as one who is guilty.[18] But the lament is not a constituent part of Christian prayer, and we can say that in a certain sense the confession of sin has become the Christianized form of the lament: *"Mea culpa, mea culpa, mea maxima culpa!"* The result of this is that both in Christian dogmatics and in Christian worship suffering as opposed to sin has receded far into the background. Jesus Christ's work of salvation has to do with the forgiveness of sins and with eternal life; it does not deal, however, with ending human suffering. Here we see the real reason why the lament has been dropped from Christian prayer. The believing Christian should bear suffering patiently and not complain about it to God. The "sufferings of this world" are unimportant and insignificant. What is important is the guilt of sin. The impression thus given is that although Jesus of Nazareth actively cared for those who suffered and took pity on those who mourned, the crucified and resurrected Lord in contrast was concerned with sin and not at all with suffering.[19]

We must now ask whether Paul and Pauline-oriented theology has not understood the work of Christ in a one-sided manner. It is not to be denied that Jesus of Nazareth understood

18. For this reason the early church and the reformers had a preference for the "seven penitential psalms" (Pss. 6, 32, 38, 51, 102, 130, 143), especially for Ps. 51 (see the article "Busspsalmen" in RGG, 3, 1959, cols. 1538f). It is extremely odd that preference for these Psalms has lasted for centuries without anyone having ever asked why, among such a large number of Psalms, there are in fact so few Psalms of repentance.

19. That thought is now beginning to be given to this point is indicated by a book review by Dorothee Sölle, "Gott und das Leiden. Ein Buchbericht zu neuer theologischer Literatur," in *Wissenschaft und Praxis in Kirche und Gesellschaft*, 62, 173, 358–372. Note, e.g., the statement, "Hedinger begins with the phenomenon of the repressed lament" (p. 268).

what he was doing for those of his time as something he was doing for those who suffered. It is not to be denied that he heard and accepted their lament. There is no passage in the Gospels which suggests that Jesus saw his task to be one of convincing the sufferer that one must bear suffering patiently. There are narratives in which Jesus combines the forgiveness of sins with healing, but there are no narratives in which Jesus puts the forgiveness of sins in the place of healing.

There is a second factor to be considered. If the gospel story of the passion is presented in the words of Psalm 22, the authors quite obviously wanted to say that Christ had taken up the lament of those people who suffer, that he too had entered into suffering. Hence, his suffering is a part of the history of those who have suffered, who have found their language in the Psalms of lament. With his suffering and dying, therefore, Jesus could not have had only the sinner in mind; he must also have been thinking of those who suffer. If, as in the New Testament, the work of Christ is described as salvation from sin and death, then (following the Old Testament understanding) by "death" we mean not only the cessation of life but the power of death at work within life which people experience in all types of suffering.[20]

On the basis of these observations we would have to decide anew whether the one-sidedness of relating the work of Christ to sin alone, to the exclusion of any relation to human suffering, actually represents the New Testament as a whole and, if so, whether that understanding would not have to be corrected by the Old Testament. A correction of this sort would have far-reaching consequences. One of these would be that the lament, as the language of suffering, would receive a legitimate place in Christian worship, as it had in the worship of the Old Testament.

7) *The lament of the mediator* is a rare but important intermedi-

---

20. Westermann, "Salvation and Healing in the Community," *International Revue of Missions* 61, 1972, 9–19.

ate form. It is a personal lament but one which deals with matters facing the nation. The individual brings before God not his own personal suffering but, through his mediation, the suffering which affects the nation. It first appears in the lament of Moses, recurs in the lament of Elisha and reaches a high point in the laments (or confessions) of Jeremiah, which then in turn point to the songs of the Suffering Servant in Deutero-Isaiah. Thus, the history of God's relationship with Israel begins with the lament of the oppressed in Egypt and reaches its climax in the suffering of one who mediates in behalf of the nation. The cry of Jesus on the cross stands in continuity with this history of the lament of the mediator as it runs through the whole of the Old Testament. In this sense it can be viewed as the goal of that history.[21]

The theological significance of the lament of the mediator can be recognized only if we look at it in connection with the lament of the nation and that of the individual. This connection is most clearly seen in the laments of Jeremiah.[22] The task that had befallen Jeremiah of announcing to his own people the defeat God had decreed was super-humanly difficult. The weight of the burden which it placed on him came to expression in his laments. These laments enable us to see rather clearly two things: (1) The language of suffering, which took form in the Psalms of personal lament, has also left its stamp on the laments of Jeremiah. As in the Psalms the three elements of the lament are determinative: The accusation against God, in which Jeremiah casts his profound despair before him; the I-lament, which expresses the loneliness and inescapableness of his situation; and, the lament against the enemy, which as in the lament psalm, is joined with a petition that God intervene

21. Soon to be completed is a Heidelberg dissertation by F. Ahuis, *Der klagende Gerichtsprophet*, containing a history of research and a complete bibliography of the literature.

22. On the laments of Jeremiah, see G. von Rad, *Theologie des Alten Testaments*, München: Chr. Kaiser Verlag, 1957, II. Band, II. Hauptteil, Kapitel Jeremia; Eng.: *Old Testament Theology*, trans. D. M. G. Stalker, New York: Harper and Row, Publishers, 1965, 2: 188–219.

against Jeremiah's enemies. (2) At the same time, however, it is Jeremiah's office and mission which speak through these laments: The enemy is not his personal adversary, but he makes them his adversary by his preaching. Like the enemy in the Psalms of lament, they want to "lay a trap" for him in order to silence his announcement of judgment. The I-lament is likewise related to his mission: Jeremiah could no longer endure his burdensome task. It had brought him loneliness, disgrace, and contempt. His bitterly caustic accusation reproaches God for the unbearable tension which he had to endure between his mission on the one hand and the absence of any realization of his message on the other. The prophet is abandoned without resistance to rejection and ridicule because God is silent. God does nothing.

When we view them this way, the laments of Jeremiah become a witness both to the history of the Psalms of lament and to the history of the prophets. In his laments Jeremiah is simply a man who suffers and who speaks the language of the suffering of his people. But he is also a prophet who was thrust into suffering by his mission and who expresses the suffering it caused through his lament. Thus we can say that the history of the lament and the history of the messengers of God meet in the confessions of Jeremiah.[23]

In purely formal terms, Jesus' lament on the cross in words from Ps. 22 corresponds with Jeremiah. In terms of content, however, there is an essential difference. The suffering which Jeremiah expresses in his laments has no apparent positive significance. The laments contain no indication whatever that Jeremiah understood his suffering to be for the nation; it is not substitutionary or expiatory suffering. Jeremiah can see no meaning in his suffering and in despair he accuses God.

Between the suffering and death of Jesus and the suffering in the laments of Jeremiah stand the songs of the Suffering Servant in Deutero-Isaiah. Here for the first time the suffering

23. W. Baumgartner, *Die Klagegedichte des Jeremia*, BZAW, 32, 1917.

of a single man takes on far-reaching and positive significance for the well-being of a whole people. The Servant's suffering is substitutionary suffering. This revolution in the lament of the mediator which occurs between the laments of Jeremiah and the Servant Songs was brought about by the intervening collapse of the state, the temple, and the empire. The message of judgment that Jeremiah proclaimed had come true; his mission and his actions were confirmed. This is precisely what the Servant Songs permit us to see; they assume the prophets labored without ostensible success (Isa. 49:4). The Suffering Servant carries on the work of the prophets, but it is now extended to all the nations (49:6); the vicarious suffering of the Servant of God is no longer limited to the borders of one nation. Thus, a second element in the lament of the mediator is now changed. In Jeremiah the laments of accusation and petition against the enemy constitute important and necessary parts of the lament, just as they do in the Psalms of lament. In the Servant Songs, however, accusation against the enemy recedes into the background; the transgressor is included in the supplication of the mediator (Isa. 53:12).

This is the clearest connection we can find between the Old and the New Testaments. The Gospel accounts of the suffering and death of Jesus follow the Servant Songs point by point. In both the suffering is vicarious; in both the one who suffers is confirmed by God in and through death; in both he intercedes for his enemies; and, in both there is a community which believes that the suffering and dying was for them.[24]

However, it makes a considerable difference whether we take the Servant Songs as isolated texts, relate them to the Christ event and then describe them as prophetic sayings which were

---

24. The suggestion that the words of a king mediating on behalf of his people can also be discerned in the Servant Songs, especially in 42:1–4, would require extensive comment. The king is representative of the people in a different way, and the suffering of a kingly mediator is something essentially different than the suffering of a messenger of God. Its meaning and significance can only be explained against the background of the whole phenomenon of the sacral kingship. In this regard, see my forthcoming article, "Sacral Kingship," in the *Encyclopedia Britannica*.

fulfilled in Christ, or whether we understand them as the end
of a path that leads through the whole Old Testament. Looked
upon in the latter way, the Servant Songs belong within the
narrow sphere of the history of the mediator which runs from
Moses, to Elijah and Jeremiah, to the Suffering Servant of
Isaiah; they belong within the wider sphere of the history of
the lament as the language of suffering experienced by the
people of God. In the narrow sphere, the Suffering Servant
belongs within the history of the mediators who had to suffer
in their office; the Servant stands in that history of the end of
the prophetic period and thus close to the laments of Jeremiah.
In the wider sphere, the Suffering Servant belongs within the
history of the afflicted who in their laments laid their suffering
before God that he might take it away.

8) In conclusion we must draw attention to a very important
phenomenon: the lament of God. The book of Isaiah (and thus
the entire collection of prophetic books) begins with God's lament over the rebellion of the people: "Sons have I reared and
brought up, but they have rebelled against me!" (Isa. 1:2). The
same lament recurs in Jer. 8:5: "Why then has this people
turned away in perpetual backsliding?" In order to show the
unnaturalness of their rebellion, both laments are followed by a
reference to the behavior of animals ("An ox knows its owner";
"the stork in the heavens knows her times"). When the redac-
tors placed such laments as these at the beginning of the prophetic books, they obviously wanted to say that the compassion
of God does not suddenly depart when he intervenes as judge
against the people he saved from slavery.

The lament of God becomes exceedingly more bitter, however, whenever it concerns a judgment which God himself must
bring upon his people. This is true of the laments in the book
of Hosea. H. W. Wolff[25] suggests that the question in 6:4 "corresponds completely with Hosea's peculiar style of proclama-

25. On this verse and 4:4–15; 5:10f.; 11:8, see *Hosea. Dodekapropheten; Biblischer Kommentar,* Neukirchen, Neukirchener Verlag, 1957, p. 151.

tion which vacillates between compassionate lament and bitter accusation"; and that "it testifies to the fact that God is wrestling with himself." These laments of God are intensified in Jeremiah. It is certainly not by chance that they stand beside Jeremiah's own laments in chapters 12, 15, and 18 (12:7–13; 15:5–9; 18:13–17). Underlying all three texts is the prophetic form employed in the announcement of judgment, but instead of a sentence there appears a lament. God mourns the destruction of the people, "the beloved of my soul" (12:7), but it is he who has given them over to the hands of their enemies! The juxtaposition of God's wrath and God's grief vis-à-vis the people in these texts is almost incomprehensible. This isn't something that is said all the time, but only when life is pushed to its ultimate limit: to the edge of annihilation which God brings upon his own people. The lament of God is not a general statement *about* God; it is rather only one of those rare and extreme possibilities for speaking of God. As such, it finds its ground in the situation itself. The incomprehensible idea that God destroys his own has its corollary in that which is equally incomprehensible, viz., that the God of wrath is also the God who mourns. The meaning of such talk about a God who laments or mourns lies not in its saying something about God in himself but about his relationship to his people. It enables those who are afflicted to hold on to an incomprehensible God, one who judges and also mourns.

On the basis of the laments of God found in the book of Jeremiah, the doctrine of the incarnation could take on new meaning. The God who becomes man would then have to be understood in terms of the history of God's relationship with his people—a history which ultimately reaches the point where God, as the God of judgment, suffers for his people.[26]

26. On the suffering of God, see Dietrich Bonhoeffer, *Widerstand und Ergebung* (München: Chr. Kaiser Verlag, 1951, 1957⁶); Eng.: *Letters and Papers from Prison,* trans. Reginald H. Fuller, New York: The Macmillan Company, 1962; Kazō Kitamori, *Die Theologie des Schmerzes Gottes,*: Göttingen: Vandenhoeck und Ruprecht, 1972; Japanese, 1946; Eng.: *The Theology of the Pain of God,* Richmond, Va.: John Knox Press, 1965; Jürgen Moltmann, *Der gekreuzigte Gott,* München: Chr. Kaiser Verlag, 1972; Ulrich Hedinger, *Wider die Versöhnung Gottes mit dem Elend,* Zürich: EVZ-Verlag, 1972; and also see ftn. 19 above.

Bibliography

PSALM COMMENTARIES AND INTRODUCTIONS

(Superior numerals indicate the edition.)

Olshausen	1853	Wutz		1925
Hitzig[2]	1863-65	Gunkel[4]		1926
Ewald[3]	1866	Gunkel-Begrich (Introduction)	1933
C. B. Moll	1869	König		1926-27
Hupfeld-Nowack[3]	1887-88	Peters		1930
Delitzsch[4]	1883	W. E. Barnes		1931
Kessler[2]	1899	A. Bentzen (Introduction)	1932
Kautzsch	1896	A. Bentzen (Lectures)	1932
Kautzsch[3]	1909	H. Schmidt		1934
Duhm	1899	J. Calès		1936
Baethgen[3]	1904	H. Herkenne *HSAT*	1936
Ehrlich	1905	J. Hylander		1937
Briggs	1907-09	M. Buttenwieser		1938
Kirkpatrick	1910	W. O. E. Oesterley		1939
Gunkel (Selections)[4]	1917	A. Weiser[2]		1939
Duhm[2]	1922	A. Weiser[3]		1950
Kittel[3-4]	1922	F. Böhl and B. Gemser	1946-49
Kittel[5-6]	1929	B. Eerdmans O.T.S. IV	1947
Bertholet *KHSAT*	1922	F. Nötscher, *Echter-Bibel*	1947
Staerk	1911	E. A. Leslie		1949
Staerk[2]	1921	E. Podechard		1949

SURVEYS

The most recent summary presentation of the work on the Psalms:

A. R. Johnson, "The Psalms" in *The Old Testament and Modern Study*, Oxford, 1951. This work gives a comprehensive listing and presentation of the literature in Psalm research in the last twenty-five years. The most recent comprehensive work in the German language is Gunkel-Begrich, *Einleitung in die Psalmen*, 1933.

A slightly older survey is Max Haller, "Ein Jahrzehnt Psalmenforschung, *ThR*, 1929, 6. It gives the literature from 1920-1929.

An important summary of the work on the Psalms is D.C. Simpson,

The Psalmists, Oxford, 1926, with contributions from A. M. Blackman, G. R. Driver, H. Gressmann, T. H. Robinson, W. H. Robinson. For the question of the sacral kingship and its significance for the Psalms, which was not handled extensively here, reference should be made to two surveys: Aage Bentzen, *Messias, Moses redivivus, Menschensohn*, Zürich, Zwingli-Verlag, 1948 (Eng. tr., *King and Messiah*, translated by the author, London: Lutterworth Press, 1955) and Martin Noth, "Gott, König, Volk im A.T.," *Z.Th.K.*, 1950, 2. Cf. H. H. Schrey, "Die alttestamentliche Forschung der sogennanten Uppsala-Schule," *Theol. Zeitschrift*, 7, pp. 321-341, Basel, 1951.

Monographs (Restricted to works important for the theme of this work):

Balla, Emil, *Das Ich der Psalmen*, Göttingen: Vandenhoeck & Ruprecht, 1912.

Barth, Chr., *Die Errettung vom Tode in den individuellen Klage- und Dankliedern des A.T.*, Zollikon: Evangelischer Verlag, 1947.

Baumgartner, W., "Die literarischen Gattungen in der Weisheit des Jesus Sirach," *ZAW* 34, 1914, pp. 161 ff.

Begrich, J., "Die Vertrauensäusserungen im israelitischen Klagelied des Einzelnen und in seinem babylonischen Gegenstück," *ZAW* 46, 1928.

Calès, J., "Les psaumes du règne de Jahwe," *Recherches de science Religieuse* 25, 1935, pp. 462-489, 583-592.

Causse, A., *Die altisraelitische Kultuspoesie und der Ursprung der Psalmen*, 1926.

Causse, A., *Les plus vieux chants de la bible*, Paris: F. Alcan, 1926.

Galling, K., "Der Beichtspiegel, eine gattungsgeschichtliche Studie," *ZAW* 47, 1929, pp. 125 ff.

Gunkel, H., *Einleitung in die Psalmen*, ed. J. Begrich, Göttingen: Vandenhoeck & Ruprecht, 1933.

Gunkel, H., "Psalmen" in *Die Religion in Geschichte und Gegenwart*, Tübingen: Mohr, 1927-1931.

Gunkel, H., "Die israelitische Literatur" in *Kultur der Gegenwart*, ed. Paul Hinneberg, Leipzig: B. G. Teubner, Teil I, Abteilung 7[1], 1906.

Gunkel, H., "The Religion of the Psalms" in *What Remains of the O.T. and Other Essays*, tr. A. K. Dallas, London: Allen & Unwin, 1928.

Gunkel, H., "Die Grundprobleme der israelitischen Literaturgeschichte: Die Psalmen" in *Reden und Aufsätze*, 1913; "Ägyptische Danklieder," *ibid*.

Gunkel, H., "Formen der Hymnen," *ThR* 20, 1917.

Gunkel, H., "Danklieder im Psalter," *Zeitschrift für Missionswissenschaft und Religionswissenschaft*, 34, 1919.

Gunkel, H., "Lieder in der Kindheitsgeschichte Jesu bei Lukas," in *Festgabe für Harnack*, Tübingen: J. C. B. Mohr, 1921.

Horst, F., "Die Doxologien im Amosbuch," *ZAW* 47, 1929.

Jacob, B., "Beiträge zu einer Einleitung in die Psalmen," *ZAW* 16-17, 1897.

Jansen, H. L., *Die spätjüdische Psalmendichtung, ihr Entstehungskreis und ihr Sitz im Leben,* Vidensskapsselskapets Skrifter II, Hist.-filos. Klasse No. 3, 1937.

Löhr, Max, *Psalmenstudien, BWAT,* NF 3, 1922.

Mowinckel, S., *Psalmenstudien,* I-VI, Kristiania, 1921-24.

Mowinckel, S., *Offersang og sangoffer. Salmediktning i Bibelen,* Oslo, 1951 (Eng. tr., *The Psalms in Israel's Worship,* tr. D. R. Ap-Thomas, Oxford: Basil Blackwell, 1962). This book, which brings together the results of Mowinckel's life work on the Psalms, appeared after the conclusion of this present work and I was thus unable to make use of it.

Oesterley, W. O. E., *A Fresh Approach to the Psalms,* N.Y.: Scribners, 1937.

Quell, G., *Das Kultische Problem der Psalmen, BWAT* NF 11, 1926.

Schmidt, H., *Die religiöse Lyrik im A.T.* Tübingen: Mohr, 1912.

Schmidt, H., *Die Thronfahrt Jahwes,* 1927.

Schmidt, H., *Das Gebet der Angeklagten im A.T., BZAW* 49, 1928.

Snaith, N. H., *Studies in the Psalter,* London: The Epworth Press, 1934.

Steuernagel, C., "Psalmen zu einem Thronbesteigungsfest Jahwes?" *Preuss, Kirchenzeitung* 22-24, 1928.

Literature not specifically dealing with the Psalms:

Begrich, J., "Das priesterliche Heilsorakel," *ZAW* 52, 1934.

Begrich, J., *Der Psalm des Hiskia,* Göttingen: Vandenhoeck & Ruprecht, 1926.

Buhl, Frants, "Über Dankbarkeit im A.T. und die sprachlichen Ausdrücke dafür," *Baudissin-Festschrift,* Giessen, 1918, pp. 71-82.

Döller, J., *Das Gebet im A.T. in religionsgeschichtlicher Beleuchtung,* Wien, 1914.

Elbogen, J., *Der jüdische Gottesdienst in seiner geschichtlichen Entwicklung,* Frankfurt, 1924.

Ginsberg, H. L., "Psalms and Inscriptions of Petition and Acknowledgment," in *Louis Ginsberg Jubilee Volume,* N.Y.: American Academy of Jewish Research, 1945.

Glueck, N., *Das Wort hesed im atl. Sprachgebrauch als menschliche und göttliche gemeinschaftsgemässe Verhaltungsweise,* Giessen: A. Topelmann, 1927.

Greiff, A., *Das Gebet im A.T.,* Münster, 1915.

Heiler, F., *Das Gebet,* 2nd ed., München, 1920 (Eng. tr. *Prayer,* tr. Samuel McComb, London: Oxford, 1932).

Hempel, J., *Gebet und Frömmigkeit im A.T.,* Göttingen, 1922.

Hempel, J., "Segen und Fluch im Licht altorientalischer Parallelen," *Zeitschrift der Morgenländischen Gesellschaft,* NF 4, 1925.

Humbert, Paul, *La terouca, analyse d'un rite biblique,* Neuchâtel, 1946.

Humbert, Paul, "Laetari et exultare dans le vocabulaire religieuse de l'ancien testament," *Revue d'histoire et philosophie religieuses.*

Köhler, L., *Deuterojesaja, stilkritisch*

untersucht, Giessen: A. Töpelmann, 1923.

Köhler, L., *Lexikon in veteris testam. Libros,* Leyden: E. J. Brill, 1948-1953.

Nielen, J., *Gebet und Gottesdienst im N.T.,* Freiburg, 1937.

Nöldeke, Th., "Hallelujah," *Baudissin-Festschrift,* Giessen, 1918.

Pedersen, J., *Israel, Its Life and Culture,* I-IV, London: Geoffrey Cumberlege, 1926-1940.

Müller, Christa, *Das Lob Gottes bei Luther,* München, 1934.

Wendel, Adolf, *Das freie Laiengebet im vorexilischen Israel,* Leipzig: Eduard Pfeiffer, 1932.

Selected literature related to "The Structure and History of the Lament in the Old Testament:

Baumgartner, W., *Die Klagegedichte des Jeremia, BZAW* 32, 1917.

Begrich, J., "Die Vertrauensäusserung im israelitischen Klagelied des Einzelnen und in seinem babylonischen Gegenstück," *ZAW* 46, 1928; also *TB* 21, 1964, pp. 168–216.

Begrich, J., *Deuterojesaja-Studien, BWANT* 25, 1938, 2d ed. 1963.

Bentzen, A., "Daniel 6," in *Festschrift A. Bertholet,* Tübingen: J. C. B. Mohr [Paul Siebeck], 1950.

Birkeland, H., *Die Feinde des Individuums in der israelitischen Psalmenliteratur,* Oslo: Grønhahl & Sons, 1923.

Castellino, R. G., *Le Lamentazioni individuali e gli inni Babilonia e in Israele,* Torino: Societa Editrice Internazionale, 1940.

Engnell, I., *Divine Kingship in the Ancient Near East,* Oxford: Blackwell, 1943, 2d ed. 1967.

Gray, J., "Canaanite Kingship in Theory and Praxis," *VT* 2, 1952, pp. 193–220.

Gunkel, H.–Begrich, J., *Einleitung in die Psalmen,* Göttingen: Vandenhoeck & Ruprecht, 1933.

Haller, M., *Die fünf Megilloth, HAT,* Tübingen: J. C. B. Mohr [Paul Siebeck], 1940.

Jahnow, H., *Das Hebräische Leichenlied im Raum der Völkerdichtung, BZAW* 36, 1923.

Johnson, A. R., "The Psalms," in *The Old Testament and Modern Study,* ed. H. H. Rowley, Oxford: At the Clarendon Press, 1951.

Kahle, P., "Die Totenklage im heutigen Ägypten," in *Eucharisterion, Festscharift for H. Gunkel,* Göttingen: Vandenhoeck & Ruprecht, 1923.

Littmann, E., "Abessinisches zum AT," in *Festschrift A. Bertholet,* Tübingen: J. C. B. Mohr [Paul Siebeck],, 1950.

Marschall, G., *Die Gottlosen des ersten Psalmbuches*, Münster i.W.: Helios-Verlag, 1929.

Mowinckel, S., *Psalmenstudien I–VI*, Amsterdam: Verlag P. Schippers, 1921–1924.

Mowinckel, S., *Offersang og sangoffer*, Oslo: Aschehowg, 1951 (Eng. tr.: *The Psalms in Israel's Worship*, New York: Abingdon Press, 1962).

Mowinckel, S., *Religion und Kultus*, Göttingen: Vandenhoeck & Ruprecht 1953.

Noth, M., "Gott, König, Volk im Alten Testament," *ZThK* 2, 1950; also in *ThB* 6, 1957, pp. 188–229.

Noth, M., *Überlieferungsgeschichtliche Studien I*, Halle: M. Niemeyer, 1943, 2d ed. 1957.

Puukko, A. F., *Der Feind in den alttestamentlichen Psalmen.* Oudtestamentliche Studien 8, 1950.

Rowley, H. H., *The Relevance of Apocalyptic*, London: Lutterworth Press, 1944, 1950.

Stummer, F., *Sumerisch-akkadische Parallelen zum Aufbau alttestamentlicher Psalmen*, Paderborn: F. Schöningh, 1922 (also New York: Johnson Reprint Corp., 1968).

Weiser, A., *Die Psalmen, ATD*, Göttingen: Vandenhoeck & Ruprecht, 3d ed. 1950 (Eng. tr.: *The Psalms*, Philadelphia: Westminster, 1962).

Wendel, A., *Das freie Laiengebet im vorexilischen Israel*, Leipzig: Eduard Pfeiffer Verlag, 1931.

Westermann, C., *Der Aufbau des Buches Hiob*, Stuttgart: Calwer Verlag, 1956, 2d ed. 1977 *Calwer Theologische Monographien* 6.

Widengren, Geo., *The Accadian and Hebrew Psalms of Lamentation as Religious Documents*, Uppsala: Almqvist & Wiksells, 1936.

Willesen, F., "The Cultic Situation of Psalm LXXIV," *VT* 2, 1952, pp. 289–306.

Literature related to "The 'Re-presentation' of History in the Psalms":

Bernhardt, K.-H., *Das Problem der altorientalischen Königsideologie im AT. VT Suppl 8*, Leiden: E. J. Brill, 1960.

Jirku, A., *Die älteste Geschichte Israels im Rahmen lehrhafter Darstellungen*, Leipzig: A. Deichert, 1917.

Kraus, H.-J., *Psalmen I, BK*, Neukirchen: Neukirchener Verlag, 3d ed. 1966.

Lauha, A., *Die Geschichtsmotive in den alttestamentlichen Psalmen*, Helsinki: Der Finnischen Literaturgesellschaften, 1945.

Noth, M., "Die Vergegenwärtigung des AT in der Verkündigung," in C. Westermann, ed., *Probleme alttestamentlicher Hermeneutik*, München: Chr. Kaiser Verlag, 1960, pp. 54–68 (Eng. tr.: *Essays on Old Testament Hermeneutics*, Richmond: John Knox Press, 1963).

Pedersen, J., "Passahfest und Passahlegende," *ZAW NF* 11, 1934, 3.

Rad, G. v., "Das formgeschichtliche Problem des Hexateuch," *Theologische Bücherei*, 8, 1958, pp. 9–86.

Widengren, Geo, *Sakrales Königtum im Alten Testament und im Judentum*, Stuttgart: Kohlhammer, 1955.

Witzel, M., *Tammuz-Liturgien und Verwandtes, An Or* 10, Rome: Pontifical Biblical Institute, 1935.

Addendum: Recent literature dealing with the Psalms:

Barth, Ch., *Einführung in die Psalmen*, BSt 32, Neukirchen: Neukirchener Verlag, 1961.

Dahood, M., *Psalms I: 1–50*, The Anchor Bible, New York: Doubleday, 1966.

Drijvers, P., *The Psalms, Their Structure and Meaning*, Freiburg: Herder, 1965.

Falkenstein, V., von Soden, W., *Sumerische und akkadische Hymnen und Gebete*, Stuttgart, 1953.

Gerstenberger, E., "Psalms" in *Old Testament Form Criticism*, ed., J. H. Hayes, San Antonio: Trinity University Press, 1974, pp. 179–224.

Kapelrud, A., "Die skandinavische Einleitungswissenschaft zu den Psalmen," *Verkundigung u. Forschung* 11, 1966, pp. 62–93.

Kühlewein, J., *Geschichte in den Psalmen*, Stuttgart: Calwer Theologische Monographien 2, 1973.

Stamm, J. J. "Ein Vierteljahrhundert Psalmenforschung," *Theologische Rundschau* 23, 1955, pp. 1–68.

Westermann, C., "Psalter" in *BHHW* III, col. 1523–1529.

Index of Biblical Passages